D1121960

STANLEY KUBRICK

Stanley Kubrick

American Filmmaker

DAVID MIKICS

Yale

UNIVERSITY

PRESS

New Haven and London

Yale University Press books may be purchased in quantity for educational,
business, or promotional use. For information, please e-mail sales.press@yale.edu
(U.S. office) or sales@yaleup.co.uk (U.K. office).

Set in Janson Oldstyle type by Integrated Publishing Solutions.
Printed in the United States of America.

Library of Congress Control Number: 2019955073
ISBN 978-0-300-22440-5 (hardcover : alk. paper)

A catalogue record for this book is available from the British Library.

This paper meets the requirements of ANSI/NISO Z39.48-1992
(Permanence of Paper).

10 9 8 7 6 5 4 3

Frontispiece: Stanley Kubrick directing *A Clockwork Orange*
(Courtesy of Photofest/Warner Bros)

For Larry and Edith Malkin

CONTENTS

CONTENTS

STANLEY KUBRICK

Introduction

"STANLEY KUBRICK told me a story about a girl he loved," Kirk Douglas recalled. "He had a big fight with her, and goddamnit! He felt macho. The hell with it! He'd had enough! That was it! He packed his bag and slammed the door. He went out. As he started walking, that bag got heavier and heavier and he couldn't carry it. He had to go back."[1]

A piquant fairy tale: male defiance is quickly foiled by fate, which brings the man back to where he started. Kubrick's anecdote is also the plot of his last and most personal movie, *Eyes Wide Shut*. In that film the man rebels by seeking sex, but most Kubrick movies are about rebellion of some kind. Usually the rebel starts to look small, despite the sizable energies he lets loose. Being a rebel is not how you solve problems, and problem solving is very close to Kubrick's heart.

When he made a movie Kubrick was obsessively focused because he had to find a solution to every problem, but he was also drawn to macho revolt, and to anything else that makes well-laid plans screw up royally. His movies are about mastery that fails. Perfectly controlled schemes get botched through human error or freak accidents, or hijacked by masculine rage. A rebellious imp of the perverse always lurks somewhere. Kubrick relishes whatever throws a wrench in the works: the antic wiles of Alex in *A Clockwork Orange* and Quilty in *Lolita*, the chest-puffing death drive of *Dr. Strangelove*'s nutjob generals, Jack Torrance's wild anger in *The Shining*, the sudden fury that conquers Barry Lyndon at the sight of his stepson Bullingdon. A zestful insanity courses through the rigid champions of order, like Drill Instructor Hartman in *Full Metal Jacket*. Finally, after all this tearing apart, Kubrick comes back home at the end of *Eyes Wide Shut*, and shows us the intimate, ordinary life of a married couple.

Kubrick's movies are outliers, and we look at them differently than most popular films. Whether the Kubrick hero is a rebel like Alex in *A Clockwork Orange* or a calm problem solver like Dave Bowman in *2001*, we observe him across a distance and with ambivalence, instead of rooting for him in classic Hollywood fashion. Kubrick likes to trap his characters, put them on display. He is an arch modernist, allergic to tearjerkers, joyous endings, and scenes full of heart. His work also argues against most film noir and outlaw movies, which prize wicked self-possession and cool, from *The Maltese Falcon* down to Tarantino. Yet for all these avoidances Kubrick's movies were and are hugely popular: *2001*, intensely slow, quiet and abstract, became one of MGM's ten biggest moneymakers. Moments from Kubrick movies are as iconic as anything in *The Godfather*, a film Kubrick loved but which, in stark contrast to his own work, achieves a classic Hollywood trifecta of pathos, violence, and male bravado.

Kubrick's detractors argue that his movies don't sufficiently champion the human soul against the constricting routines they depict. Kubrick seems to them to be on the side of oppression, his movies cold, ponderous, and heavy-handed, extreme in all the wrong ways. One could, of course, say the same of Kafka's writing—and Kubrick was a devoted reader of Kafka. The deep-frozen impersonality that some claim to see in Kubrick is really his rejection of Hollywood pathos: the hero who drinks because he can't get over a dame, the brave heroine blinking back tears. Kubrick doesn't do what the movies are supposed to do, give you satisfying cathartic jolts. Nor is he austere in the manner of the European art film, though he admired Antonioni and, especially, Bergman. Film critic James Naremore writes that Kubrick's crystal-clear images give "a sense of authorial understanding without immersion, as if volcanic, almost infantile feelings were being observed in a lucid, rational manner."[2]

Kubrick's aloofness coexists with a kid's heart and a kid's upsetting energy. His movies show an odd mating of hyper-aware adult rationality and the raw feelings of a child. Childhood is telling: Kubrick the mischievous, stubborn little boy is at the core of his films, along with the grown-up director, calm and in control, who liked nothing better than staying home and making movies.

There's a home movie of Stanley Kubrick clowning around, probably at about age eight, hamming it up for his kid sister Barbara. Wearing oversized pants, he does a slapstick dance routine. At one point his grin looks a little like Alex's: malicious delight. Little Stanley got poor grades in conduct and playing with others. He had a strong Bartleby side: he never had a bar mitzvah, from sheer lack of interest.

Stanley's childhood rebellion began early. In first and second grade he often refused to go to school, attending only about 60 percent of the time. Headstrong and utterly sure of himself, the boy must have baffled his first-generation immigrant Jewish parents, who owed their middle-class lifestyle to taking education seriously. Remarkably, his doctor father, Jack Kubrick, seems to have given him leeway to stay home with his mother Gert, while remaining as mystified by his self-assured child as Jack is by Danny in *The Shining* or we are by *2001*'s Starchild. Stanley's independent streak would only become more marked as he grew older.

Young Stanley grew up on the Grand Concourse, the Champs Élysées of the West Bronx. The great boulevard was eventually ruined, long after Kubrick left, by Robert Moses's Cross Bronx Expressway. Among the Grand Concourse's monumental features was a temple of cinema called Loew's Paradise. (Another, the RKO Fordham, was just east of the Concourse.) Loew's was a vast and sumptuous faux-baroque theater with projected clouds moving across its ceiling. The neighborhood also had the usual soda fountains, Chinese restaurants, and bars, a Bickford's diner with its cluster of bookies, and the Villa Avenue Gang, Italian-American delinquents that Jewish kids like Kubrick had to watch out for.

"I was such a misfit in high school," Kubrick told an interviewer years later.[3] The other teenagers belonged to clubs with names like the Zombies and the Hurricanes, and played stickball and baseball in the streets. What consumed Stanley instead, from the time he was twelve, was photography. That year his father gave him a Graflex camera, a big antediluvian box that you had to look down into so that you could see the image on the ground glass. Stanley fitted it with a 35mm lens, and he was off. The next year Jack Kubrick taught his son chess, and this too became a passion.

Jack Kubrick was "a very nice man, a bit conservative and a worrier," Kubrick's widow Christiane remembered in an interview. His mother was Stanley's source of strength, Christiane added: "He was a gifted boy, brilliant and independent, and she, in her wisdom, succeeded in implanting in him a strong belief in himself."[4] While Stanley's father seems nothing like that flamboyant ogre Jack Torrance, both Jacks were serious worriers. Kubrick's father didn't understand his ambitions, and hopelessly wanted him to become a doctor; his mother realized that Stanley was on his own path.

Steven Marcus, later a literature professor at Columbia, was Stanley's classmate at William Howard Taft High School, where Kubrick asked day after day to copy Marcus's homework. When Marcus finally asked, "Stanley, why aren't you doing your homework?" Kubrick responded, "Well, I'm not interested."[5] Stanley just didn't respond to education by command. If he liked something, he threw himself into it. If not, he was hopeless.

Along with photography and chess, movies possessed Stanley. He attended Loew's and the RKO religiously, often skipping school to see a double feature. This was the early forties, a shining summit for Hollywood movies. Among Kubrick's favorites from those years, he told *Cinema* magazine in 1963, were Welles's *Citizen Kane*, William Wellman's *Roxie Hart*, Olivier's *Henry V*, and Edward Cline's *The Bank Dick*, with W. C. Fields. Stanley liked jazz, too, and drummed in a band fronted by a teenage Eydie Gorme, a Taft classmate.

Stanley graduated Taft with a 70 average, too low to get into college in the GI Bill years. He was no slacker, though; he knew what he wanted. "Stanley had a demonic belief in his own capacity. Demons were driving him. Nothing could stand in his way," said Marcus. Michael Herr, who knew the grown-up Kubrick, concurred: "You'd have to be Herman Melville to transmit the full strength of Stanley's will."[6]

The teenage Stanley was disheveled, a bohemian in too-large pants and jacket and uncombed hair. After high school, when he married his sweetheart Toba Metz and moved to

Greenwich Village, he fit right in. He played charades at Diane Arbus's house on Saturday nights, and he got to know Weegee, James Agee, and Dwight Macdonald.

Early on, Kubrick gravitated to the world of New York artists and intellectuals. But he wanted to do more than make rarefied art house films. His goal was to speak to mainstream America, and he reached it by making the art house sensibility mainstream, especially in *2001: A Space Odyssey*. He shared with Coppola, Spielberg, and Woody Allen—all directors he admired—the need for his work to be iconic, central to the culture. Central means chasing something crucial about America, the cinematic equivalent of *Huckleberry Finn*, or *The Scarlet Letter*, or *Moby-Dick*. Kubrick is, as my subtitle implies, an American director, in spite of his decades-long exile in his country estate in Childwickbury, England. He had videotapes of American pro football flown to him across the Atlantic, and he particularly liked the Super Bowl commercials. He read the *New York Times* every morning. "I don't feel that I'm not living in America," he told an interviewer.[7]

Kubrick has often been called an ice-cold filmmaker. A longtime critical enemy, Pauline Kael, liked to refer to his "arctic spirit." When he died in March 1999, just after finishing *Eyes Wide Shut*, the adjectives "cold" and "chilly" surfaced frequently in his obituaries. The charge is misguided. The week of his death the music critic Alex Ross said about Kubrick's movies, "They make me happy, they make me laugh. . . . If this was cold, then so was Fred Astaire." Cinema scholar Robert Kolker writes that Kubrick's films "are in fact deeply moving, but the emotions need to be accessed through the intellect: by seeing more, understanding more." Kubrick "seems to want us to see everything," Kolker adds, but we can never quite make full contact with his films.[8] They tantalize, and so we go back and watch them over and over.

Kubrick's career was made possible by the plunge in the

popularity of movies after 1948, when American households flocked to the TV screen, captivated by the new invention. Between 1948 and 1954 the movie audience declined by about forty million. With the major studios in trouble, the movie business opened up as it would again decades later in the seventies. Hundreds of art house cinemas sprouted up in cities and college towns during the early fifties. Foreign films were in, and "arty" became a term of praise. Many of the movies had sexual content that Hollywood hadn't dared to include since the pre–Production Code years, and that didn't hurt audience loyalty either. Week after week foreign film fans kept coming back. For most of his career Kubrick relied heavily on the art house audience, which had by the late sixties colonized huge swaths of middle America. He never churned out blockbusters aimed at a preteen audience, like those seventies whiz kids Steven Spielberg and George Lucas. *2001* was the ultimate art house triumph: no one knew what it meant, yet everyone saw it and talked about it.

Kubrick's great sixties–early seventies trio of iconic films, *Dr. Strangelove*, *2001*, and *A Clockwork Orange*, rode on another revolution in Hollywood. After Hitchcock's *Psycho*, the Production Code fell apart, and films could be more shocking, violent, and sexual. Like Hitchcock, Kubrick broke taboos, but in contrast to the sophisticated master of suspense, he rarely winks at the audience. *Dr. Strangelove*, with all its *MAD* magazine–style antics, is anything but a game; *2001* even risks solemnity, and wins. Unlike Hitchcock or Orson Welles (who called the young Kubrick a "giant"), Kubrick is rarely ingenious: his shots have the rightness of perfect design, but he doesn't play tricks. His madcap scenes never descend to devil-may-care whimsy, like so many sixties movies (think Richard Lester's *Help!*). Kael called *A Clockwork Orange* the work of a Teutonic professor, and so be it. Kubrick is always in earnest.

Inner torment is never glamorous or sexy in a Kubrick

movie. Instead it feels like a malfunction. That's why the awkward Tom Cruise, who lacks a hero's grace, was the right choice for *Eyes Wide Shut*. Kirk Douglas, who starred in *Spartacus* and *Paths of Glory*, has a streak of the maladroit too, and a grinding quality that pushes away subtlety. These two actors show their need to be in control, and so their control starts to wobble. In Kubrick's canon only Malcolm McDowell as *Clockwork*'s Alex feels assured in his playful masculinity. Kubrick's other leading men are stymied rather than stylish, pushed and pulled from within and without.

Kubrick required endless devotion from the people who worked on his films. His perfectionism could be maddening, since his own dedication to his art was total. Michael Herr, who cowrote *Full Metal Jacket*, said, "Everyone earned their pay with Stanley . . . but nobody earned their pay the way Stanley earned his pay." Dan Richter, who played Moonwatcher, the lead ape in *2001*, remarked, "What would be compulsion in others is single-mindedness in Stanley." Ken Adam, Kubrick's art director for *Dr. Strangelove*, said, "We were expected to obey his orders like Rommel's Afrikakorps. He was somewhat of a sadist, especially with people he loved." Terry Southern, who worked on the *Dr. Strangelove* script, remarked that Kubrick "scarcely let as much as a trouser pleat go unsupervised." For Kubrick there was "no detail too mundane, all the way down to stationery and paper clips," Herr agreed. Lisa Leone, who worked on *Eyes Wide Shut*, said, "As much as you gave, it was always more, and more, and more." "He's a genius, but his humor's black as charcoal. I wonder about his . . . *humanity*," McDowell muttered. And then there was Kirk Douglas, who groused, "Stanley Kubrick is a talented shit."[9]

Kubrick had his Rasputin side, no doubt about it. Those pitch black, sleep-deprived eyes bored right into you. Kubrick did not tolerate fuckups, and he inspired real fear. But he was also "congenial, accessible, bemused, sardonic," said the young film critic Jay Cocks (later a screenwriter for Martin Scorsese), and he could be a pal on the set, too. "When you shook hands with Stanley it was warm and gentle, it was just like a buzz went through you," said Leon Vitali, who played Bullingdon in *Barry Lyndon* and then became Kubrick's assistant for the next thirty years.[10]

Kubrick talked eagerly about a lot of things, from Wittgenstein to pro football, but most of all he knew about making movies. Geoffrey Unsworth, *2001*'s director of photography, admitted that he learned more from Kubrick in six months than he had in twenty-five years as a top British cinematographer. "He is an absolute genius," Unsworth marveled. "He knows more about the mechanics of optics and the chemistry of photography than anyone who's ever lived." Kubrick had a spooky, preternatural grasp of camerawork, lighting, sound, and, it seemed, every other technical aspect of filmmaking. On the set of *Full Metal Jacket*, actor Arliss Howard remembered, "He could come into a room and say, 'We're two stops off in this light.' They'd say, 'No, we just checked the camera.' He'd say, 'We're two stops off,' and they'd be two stops off."[11]

Kubrick had in spades the toughness that moviemaking requires. He could throw a screaming fit if it served his purpose, but he was mostly a calm problem solver. Steven Berkoff, who played Lord Ludd in *Barry Lyndon*, remarked, "Stanley has a kind of slightly rabbinical air. . . . He's an intellectual, and intellectuals don't get riled."[12] Kubrick, who started as a photographer for *Look* magazine, said that photography was perfect preparation for moviemaking because it made you figure things out. Playing chess, he added, also taught him how to evaluate ideas practically, to solve problems.

Problem solving in Kubrick can be creative, as when Dave outmaneuvers HAL in *2001*. But problem solvers, who love to be in control, often destroy human beings for the sake of an idea. The scientists of *A Clockwork Orange* clear up the question of evil through behavioral programming. Lieutenant Hartman of *Full Metal Jacket* reshapes teenagers into robotlike savages. For Strangelove, like the generals in *Paths of Glory* and HAL in *2001*, humans are expendable. Ziegler in *Eyes Wide Shut* stands for all the powerful men who see and manipulate without being seen. These are all examples of chilling uncreative mastery, in contrast to the masterful director Stanley Kubrick, who was always ready to draw on actors, writers, and the other filmworkers who clustered around him.

Kubrick once compared filmmaking to writing *War and Peace* in a bumper car. Yet he loved bouncing off other people's ideas. Every great director knows how to collaborate, but Kubrick took particular pleasure in the joint work of moviemaking. His actors suggested key moments in many of his films, like the "Singin' in the Rain" routine in *A Clockwork Orange* (McDowell's idea) and HAL's lipreading in *2001* (suggested by Gary Lockwood).

All work and no play makes Jack a dull boy. That's Jack Torrance typing away in *The Shining*, a hollow man who doesn't know how to work or how to play. Kubrick, when he made his movies, did both at once. One of Kubrick's favorite parts of moviemaking was developing a story in cahoots with writers like Michael Herr (*Full Metal Jacket*) and Diane Johnson (*The Shining*).

Such companionable work-as-play is usually absent from Kubrick's films themselves. A Kubrick movie is often a highly programmed world that severely controls the people in it. Their responses radically altered, they become captive to this world's emptiness. We see initiation into the soldier's ritual brutality (*Full Metal Jacket*), absurd military gameplaying (*Paths of Glory, Dr. Strangelove*), behavioristic social control (*A Clockwork Orange*), an aristocracy ruled by rigid customs (*Barry Lyndon*), a hotel that possesses its inhabitants (*The Shining*), and a secret society that claims the power of life and death (*Eyes Wide Shut*).

Kubrick's vistas look narrow and constraining even when their scope is vast, like the spacescapes of *2001*. A number of Kubrick movies end with the hero trapped or immobilized: *The Killing, Paths of Glory, Lolita, The Shining*. Others present in their last scenes an ambiguous rebirth that feels at once freeing and frightening: *Dr. Strangelove, 2001, A Clockwork Orange, Full Metal Jacket*. Only Kubrick's last testament, *Eyes Wide Shut*, and his first mature film, *Killer's Kiss*, offer a humane encouragement in their final moments.

More than any other director I can think of, Kubrick makes us work to grasp the relationships among his films. Each Kubrick movie is a world unto itself, yet deeply and cryptically related to the others. Dave Bowman's trip through the Stargate transforms Major Kong's whooping ride on his warhead in *Dr. Strangelove*, just as Bowman's rebirth as the Starchild answers Strangelove's rise from his wheelchair to salute the new nuclear day. And when Alex turns his eye on the audience at the start of *A Clockwork Orange*, he echoes the Starchild's uncanny gaze.

Because Kubrick is so lucid yet at times so enigmatic, a few of his movies seem tailor-made for conspiracy theorists. This makes a strange kind of sense, given his focus on obsession and problem-solving. Legions of web-based crackpots long ago fell in love with *The Shining*, which is said to prove that Kubrick faked the *Apollo 11* moon landing for NASA. Now they adore *Eyes Wide Shut* because it warns us about the Illuminati, or Hollywood pedophile rings. More subtly, *The Shining*, we are told, is "really" about the Holocaust. But Kubrick's films cannot be decoded in this way. They are open-ended works of art, not puzzles waiting to be solved.

Kubrick was a Jewish director, though he would never have said so. He read obsessively about the Holocaust, and came close to making a movie about it based on Louis Begley's haunting novel *Wartime Lies*. "In a sense Kubrick even married into the Holocaust," remarks Kubrick scholar Nathan Abrams. Kubrick's third wife, Christiane, his companion for the last forty-two years of his life, was the niece of Nazi filmmaker Veit Harlan, who directed the antisemitic propaganda movie *Jud Süss*. Before Kubrick met Harlan in 1957, he drank a big glass of vodka, and he told Christiane, "I'm standing here . . . looking like ten Jews." Among fellow directors he felt closest to Allen and Spielberg, who completed Kubrick's project *A.I.: Artificial Intelligence* after his death. The smart-alecky black humor of *Dr. Strangelove* aligns him with Lenny Bruce, Joseph Heller, and the sacred-cow bashers at *MAD*. Christiane said that "the girls [the Kubricks' daughters] and I used to tease him by saying his body language was like that of Tevye the Milkman—he would clasp his hands and sigh . . . with a big 'ochhh' while looking up toward God with accusation and melancholy. We imitated him and laughed."[13] As a Bronx Jew on his country estate in Hertfordshire, England, Kubrick must sometimes have felt just as out of place as that Irish upstart Barry Lyndon.

Kubrick tackled most of the crucial American genres: film noir, historical epic, war, science fiction, horror, and what philosopher Stanley Cavell calls the comedy of remarriage, about the reconciliation of a couple on the rocks. The remarriage theme is most noticeable in Hollywood's screwball comedies, but Kubrick transmutes it in his uncanny and troubled last film, *Eyes Wide Shut*.

A Kubrick film provokes thought without being at all fake-intellectual, like certain anomie-laced European movies that incline us toward a predictable brooding over human malaise. Kubrick the American is attuned to the cultural neuroses that mark our culture for better and worse: the self-made man stuck in a hollow life, adolescent rebellion, regeneration through violence.

Yet there is another side to Kubrick too, a European one. Stanley Kubrick, the second child of Jacques (Jack) Kubrick and Gertrude Perveler Kubrick, was born in New York City on July

26, 1928. But his sensibility, as critic Michel Ciment points out, comes from eighteenth-century Europe, which dreamed of reshaping humanity along strictly rational lines. From *Dr. Strangelove* to *2001*, *A Clockwork Orange*, and *Full Metal Jacket*, he is fascinated by schemes to radically manage or transform human nature. Kubrick, like the Enlightenment philosophers, knows that the schemes all fail, since reason turns out to be dangerously extremist, and therefore irrational.

Reason keeps on metamorphosing us, from the Stone Age to the cyberspace present. Now, in the twenty-first century, new machines are infiltrating our emotional lives, and the self might soon be modeled on the computer's algorithms. Kubrick appeals to our ambiguous shudder, both excited and fearful, when we confront reason once again remaking our inner world.

Choosing the greatest movie ever made is a mug's game, but still the choice reveals a critic's taste. For me two films are tied for first place, and they couldn't be more different: *2001: A Space Odyssey* and *The Rules of the Game*. Renoir's film is humane, funny, and grandly touching, reassuring in its dignity and ease. Kubrick's *2001*, static and sublime, is none of these things: it goes beyond the human, and courts uncharted spaces. Since I first saw it at age twelve, a few years after its release, it has chilled and inspired me like nothing else on a movie screen.

Kubrick belongs to the school of alienation, rejecting the warm humanity that Renoir prizes. With his clean, contoured style he knows as well as Antonioni and Bergman how to value empty spaces. Kubrick rejected Hitchcock's stylish adeptness and inclination to charm and Welles's taste for grandeur, but he absorbed from these two masters a will to control the information we get as viewers.

Think of the antiques that clutter Charles Foster Kane's mansion after his death, a setting Kubrick echoes when he depicts Quilty's house in *Lolita*: everything gets in the way of grasping the mystery of the man. Kubrick, like Welles and Hitchcock, Bergman and Antonioni, makes sure we know only what he decides to tell us, and that we remain aware of this constraining power. He is the antithesis of a Renoir, who seems to open the world to us.

In his acceptance speech for the D. W. Griffith Award given by the Directors Guild of America, Kubrick noted that Griffith, who liked to do things his own way, was sometimes compared to the hubristic Icarus. "But at the same time," Kubrick continued, "I've never been certain whether the moral of the Icarus story should only be, as is generally accepted, 'Don't try to fly too high,' or whether it might also be thought of as 'Forget the wax and feathers and do a better job on the wings.'"[14] Kubrick's patient, perfectionist artistry allowed him to fly higher, and more securely, than the other filmmakers of his time. His movies, like that black monolith, will be objects of fascination as long as cinema is still an art form.

1

I Know I Can Make a Film Better Than That:
Killer's Kiss, The Killing

PRESIDENT ROOSEVELT DIED on April 12, 1945, nine months
before Stanley Kubrick graduated from high school. The next
day Stanley walked past a news kiosk displaying the headline
FDR DEAD. Stanley coached the newsdealer into a dejected pos-
ture and snapped a photo, which he promptly brought to the
offices of *Look* magazine. *Look*'s photo editor, Helen O'Brien,
took a chance on young Kubrick, and before long he was a staff
photographer.

Still only seventeen, Kubrick had snagged what he later
called a "fantastically good job" at *Look*, and he would stay there
for the next four years. Meanwhile, he was having trouble getting into college. "My father, who was an alumni [*sic*] of NYU
uptown, took me to see the Dean. . . . Nothing worked," Kubrick remembered. But skipping college turned out to be a huge
plus. Photography "gave me a quick education in the way things
happen in the world," Kubrick later said.[1]

Look, unlike its more wholesome rival *Life*, specialized in the gritty and pessimistic. Spurning *Life*'s feel-good stories, it often featured grim cityscapes. The magazine was full of "unemployment, alcoholism, juvenile delinquency, divorce," notes the journalist Mary Panzer.[2]

In his photos for *Look*, Kubrick loved depicting limbolike places: a dentist's waiting office, a subway platform. Sometimes the pallid, confrontational feel of the photos echoes Diane Arbus, as when Kubrick photographs a row of artificial limbs at Walter Reed hospital. A stolid man stares straight into the camera, his pencil behind his ear, while a soldier on crutches haunts the background. In one Kubrick photo a boxer down for the count, foreshortened like Mantegna's Christ, groans in agony. In another, two young men in ties face the camera, one solemnly adjusting his pompadour, the other staring right at us.

Kubrick also photographed stars for *Look*. He profiled Leonard Bernstein in August 1949. Here's Lenny clowning in swimming trunks, making a Hitler moustache with one hand and heiling with the other; sitting in his bathrobe, abstracted; pensively holding a book by Erich Fromm. In March 1949 Kubrick showed Monty Clift, then twenty-eight, in his New York apartment, sitting blankly in front of a bowl of cereal and a glass of milk, then lying on the floor next to an unmade bed, legs splayed, pretend-drinking from a wine bottle. Kubrick also shot Frank Sinatra and Rocky Graziano, George Grosz and Jacques Lipchitz, and the radio star Johnny Grant, "Johnny on the spot." (Not all those photos made it into print.)

In his work for *Look*, Kubrick used canted camera angles and, often, artificial lighting. He brought lights into a Central Park West subway stop for a noirish shot of an embracing couple. In 1947 he photographed the shooting of Jules Dassin's *The Naked City*. Dassin's film was deadpan and evocative, and a clear influence on Kubrick's noir films of the fifties.

Kubrick's photographic style is stark and clean, foreboding

From a Kubrick feature on the circus for *Look* magazine
(Courtesy of Museum of the City of New York)

in its precision. But it also had room for drama. He did a series
on the socialite Betsy von Furstenberg, featured in the May
1950 *Look*. In one shot she is lolling, fashionably bored, on a
couch with a young man in a tuxedo, with Picasso's painting of
Angel Fernández de Soto staring out at us from the wall above.
Betsy in shorts, sitting in a window with a script—she was an
aspiring actress—looks like *Lolita*'s Sue Lyon. She does an impression of rapture while clutching the script to her chest, ab-
sently scratching a cat's head with one hand, her painted toe-
nails curling.

In June 1946 Kubrick shot another dramatic photo spread

Kubrick's shot of a couple embracing in the subway
(Courtesy of Museum of the City of New York)

showing what goes on at a handwriting analysis booth. In just six images, he gives us a full-fledged encounter, with emotions that run the gamut. He focuses on a young serviceman and a woman handwriting analyst who seem to be heading toward a first date: we see their rhythm of shy flirtation, averted eyes, fervent appeal, indecision. (*Look* published only one of these photos, the following summer.)

Kubrick the photographer liked visual parables: people raptly gazing into a monkey house, with the monkeys off-camera. There is something parabolic, too, about a shot from his series

Betsy von Furstenberg, by Kubrick, for *Look*
(Courtesy of Museum of the City of New York)

on student life at the University of Michigan: outlined by the
stark artificial lighting that Kubrick liked to use, a woman lights
a man's cigarette. Above all, Kubrick knew how to convey a
sense of closed-off emotional turmoil. For a photo essay called
"First Loves of Teenagers" he shot a girl with her back to us,
her face hidden. She has just scrawled I HATE LOVE! in lipstick
on a wall, and the hand holding the lipstick droops in defeat.

In May 1948 the twenty-year-old Kubrick married his high
school sweetheart, Toba Metz. Kubrick's friend Gerald Fried,

Kubrick's photo of Aaron Copland and Oscar Levant at a party
(Courtesy of Museum of the City of New York)

who later wrote the music for his early movies, commented that when Stanley and Toba began their relationship, "they were still in their teens—it almost didn't count. It was a legal marriage, but they were, like, dating. There was no exchange of any deep affection."[3] The couple moved to Greenwich Village, where Kubrick tagged along with the bohemian intellectual scene. He also sat in on literature classes at Columbia taught by Mark Van Doren and, probably, Lionel Trilling. He got to know some of the *Partisan Review* crowd, like Dwight Macdonald and James Agee, as well as Weegee and Arbus.

Kubrick had now plunged into reading literature and philosophy, and after a few years he could give the high-octane

New York intellectuals a run for their money. "I spent an interesting three hours with Stanley Kubrick, most talented of the younger directors," Macdonald wrote in 1959, "discussing Whitehead, Kafka, Potemkin, Zen Buddhism, the decline of Western culture, and whether life is worth living anywhere except at the extremes—religious faith or the life of the senses; it was a typical New York conversation."[4]

By 1950 Kubrick was becoming dissatisfied with his job at *Look*. In four years at the magazine, he pulled in no more than $150 a week. ("They pay lousy salaries, anyway. Off the record," he told interviewer Robert Ginna years later.) Even apart from the low pay, Kubrick was restless. As a child he had dreamed of being a writer like Conrad, but now he knew he wanted to make films. "For a period of four or five years I saw every film made," he remembered. "I sat there and I thought, well, I don't know a god-damn thing about movies, but I know I can make a film better than that."[5] A friend reported that Kubrick sometimes read the newspaper in the movies when he got bored by what was on screen.

The young Kubrick taught himself how to make movies, a rare thing among major directors. He read Pudovkin on film editing and Stanislavski on acting. "In those days there were no film schools," remembered Gerald Fried. "We had to learn by going to movies. Our discussions after seeing them were primarily listening to Stanley kind of smirking at the tasteless sentimentality of most pictures."[6] As an antidote to Hollywood sentiment, Kubrick had also seen all the foreign films at the Museum of Modern Art, most of them more than once. Now he was ready.

In 1950 the twenty-one-year-old Kubrick made his first movie, *Day of the Fight*, a 12½-minute newsreel about a boxer named Walter Cartier. Kubrick's high school friend Alex Singer worked the camera. Kubrick made *Day of the Fight* for about thirty-nine hundred dollars and sold it to RKO-Pathé for four thousand. This was much less money than he and Singer had expected, but still he was elated. *Day of the Fight* still holds up. Cartier's knockout punch at the end is spectacular, but it seems almost an afterthought. Before that Kubrick grips the viewer with Cartier's routine in the hours leading up to the fight. He wakes up next to his identical twin brother, goes to morning mass, where he gulps anxiously before he receives the communion wafer, carefully examines his nose in the mirror, and goes to the doctor for his prefight checkup. Kubrick makes tense human drama out of these details. "Time has a way of staring you in the face as it barely moves along," a voice-over intones as Vince, the twin brother, gives Cartier a rubdown before the fight. Cartier is a twenty-four-year-old kid, hopeful and anxious, the first in Kubrick's line of young men trying to make their mark: Barry and his stepson Bullingdon in *Barry Lyndon*, *Clockwork Orange*'s Alex, Joker in *Full Metal Jacket*, and finally, that boy in a man's marriage, Dr. Bill Harford in *Eyes Wide Shut*.

Nine months after *Day of the Fight*, Kubrick quit *Look*, determined to make it as a director. He went on to make another short for RKO-Pathé, *The Flying Padre*, about a priest in New Mexico who visits his flock by airplane.

Meanwhile, he searched for cash to make a feature film.

Kubrick shot his first feature, *Fear and Desire*, in southern California in early 1951, after raising ten thousand dollars, mostly from his uncle Martin Perveler, who owned a string of pharmacies in LA. Perveler demanded that Kubrick give him a percentage on all his future films, but when Stanley refused he gave him the money anyway. Paul Mazursky, who acted in the movie, remembered driving with Kubrick to visit Perveler. "He needed another $5,000 to finish the film, and he says, 'I'm gonna get the money from him no matter what—I can tell you that right now.' And he spat at the windshield from inside the car. I'll never forget that. He got the money."[7]

Released in 1953, *Fear and Desire* is a deadly serious Conrad-style tale about four soldiers stranded behind enemy lines in an unnamed war. Years later Kubrick mercilessly derided his first feature film and tried to keep it from being shown. He said to an interviewer, "I wasn't satisfied to just make an interesting film, I wanted it to be a very poetic and meaningful film. It was a little like the Thurber story about the midget who wouldn't take the base on balls and decided to swing. . . . It opened at the Guild Theatre in New York and it was pretty apparent it was terrible."[8]

Fear and Desire is fatally adolescent, as Kubrick later realized. There is a grandly portentous voice-over, and in one scene a shadowy figure called the General, who topples over into death like one of Welles's hero-villains. Kubrick wouldn't give us this kind of hokum again. The movie contains only one memorable scene, when the four soldiers kidnap a girl from the enemy side and tie her to a tree. Sidney (Paul Mazursky) dances around the impassive girl, whose face remains blank, and delivers a demented Bergmanesque monologue referencing Shakespeare's *The Tempest* (later the basis for a disappointing film by Mazursky). The girl slips her bonds and runs, and Sidney shoots her dead.

The soldier's showdown with a silent and implacable woman makes up *Fear and Desire*'s hot emotional center. It has echoes in some later Kubrick: when Jack in *The Shining* embraces a nude beauty only to find her transformed into a cackling, pustule-ridden hag, when Joker shoots the teenage Vietnamese sniper in *Full Metal Jacket*, and when Bill in *Eyes Wide Shut* faces off against a masked woman at an orgy. *Fear and Desire* is a hopeless muddle, but even here Kubrick begins working through what men see in and do to women, a frequent theme of his later movies.

Joseph Burstyn, a crucial distributor of foreign films in America, booked *Fear and Desire* into New York art house theaters like the Guild, on 50th Street near Radio City. It played in a handful of other big cities too. In the sixties Kubrick took the movie out of circulation. When it was screened against his wishes at Telluride and at New York's Film Forum thirty years later, he announced to the press that it was a "bumbling, amateur film exercise . . . a completely inept oddity, boring and pretentious."[9] Kubrick was right to trash his first feature; only hardcore Kubrick fans will seek it out. Yet the movie gives us some important clues about who Kubrick was.

Toba Metz, dark-haired and pale, with beatnik bangs over her dark eyes, appears briefly in *Fear and Desire*. Shortly after the film was finished, in late 1951, the couple returned from California to New York, and soon after they separated. Their hand-to-mouth existence no doubt weighed on her. Kubrick had to scrounge for a living, playing chess for quarters in Washington Square Park. He was the fifth- or sixth-best player in the park, he told the journalist Jeremy Bernstein. "It was a whole lot of potzers, and semi-potzers, and people who put up fierce struggles but invariably lost," Kubrick said.[10] While waiting for an answer about a movie, he would arrive at the park at noon and leave at midnight, with quick breaks for meals. Years later Kubrick fantasized that he could have been as great as Bobby Fischer, good enough to beat the Russians, if only he had been able to study chess nine hours a day.

Kubrick met the dancer Ruth Sobotka in 1952 while he was editing *Fear and Desire*, and the two quickly began an affair. Stanley and Ruth married in January 1955, after living together in the Village for three years. This marriage, like Kubrick's first, didn't last long. Stanley and Ruth split the next year, legally separated in 1958, and divorced in 1961. But while they were together Sobotka was a serious intellectual presence in Kubrick's life. Nearly three years Kubrick's senior, she was far beyond him in her artistic career. Sobotka had ties to the avantgarde: in 1947 she had appeared in Hans Richter's film *Dreams That Money Can Buy*, which contained sequences designed by Calder, Man Ray, Duchamp, Ernst, and Léger. Ruth had studied with Lee Strasberg and acted on the stage in New York. When Kubrick met her, she was a dancer with George Balanchine's New York City Ballet, and a designer as well. In 1951 Ruth designed costumes for and danced in *The Cage*, the sensational Jerome Robbins ballet that depicted a praying mantis–like female devouring her male brood. The dance, hieratic and bloody and as puzzling as Kafka, must have made a strong impression on Kubrick, who no doubt saw it when it was revived by Balanchine's company.

A dancer friend remembers Sobotka wearing a voluptuous full-length red bathrobe with a fur collar, "like something out of 'Anna Karenina.' She was incredibly beautiful."[11] A Viennese Jew, daughter of a well-known actress, Gisela Schönau, and a famous architect and designer, Walter Sobotka, Ruth had fled Austria with her family after Hitler's *Anschluss* in 1938, when she was twelve.

Unlike Toba, Ruth Sobotka was Kubrick's artistic collaborator. Along with a brief role in *Killer's Kiss* (1955), she made storyboards for *The Killing* (1956), his third movie, and a United Artists press release called her "Hollywood's first female art director." Like Kubrick, she was a perfectionist. One friend said that when she married Kubrick, she "learned to play chess with no less commitment to the task than studying ballet or acting." Gerald Fried said about Stanley and Ruth that "there was a lot of sparring, but I thought they were quite perfect for each other."[12]

Ruth Sobotka, emissary from the *Mitteleuropäische* artistic world, left a lasting mark on Kubrick. She may even have told him about *Traumnovelle* (Dream Story), by another Viennese Jew, Arthur Schnitzler, a book that obsessed Kubrick for decades before he filmed it as *Eyes Wide Shut*.

The words "film noir" conjure up muffled gunshots in the dark, rain-drenched city streets, and dizzying, recursive plots. Plus maybe a traumatized ex-con, a hard-drinking detective, or a devilish dame; not to mention the bitter taste of black coffee, and the shadow of the gallows. In film noir tough guys usually get outmaneuvered, shown up as hapless pawns. It's the flip side of that American icon, the lone hero carving out his destiny.

Kubrick's first two mature films, *Killer's Kiss* (1955) and *The Killing* (1956), are certainly noir, but they don't share the genre's glamorous dark moodiness. His protagonists lack the seductive sheen of most noir heroes. Instead they are busy trying to get a grip—on what, they're not so sure.

Kubrick sides with noir's hallucinatory sense that life is a dark illusion even when it seems most real, that the boldest of actions can look passive and dreamlike. In Anthony Mann's *Raw Deal* (1948), a character says, "I suddenly felt, I don't know, big and small at the same time." Noir draws an ironic frame around our fantasies of significance, and Kubrick appreciated the irony.

Kubrick made *Killer's Kiss* in New York in 1954. The shooting took thirteen weeks, a long time for a low-budget picture. There is much that predicts later Kubrick in *Killer's Kiss*, starting with the title, which ranks with *Full Metal Jacket* and *Eyes Wide Shut* in its poetic snap. (Two earlier versions of the title were *Kiss Me, Kill Me* and *The Nymph and the Maniac*.)

Killer's Kiss begins with two lonely New Yorkers observing each other from the facing windows of their apartments. The woman, Gloria Price, is a taxi dancer (in other words, a prostitute) in a seedy Times Square club called Pleasure Land. The man, Davey Gordon, is a boxer getting ready for what will turn out to be his last bout. They begin a romance, which is threatened by Gloria's boss, Vinnie Rapallo, a middle-aged brute who wants Gloria for himself.

Killer's Kiss is about ordinary, minor-scale people. No one is neurotic, demonic, or flagrantly doomed as in some film noir. Jamie Smith, who plays Davey, seems passive yet alert, and as devoid of personality as Keir Dullea, Dave Bowman in *2001*. Irene Kane as Gloria is slightly feral and shy. Pursued by Rapallo, Gloria can't be had, but not for the usual noir reasons. She's not perverse or deadly, certainly no femme fatale, and not baby-doll girlish either. "Her Soft Mouth was the Road to Sin-Smeared Violence," screamed the lurid poster for *Killer's Kiss*, but this was false advertising. *Killer's Kiss* is a remarkably chaste film: Gloria is too jumpy and evasive to be sexy, and Davey too cautious, too stunned by life, to thirst after her. There is something off about them, in the same way there is something off about certain people you know.

Killer's Kiss has a makeshift quality influenced by New York school photography and cinéma vérité. Gerald Fried's jittery, jazzy score keeps the audience on edge. Kubrick makes the streets of New York look tawdry and dreamlike, full of gritty urban oddities. He cuts from the flashing neon signs of Broadway to hot dogs on a grill to a toy baby floating in a tub in a dime store window.

Kubrick later disparaged *Killer's Kiss*, saying that it had a "silly" story and that it was "still down in the student level of filmmaking." The story was "written in a week," he told the interviewer Robert Ginna.[13] True, there is something crude about the movie, but this lack of polish gives *Killer's Kiss* its offbeat charm. From *Killer's Kiss* on Kubrick would become increasingly precise in his filmmaking, bearing down on each nuance of lighting, composition, and sound. *Killer's Kiss* is the last homemade-looking Kubrick film.

The movie's ending reprises its first shot, with Davey, who is waiting for Gloria, nervously pacing beneath the cavernous vault of New York's Penn Station. Then the unexpected happens. In the last minute of *Killer's Kiss* Gloria runs to Davey and embraces him.

Kubrick's second full-length movie is that rare thing, a film noir with a happy ending. The hero gets the girl, but this finale feels tentative rather than celebratory. Kubrick refrains from the usual close-up clinch at the end: the lovers are seen from far off, in the diminuendo of a long shot.

Killer's Kiss, the first mature Kubrick movie, is the only one until his last, *Eyes Wide Shut*, that ends with a renewed romantic connection between a man and a woman. In both movies, the connection is exactly as hopeful as it is tenuous.

Killer's Kiss has a peculiar set piece at its center, showing the crucial place of Ruth Sobotka in Kubrick's vision. Sobotka dances a pas seul while Gloria's voice-over tells the story of her doomed sister Iris, who gave up her career as a ballet dancer at her husband's insistence and then devoted herself to her dying father. In the end Iris killed herself in protest against what her father and her husband had done to her. Gloria throws herself into a degrading job at Pleasure Land, proving that she too can be self-destructive. "Every night I worked in that depraved place, a human zoo," she says.

It's hard not to see in Ruth's *Killer's Kiss* dance solo a premonition about the future of her relationship with Stanley. Iris gives up her dancing for her husband's sake. In 1955, the year after *Killer's Kiss*, Ruth left ballet so she could move to Los Angeles with Kubrick. She quickly grew to hate the city. In a newspaper interview she said, "I liked working on a movie, but would not like to live in that city of false values. Success in Hollywood is measured in terms of money or notoriety, and what is important to those people is not what is important to me." She added that "many dancers I considered good had become slovenly since living in Hollywood."[14]

Sobotka was listed as art director on *The Killing*, as she had been on *Killer's Kiss*. But though Ruth dreamed of being Stanley's full artistic partner, such a collaboration was not to be. When *The Killing* was being shot, Stanley would often leave Ruth at home while he went to the set.

In *Killer's Kiss* Iris remains alien to the drama: a vision intruding from the past, a pure artist who destroys herself. The movie sidelines her much as Ruth Sobotka, who plays Iris, would find herself shunted aside by Kubrick's burgeoning career. After she performs her lonely virtuoso turn, the movie leaves her behind like a forgotten dying swan. The story of Davey and Gloria shuts out the memory of Gloria's sister, who lived for art.

In a screenplay treatment called The Married Man from 1954–56, when Kubrick was having marital trouble with Ruth, he wrote,

> Marriage is like a long meal with dessert served at the beginning. . . . Can you imagine the horrors of living with a woman who fastens herself on you like a rubber suction cup? Whose entire life revolves around you morning, noon and night? . . . It's like drowning in a sea of feathers. Sinking deeper and deeper into the soft, suffocating depths of habit and familiarity. If she'd only fight back. Get mad or jealous, even just once. . . . Look, last night I went out for a walk. Right after dinner. I came home at two in the morning. Don't ask me where I was.[15]

The anecdote that Kubrick told Douglas, in which he returned home after futilely trying to leave, his suitcase getting heavier and heavier, must have been about his life with Sobotka, one guesses. "Just tell me where my suitcase is, I'm getting out of here," the husband says in The Married Man.[16] His wife (named Alice, as in *Eyes Wide Shut*), is a "saint," "practically Mary Magdalene in blue jeans," and he finds her straitlaced virtue intolerable.

Two other treatments by Kubrick from the same years, Jealousy and The Perfect Marriage, are about desperate, discontented spouses like Kubrick himself. In Jealousy, a husband, convinced his wife is unfaithful, "meets a trampy looking girl and eventually winds up at her apartment. There is a sexy scene of some sort which is climaxed by the man walking out"—just as Bill Harford will do several times in *Eyes Wide Shut*. In The Perfect Marriage, the husband holds his wife's "wild" past against her, and claims that he's faithful, but "she asks about recent trips when he didn't answer [the] room phone." Kubrick sketched out a series of notes about the couple's catastrophic fight: "YOU'LL BE SORRY . . . HYSTERIA VENOMOUS . . . ADMIT INFIDELITY. LOUSY LOVER. SCREAMING[.] HUSBAND LEAVES." Kubrick also drew up a scene in which the wife abandons her husband, who "sobs like a frightened child" and then calls his mother. Outlining another movie idea, under the title The Famished Monkey, Kubrick writes, "The development of this marriage should be a kind of sado-masochistic Dostoyevskian set up" in which the husband wants "to humiliate the worshiping girl and as a result lacerate him self." This outline's scene titles convey marital trauma: "Fuck or fight," "Colored girls," "Trapped and bored after a screw."[17]

Kubrick expressed his discontent more subtly in *Killer's Kiss*, where Ruth plays the doomed figure of Iris, dancing her pas seul and then giving up her career for a man, as Ruth did for Stanley. Ruth is outstripped by the mature romantic couple who have a future because their relations are still tentative, in marked contrast to the self-sacrificing Iris.

Shortly after making *Killer's Kiss*, Kubrick encountered the creative partner he was looking for and hadn't found in Ruth Sobotka. In 1955 Kubrick met James B. Harris, known as Jimmy, an army friend of his high school buddy Alex Singer. Harris wanted to produce movies, and he was impressed with Kubrick's first two features. So the two men formed Harris-Kubrick Productions.

Harris had a languid, stylish handsomeness that contrasted with Kubrick's careless bohemian look. They became close buddies. "He was, above all, my friend," Harris remembered. "We loved to play football and poker together. . . . We shared the same troubles in our lives and the cinema was an outlet, a reason for being and a means of escape."[18] Kubrick had played drums in high school, and Harris was also a jazz drummer, who had studied at Juilliard. Both were Jewish, and both from New York. They were the same age, too, born just eight days apart.

There was no love lost between Jimmy Harris and Sobotka. Harris said, "Ruth was an over-the-hill ballet dancer who wanted to be an art director. So Stanley indulged her in that stuff. She couldn't understand why her name wasn't on the door of our office because Stanley's and my name were on there. They split up and he left. We left our wives together. He was rehearsing me on how to break the news."[19] By December 1956 Ruth was back in New York, where she returned to the New York City Ballet.

Both before and after the split with Ruth, money was tight. Every Friday afternoon Kubrick shut down production on *Killer's Kiss* so he could go to the unemployment office and pick up his check. The crew and actors grumbled at the low pay, but Kubrick was under financial pressure. He took no salary for himself on *Killer's Kiss*, and he wouldn't on his next movie either. He survived on those unemployment checks, and on loans from Jimmy Harris.

Harris had come across a novel called *Clean Break* (1955) by Lionel White, about a plan to rob a racetrack. He optioned the story for ten thousand dollars, thinking it could be Harris-Kubrick's first movie. Harris and Kubrick rechristened it *The Killing* and got to work. *The Killing* was another Kubrick adventure in noir, smoother and more assured than *Killer's Kiss*.

The Killing is an intellectual puzzle akin to a chess game. The idea is simple: a criminal's plan to knock over a racetrack gradually explodes. There is no thrill in the heist, only the constant twitch of anxiety. No wily antagonist dooms the hero, as in *Double Indemnity* or *Out of the Past* or *Gilda*, to name a few of the canonical noir movies. Bad luck and a little loose talk are all it takes for the scheme to fall to pieces. The director sacrifices his criminals like pawns for his final combination, when Johnny Clay, the gang's leader, stands hopelessly checkmated.

The poster for *The Killing* boasted, "Like No Other Picture since Scarface and Little Caesar!" But *The Killing* is no gangster movie with a flashy bad-guy hero. Instead it shows how a criminal scheme swirls slowly down the drain. The heist itself, rather than the characters, takes center stage.

To help write the screenplay Kubrick recruited Jim Thompson, the pulp novelist who had created some of the most disturbing noir fiction, including *The Killer Inside Me* (1952), a Kubrick favorite (in a blurb, Kubrick called Thompson's novel "probably the most chilling and believable first-person story of a criminally warped mind I have ever encountered"). In *The Killer Inside Me* the hero is a perverted romantic Satan, captivating and appalling by turns. *The Killing*'s Johnny Clay is just the opposite, the criminal as ordinary Joe, and the men he looks for to join his heist are just as undistinguished. "None of these men are criminals in the usual sense. . . . They all live seemingly normal, decent lives," he tells his girlfriend Fay.

Kubrick was a little wary around Thompson, a hard drinker who invariably pulled a bottle of liquor out of a paper bag before sitting down at his typewriter. Kubrick and Thompson spent their writing days in a tiny office on West 57th Street in Manhattan, and Kubrick, with his sloppy jacket and drooping white socks, sometimes went to Thompson's two-story home in Flushing, Queens, for dinner. Thompson's daughter Sharon said, "Stanley came out to our place and just drove us all insane.

He was a beatnik before beatniks were in. He had the long hair and the weird clothes."[20]

Kubrick and Harris ran into one problem with *The Killing*: no racetrack wanted to be the setting for a film about robbing a racetrack. For the initial footage of the racehorses, Alex Singer lay down with his portable Eyemo Mitchell camera in the middle of the track at San Francisco's Bay Meadows just as the horses left the starting gate. When track employees spotted him, the race was stopped. But Singer, who somehow escaped being arrested, had his footage.

Otherwise, the shooting went smoothly. *The Killing* was shot in twenty days, mostly on the studio lot. Kubrick and Harris handled postproduction together, with Kubrick calling the shots. ("I was always right next to him in the editing room," Harris said.) The film cost $330,000, but UA supplied only $200,000, so Harris made up the difference. "At the time, [Kubrick] didn't really know how to find money. I did," Harris remembered.[21]

Harris and Kubrick needed a star, and they found one in Sterling Hayden. The tall, rugged, and rambling Hayden came to acting late. He was working as a fisherman off the coast of Massachusetts when a local newspaper photographed him: "Gloucester Fisherman Looks Like Movie Idol," the caption said. In 1933, when he first came to LA, Hayden lived in San Pedro on a schooner. Then he served in the Second World War: "I was in Yugoslavia with Tito's partisans, and I liked everything I saw," Hayden remembered decades later. He made "ten-day westerns," then hit it big in 1950 with *The Asphalt Jungle*, John Huston's meticulous heist flick. A few years later Hayden's agent told him, "There's some weirdo out from New York who's supposed to be a bloody genius."[22] And so Hayden agreed to star in *The Killing*, for a salary of $40,000.

"What did Kubrick see in you?" an interviewer once asked Hayden, who gave a loaded response: "Why is a man a two-bit hood . . . maybe the weakness?" When Hayden was called up in 1951 before the House Un-American Activities Committee to testify about Communists in Hollywood, he named names. "I was a rat," he admitted.[23] Hayden's shame at giving in to HUAC comes through in the character of Johnny Clay, who remains insecure beneath his brusque armor.

We first see Hayden as Johnny Clay in a remarkable tracking shot that Kubrick would use again in *Lolita*. The camera, following Johnny, sweeps through the rooms of his apartment as if they had no walls. Hayden, his long stride eating up the space in front of him, looks utterly confident, but this soon fades. The moment he launches his plot, the net starts to close around him. Without exactly knowing how, we sense that he will lose this one.

Johnny and his girlfriend Fay echo the pair played by Hayden and Jean Hagen in *The Asphalt Jungle*. In Huston's movie Hayden snaps at the pliable Hagen, "Shut up and get me some bourbon." In the first scene of *The Killing* Fay, similarly obedient, reminds Johnny matter-of-factly, "I'm not pretty and I'm not very smart." Kubrick gives Johnny no reaction shot: she doesn't register with him, not even as an annoyance.

Johnny and Fay might also put us in mind of Stanley and Ruth. It's hard not to see an image of Kubrick's wish to escape his marriage to Ruth when Johnny shrugs off his girlfriend so he can plan the heist along with his men-only team.

Johnny cooks up the racetrack robbery as a get-rich-quick scheme. He wants to "have it made," but the phrase sounds empty in his mouth. He is joined by a ragtag band of partners, including Elisha Cook Jr., well known to moviegoers as the clumsy, cheap hood Wilmer in *The Maltese Falcon*. In *The Killing* Cook plays George, a milquetoast husband hounded by his wife, who is having an affair with the hunky Val (played by Vince Edwards, one of Kubrick's poker buddies).

Marie Windsor plays Sherry, wife of the hapless George,

with a viperish contempt. Kubrick had seen Windsor in *The Narrow Margin* (Richard Fleischer, 1952), where she gets called a "60 cent special, cheap, flashy, strictly poison." In *The Killing* as in *The Narrow Margin*, Windsor is some kind of a dame, hard as nails, a jarring, unquiet spirit. She has a touch of Joan Crawford about her, and she can remind you of Lana Turner when her almond-shaped eyes slide slowly, like billiard balls, to the bottom edge of the screen. But unlike those doyennes Windsor remains a bit player. She lacks Turner's intimacy with fate, or the alien force of Crawford's stark, staring rage.

Windsor's Sherry gets *The Killing*'s snazziest dialogue, no doubt courtesy of Jim Thompson. When she tells her boyfriend Val that her wimp of a husband will be their road to riches, he sneers, "That meatball?" "Meatball with gravy, Val," she snaps. In the end, Sherry turns the heist into a disaster by spilling the beans and then gets herself spectacularly killed, which might be Kubrick's revenge on Ruth for inserting herself into her husband's filmmaking, here analogous to Johnny's crime scheme. Women spell trouble, is this picture's implication. With Harris and Kubrick at the helm, your project comes off perfectly; if you let Ruth meddle, you risk catastrophe.

Early on in *The Killing*, the burly Kola Kwariani, one of Kubrick's chess buddies, tells us why Johnny is not the existential hero of noir but instead a walking emptiness. At a midtown chess and checkers club, Kwariani, playing a character named Maurice, brushes off a bad chess player with "Shut up, potzer." Then he tells Johnny,

> I have often thought the gangster and the artist are the same in the eyes of the mass. They are admired and hero-worshipped, but there is always present underlying wish to see them destroyed at the peak of their glory.

This speech, riffing on New York intellectual Robert Warshow's famous essay on gangster movies, goes right over the confused

Johnny's head. He is not the glorious artist-gangster but instead a mediocrity. His blankness finds an echo in some later Kubrick heroes: Dave in *2001*, Barry Lyndon, Bill Harford. In this crew only Dave has native intelligence. Kubrick liked his protagonists baffled and beaten, and not overly smart.

The Killing's denouement arrives quickly. After a chaotic shootout, only Johnny is left alive from the gang, and he has a suitcase full of money. And now Kubrick makes something brilliantly calamitous happen. In a Hitchcockian touch, an airport luggage cart carrying the million-dollar suitcase gets overturned by a middle-aged lady's yapping poodle, and Johnny watches all those dollars swirl through the air like a leaf storm. Johnny's plot has come to a dead end, as we suspected it would.

With the spectacular ending of *The Killing*, as in its fight scene where the bare-chested Kwariani struggles with eight cops, Harris and Kubrick stole a page from Huston's *Treasure of the Sierra Madre* (1948), one of Kubrick's favorite movies. Like Johnny Clay's dollars, the gold that Huston's Fred C. Dobbs (Humphrey Bogart) thirsts for gets blown away in the wind, gone forever. But Johnny is no Dobbs. Bogart turns Dobbs into an allegorical figure of avarice, a hunched-over gargoyle chortling madly. Johnny has none of Dobbs's aggressive quirks: he is more or less a dud, as Kubrick intended him to be. The noir films most similar to *The Killing* have inconspicuous, muddled heroes: think Edgar Ulmer's *Detour* (1945) or Jules Dassin's *Night and the City* (1950).

The Killing is a comic film, though it's not very funny: Kubrick doesn't enjoy absurdity the way Hitchcock does. The movie employs a complex recursive time scheme that forecasts Tarantino's *Pulp Fiction*, and, like many Kubrick films, a voiceover. In *Killer's Kiss* the longed-for escape from the urban trap actually took place, but in *The Killing*, Kubrick obeys the laws of his chosen genre. In noir the quest for freedom must fail, and irony rules.

The Killing ends with a flat hopelessness. The money has just blown across the airport runway. "Johnny, you've got to run," Fay says to him. "Ah, what's the difference," he groans. Two cops wait for him, symmetrically framing the screen, the caryatids of Johnny's commonplace doom. There they are with guns drawn facing Johnny, and facing you, the viewer. Then comes the signature: "A Harris-Kubrick Production."

2

Keep Doing It Until It Is Right:
Paths of Glory, Spartacus, Lolita

"ENOUGH OF WAR FILMS. They're death at the box office. Poison," said MGM's head of production, Dore Schary, to the twenty-seven-year-old Kubrick in 1956.[1] Kubrick and Jimmy Harris were trying to get MGM interested in making *Paths of Glory*, Humphrey Cobb's 1935 novel about the French army in World War I. *Paths of Glory* was one of the few books that Kubrick had read during high school. He devoured Cobb's saga sitting in his father's waiting room while Jack Kubrick saw his patients. Kubrick wasn't drafted during the Korean conflict because he was married, but Harris was a vet, and now the two wanted to make a movie about war.

Schary wasn't biting. He had been on the hook at MGM for the box office failure of John Huston's *The Red Badge of Courage* (1951), and he wasn't going to make the same mistake twice. War movies were verboten in Schary's lexicon, but he was impressed by *The Killing*. Though the movie had flopped, losing the hefty sum of $130,000 for United Artists, it made several reviewers' top ten lists. So Schary told Harris and Kubrick, "We have a room full of properties we own. There must be something in there you boys want to do."[2]

Kubrick and Harris were now under contract at MGM, thanks to Schary, and they had forty weeks to produce a feature film. They started rifling through MGM's junk heap of old novels and screenplays. When they got bleary-eyed from long hours of reading, they would play ping-pong or watch a movie in one of the studio's screening rooms.

One day Kubrick found a gem: *Burning Secret* (1911) by Stefan Zweig, the Austrian Jewish writer who committed suicide in Brazil in 1942 after fleeing the Nazis. ("We talked a lot about two writers, Arthur Schnitzler and Stefan Zweig," Harris remembered.)[3] *Burning Secret* tells the story of a beautiful Jewish woman who goes on vacation with her twelve-year-old son while her husband remains back at home in the city. A baron staying at their hotel seduces the mother, and the boy eventually discovers the secret affair. Shocking, subtle, and above all suspenseful, Zweig's novella is perfect movie material. (In fact, it had already been filmed twice in Germany, in 1923 and 1933, and would be made again by Kubrick's assistant Andrew Birkin in 1988.)

In the end, Kubrick never made *Burning Secret*. MGM canceled Dore Schary's contract in 1957 when his latest pictures turned out to be big losers. When MGM found out that Harris and Kubrick were working on not just the Zweig script but also *Paths of Glory*, they too were fired, for breach of contract.

Kubrick enlisted Calder Willingham, the prickly, talented southern novelist, to write the *Burning Secret* screenplay with him, and they seem to have worked on it for the better part of a year. The script was thought to be lost, but a copy of the script, dated November 1956, recently turned up in Gerald Fried's archives. Kubrick did with *Burning Secret* what he did four decades later with Schnitzler's *Dream Story*, the basis for *Eyes Wide Shut:* he relocated it to America and removed nearly all traces of Jewishness, much as Arthur Miller removed Jewishness from *Death of a Salesman.* (There is a fleeting glimpse of a knish bakery in *Eyes Wide Shut*, but that's about it.) "He takes a Jewish story and turns them all into goys," as Kubrick scholar Nathan Abrams puts it.[4] The married woman is no longer a voluptuous Jewish beauty but a 1950s American housewife named Virginia. Her husband is called Roy, her son Eddy, and the baron becomes a distinctly nonaristocratic seducer named Richard. The hotel is in the Appalachian Mountains.

"Some of the *Burning Secret* dialogue seems to have found its way into *Eyes Wide Shut*," Abrams reports. "Not word for word, but the essence: the seducer makes the same pro-adultery arguments that Sandor does"—the handsome Hungarian that Nicole Kidman dances with in *Eyes Wide Shut*, in a spellbinding scene straight out of Max Ophüls's *The Earrings of Madame de* . . . (1953).

Burning Secret is one of a long list of unmade Kubrick films. The Kubrick archives contain his script taken from Nabokov's novel *Laughter in the Dark* (1932), along with a World War II drama, *The German Lieutenant*, about a last-ditch German mission behind enemy lines (written with a former paratrooper, Richard Adams). There is also *I Stole Sixteen Million Dollars*, based on the 1955 memoir by Baptist-minister-turned-bankrobber Herbert Wilson. Kubrick wanted to make a movie from H. Rider Haggard's hoary Viking epic *Eric Brighteyes* (1890), a book he loved deeply. And he planned to make Zweig's stunning *Chess Story* (1941), which might have been the first great film about chess, given Kubrick's passion for the game.[5]

Zweig's *Burning Secret* resembles King's *The Shining* (1977) and Louis Begley's novel *Wartime Lies* (1991), the basis for *The Aryan Papers*, another movie Kubrick never made. In all of these a child decodes the dangerous adult world, then takes on the responsibility of a grown-up. Here is a key to the Kubrick universe. His films have the aura of the kid who has spent his time thinking and tinkering, trying to get things exactly right—a skill you need in both chess and photography. But when the grown-up world looms and boyhood hobbies yield their place to the facts of life, which include not just sex (as in *Lolita*, another movie about a child) but war and mass death, then you grow up fast.

If Stanley Kubrick had made only *Fear and Desire*, *Killer's Kiss*, and *The Killing*, he would be known as a minor noir director, less significant than Jacques Tourneur or Jules Dassin, but interesting nonetheless. With *Paths of Glory* (1957), his next movie, Kubrick vaults into the pantheon. *Paths of Glory* is sometimes called an antiwar movie, but war is merely the setting for the director's inquiry into what men do for success and power. The film mostly shies away from battlefield gore, unlike Hollywood's most famous World War I movie, Lewis Milestone's *All Quiet on the Western Front* (1930). Kubrick's battlefield scenes are lucidly designed, and—a rare thing in a war movie—they convey clarity, not chaos, as critic Gary Giddins notes.[6]

Like *The Killing*, *Paths of Glory* deals with plotters. Here the plot requires sending masses of men to their deaths. At the beginning of the film, General Broulard, played to polished, insidious perfection by Adolphe Menjou, entices another general, Mireau (George Macready) to try to take the Anthill, the Germans' bastion. The attack is clearly futile: everyone knows the French soldiers will simply die in no-man's-land. Colonel Dax, played by Kirk Douglas, protests that the assault on the Anthill is useless, but he goes along with it.

Dax's men, pinned down by enemy fire, don't even make it out of the trenches. And so Mireau demands that some of Dax's soldiers be executed for cowardice. Three are chosen: the eccentric Private Ferol (Timothy Carey), Corporal Paris (Ralph

Meeker), and Private Arnaud (Joseph Turkel). The long, drawn-out scene in which the three men face the firing squad is one of Hollywood's most wrenching depictions of capital punishment, comparable to the gas chamber death of Susan Hayward in Robert Wise's *I Want to Live* (released a year after Kubrick's film, in 1958).

Paths of Glory had greater star power than *The Killing*, since Kirk Douglas played the hero. Douglas, much more expensive than Hayden (he was to earn $350,000 on *Paths of Glory*), was fresh from Vincente Minnelli's *Lust for Life* (1956), which had done poorly at the box office despite critical plaudits. But Douglas had a long track record as a moneymaker. In early 1957, Douglas told Harris and Kubrick that he was ready to start on *Paths of Glory* if they agreed to make a deal with his company, Bryna Productions (named after Douglas's mother, so that he could put her name in lights). Harris remembered that Douglas's agent, Ray Stark, "killed us with that deal. He just *buried* us. He was a tough agent and we were desperate."[7] Harris and Kubrick agreed to make five pictures with Bryna.

United Artists didn't want *Paths of Glory*. The studio predicted correctly that a downbeat movie about corrupt generals would do badly at the box office, and also that it would be banned in France. But Douglas was a shrewd negotiator. He pushed through *Paths of Glory* by threatening to pull out of another project, *The Vikings*, which promised to be (and was) a commercial juggernaut for UA.

Gerald Fried, whom Kubrick had known since high school, wrote the music for *Paths of Glory*, as he had for Kubrick's three earlier features. Fried's score is superb, with tense bouts of percussion punctuating the battlefield forays. The film's director of photography was Georg Krause, who had worked with Elia Kazan, but Kubrick told Krause exactly what to do, as he had told Lucien Ballard, his cinematographer on *The Killing*. In fact, Kubrick operated the handheld camera himself, here used for Douglas's unsteady-looking crawl across no-man's-land. In his later movies, too, Kubrick always reserved for himself the handheld camera sequences, with their rough, jostling feel.

Kubrick once again enlisted the oddball character actor Timothy Carey, who shot the racehorse in *The Killing*. Carey returns in *Paths of Glory* as one of the three condemned men. In all his roles, Carey gives off a slightly psychotic vibe. He enraged Douglas, and frustrated Kubrick, by indulging in offbeat improvisations. The scene where Carey rips apart his last meal, a duck dinner, required five hours, sixty-four takes, and eighteen ducks. But in the end Carey succeeded brilliantly. He steals the show with his slobbering, sobbing breakdown as he staggers toward the firing squad, leaning on the shoulder of a priest (Emile Meyer, who usually played thugs). "You better make this good, Kirk Douglas doesn't like it," Kubrick shrewdly said to Carey before he filmed the scene, and the strategy worked.[8]

Paths of Glory was filmed in Geiselgasteig studios, near Munich. This was Douglas's shrewd idea. Germany was an inexpensive place to make a movie in 1956, and Schloss Schleissheim, the vast château where the generals confer, was near the studio.

Like most war films, *Paths of Glory* needed a swarm of extras. Kubrick hired six hundred German policemen to play the French soldiers. When the director told them to move slowly and with great difficulty through no-man's-land, they shared a joke: oh, we get it, he wants us to advance like Frenchmen!

Kubrick took a month to prepare *Paths of Glory*'s battlefield, and he was meticulous about the special effects. Erwin Lange, an old hand from UFA, the German film studio, designed explosions that would cast up torrents of debris and shrapnel, rather than the clouds of dust usually seen in Hollywood war movies.

In Geiselgasteig, Kubrick said, "I found the last sad remnants of a great filmmaker": the "cracked and peeling" sets of

Lola Montès (1955), Max Ophüls's final movie. Ophüls, who was famous for his elaborate tracking shots and the sophisticated continental mood of his films, was Kubrick's favorite filmmaker, he said in an interview just after *Paths of Glory*. He confessed he had seen Ophüls's *Le Plaisir* (1952) "countless times."[9] On March 26, 1956, the day Ophüls died, Kubrick dedicated a key shot to his memory: the camera tracks in an Ophüls-like intricate curling web around Mireau and Broulard, who are chatting in the sumptuous castle that is army headquarters. This is the movie's first scene, our introduction to the two generals, and Kubrick's sinuous camera reflects their Machiavellian maneuvering.

The romantic, humane cynic Ophüls would have given his officers an air of old-world aristocracy. In Kubrick's hands their dignity is too brisk to be impressive. Efficient and self-centered, Broulard and Mireau rule over a world in which ordinary men die en masse so that a general can score a promotion. Everything they do is a calculated dance, a self-serving game.

Paths of Glory gives war a stark, ascetic look. We never see the enemy, and there are no soldiers croaking out dying words. In an early scene, the battlefield is empty like the dark side of the moon, scarred by shrapnel and craters. The château seems equally cavernous and soulless, and the trenches lined with soldiers transmit quiet dread.

While Broulard and Mireau confer in their palatial headquarters, the camera winds around them, but when Dax strides through the trenches, it tracks boldly forward with him. (Jack in *The Shining*'s snowy maze will also get this "Don Juan" shot: the camera is in front of the actor looking back at him, and both are moving forward.) Kubrick, usually a stickler for such details, departed from historical fact and widened the trenches to six feet so that the camera dolly could fit.

Douglas's Dax is straightforward, square-jawed, and solidly virtuous. When he leads the attack through no-man's-land, the camera follows him in a steady tracking shot, threading past wounded soldiers. His outrage about the battle plan, like his later ardent defense of the three soldiers in a military trial, allows Douglas to proclaim his liberal ideals. He must have insisted on Dax's righteousness much as he demanded—so the rumor goes—that his character had to appear shirtless in at least one scene (an early one, washing up in his quarters). Douglas thrusts and struts, gritting his teeth with frustrated heroism, in contrast to the serpentine Macready and Menjou, who specialize in hooded glances and suave insinuations.

Menjou and Macready are both exceptionally fine, never overplaying and never making their brand of corrupt evil seem too refined. Douglas, by contrast, overdoes it at times, as when he lets loose his fury at Broulard and calls him "a degenerate, sadistic old man." Dax's parting shot, "I pity you," spoken from the heights of his moral superiority, misfires badly. Broulard in his own eyes is simply doing what generals do. After the execution he remarks, "The men died wonderfully"—for him it's all an admirable spectacle. When Broulard realizes that Dax is not angling for a promotion by denouncing Mireau, but is instead genuinely indignant, he calls him an "idiot." Gary Giddins remarks that in this scene the superb Menjou sounds "neither verbose nor practiced": he is utterly genuine, and utterly corrupt.[10] Broulard wins this one: this is his world and his war.

Kubrick's practicality and shrewdness were evident in his dealings with the prickly Menjou. Kubrick had to trick Menjou to get him to appear in *Paths of Glory*. He told him that he would have the starring role and that Broulard was a "good general who does his best." There was friction between the two on the set as well. One day Menjou, frustrated by the number of takes Kubrick wanted, threw a temper tantrum and told the twenty-nine-year-old director that he lacked experience "in the art of directing actors." Calmly and quietly as usual, Kubrick said to Menjou, "It isn't right, and we are going to keep doing

Kubrick on the set of *Paths of Glory*, possibly with Adolphe Menjou
in the foreground (Courtesy of Photofest/Warner Bros)

it until it is right, because you guys are good.'"[11] There's a
touch of boyish naïveté here that the young tyro Kubrick used
to his advantage: "You guys are good," said to a seasoned star
like Menjou!

Kubrick cleverly managed not only Menjou, but also his
star, Douglas. Kubrick had to be quite adroit in both serving
Douglas's wish to be the courageous hero of *Paths of Glory* and
betraying him by suggesting an ironic frame around the story:
the ironist is Menjou's Broulard, who presages that later powerful cynic Ziegler in *Eyes Wide Shut*. Douglas loved the finished
film nevertheless.

At the end of *Paths of Glory* we learn that Dax's men will
return to the front. Everything will be futile as before; the executed soldiers are in the end forgettable, like all the war dead.
In every meaningful way Dax has lost. Kubrick refused to grant

Douglas his catharsis, the victory of humane ideals over the sinister higher-ups who oppress the common man. The oppressors, Mireau and Broulard, fit into the Kubrick universe, while Dax remains a naïve outlier.

This no-exit ending saves *Paths of Glory* from Stanley Krameresque liberal piety, along with the futility of Dax's leading his men to slaughter on the Anthill, even though he knows full well that the battle cannot be won. The casual viewer will identify with Dax's high-handed denunciations, not quite realizing that he serves the war machine just as Mireau and Broulard do. But Kubrick still drives his point home: because the war requires enormous bloodshed for minute or merely symbolic gains, all soldiers are expendable.

During the final minutes of *Paths of Glory*, a captive German girl is forced to sing in front of a group of French soldiers at an inn. The innkeeper pushes her on stage, bewildered and helpless. At first the soldiers taunt her, but she quickly reduces them to tears with her song.

Christiane Harlan, listed in the credits under her stage name Suzanne Christian, plays the girl. With her short blond hair and sympathetic dark eyes, she is frightened yet also comforting. The catharsis that Kubrick denies us with the terrifying execution of the three soldiers he gives us in the song, the poignant "Der Treue Hussar" (The loyal hussar), an old German favorite chosen by Harlan. (Louis Armstrong sang it in English on *The Ed Sullivan Show* in 1956.) Harlan is both girlish and maternal, and as the only woman in the movie, she voices the sorrow that the men cannot themselves express.

Jimmy Harris remembered how Kubrick invented this final scene. "You know, the picture needs something more at the end," he mused to Harris. "How about a German girl forced to sing a song?" "You're gonna turn this into a musical?" the surprised Harris responded. "Anyway, how do we find the girl?" "I have just the right person," Kubrick answered with a little smile.

"Oh God, Stanley, oh no, how could you possibly suggest a girlfriend," Harris exploded. "Okay, let's shoot the scene, and if you don't like it, we won't use it," Kubrick coolly said.[12] As it turned out, Harris was as moved as everyone else when the scene was shot, and it stayed in the picture.

Harlan was in fact Kubrick's girlfriend, just as Harris guessed. Kubrick first saw her one night on German television and was bowled over. A few days later he went to see her perform at the Kammerspiel theater in Munich. Fascinated, he then sought her out at a Red Cross benefit during Fasching, Munich's rowdy carnival season. "He was not exactly a drunken ball person," Harlan remembered: Kubrick was the only one there without a costume. "At a German carnival you get real retro drunks, the lowest of the low. There was a river of pee. He felt very scared. Stanley never forgot it."[13]

The carnival tumult might have reminded Kubrick of Ophüls's *Le Plaisir*, which features an uproarious masked ball filmed with stunning, swift fluency. There, a dancer boldly kicks up his legs, then faints and is revealed to be an old man who cannot keep up the youthful pace. Kubrick, led by his desire for Harlan, was a different kind of outsider at the revelry. Like the unmasked Bill Harford in the orgy scene of *Eyes Wide Shut*, Kubrick felt out of place and endangered in Munich.

Before her scene was filmed, Harlan was already living with Kubrick. Early the next year, 1958, she became his third wife. Stanley and Christiane stayed with each other for more than forty years, until the end of his life.

Harlan had one notorious relative, her uncle Veit Harlan, director of *Jud Süss* (1940), one of the Nazis' most famous propaganda films. "Stanley and I came from such different, such grotesquely opposite backgrounds," Christiane told an interviewer. "I think it gave us an extra something. I had an appalling, catastrophic background for someone like Stanley. . . . For me, my uncle was great fun. He and my father planned to join the circus. They were acrobats. They threw me around. It was a complete clown's world. Nobody can imagine that you can know someone who was so guilty so intimately—and yet not know."[14]

Kubrick briefly considered making a movie about Veit Harlan and *Jud Süss*, a striking way of managing the disturbing fact that Christiane was connected, via her uncle, to the evil of Nazism. Without telling his wife, Kubrick also began a script about a ten-year-old German girl, similar in age to Christiane during the war, who sees Jews hunted by the Nazis. ("I was the little girl who moved in where Anne Frank was pushed out," Christiane told an interviewer many years later.)[15]

Kubrick enjoyed Germany, Christiane remembered, though he was anxious about being there as a Jew so soon after the war. He especially liked her relatives, "a noisy, well-dressed crowd," most of them theater and film people. (Her parents were both opera singers.) "They were showboats, and they looked and acted it, and I was a little embarrassed," she recalled. "Stanley liked them because they were fun, real fun—my film star auntie was a Swede [Kristina Söderbaum], and boy could she drink you under the table, and she was a sweetie—he got on with her, and she sort of introduced him to everybody." Christiane adds that Kubrick was glad that his future wife "wasn't really that kind of person, I wasn't a dance on the table type."[16]

When I talked to her in England in the summer of 2018, surrounded by her paintings, Christiane, at age eighty-six, was still the woman Stanley Kubrick had fallen in love with. She is a warm, witty, fast-talking storyteller with perfect comic timing, whose mordant sensibility matched Kubrick's own.

In late 1957 Kubrick returned from Germany to Los Angeles with Harlan and her three-year-old daughter Katharina from her previous marriage. "We both had been miserably married and decided never to marry again, we were all bitter and twisted," Christiane said. "And then we married immediately, so it must be love."[17] (Stanley and Christiane married on April 14, 1958, in Las Vegas, though it wasn't until 1961 that New York State issued his divorce decree from Ruth Sobotka.) In LA Christiane studied painting, drawing, and English at UCLA. She had always seen herself as an artist, despite her acting career, and after *Paths of Glory* she never acted again. But her paintings play a significant role in several Kubrick movies, including *A Clockwork Orange* and *Eyes Wide Shut*.

After *Paths of Glory* "we were penniless in Beverly Hills," Christiane recalled. Kubrick's mother, Gert, who was "up on films," was still buying his clothes. Before *Spartacus*, Kubrick made money playing poker. "I was a nervous wreck, I thought oh God I've landed in the Wild West, my husband makes money from poker to put dinner on the table."[18] Kubrick insisted that his cardplaying buddies, who included Martin Ritt, Calder Willingham, and Everett Sloane as well as Jimmy Harris and Vince Edwards, read Herbert Yardley's *Education of a Poker Player*, a piquant autobiography containing much clever advice and some very exact probability tables. Kubrick made his poker gang write down the probability tables on notecards.

Meanwhile, Kubrick was having a dry spell with the studios. He told Michael Herr years later that "the way the studios were run in the fifties made him think of Clemenceau's remark about the Allies winning World War I because our generals were marginally less stupid than their generals."[19] By the end of the decade Kubrick would carve out substantial independence from the studio system, but first he had to prove he could make money for them.

Paths of Glory opened on Christmas Day, 1957. Bosley Crowther of the *New York Times* panned it, but his dislike of the movie was nothing compared to that of the French government, which banned it until 1974. The French seem to have been particularly incensed by Gerald Fried's use of the Marseillaise in his score. In the British sector of Berlin, French soldiers disrupted the screening by throwing stink bombs. Even worse, the Berlin Film Festival buckled to French pressure and refused to show *Paths of Glory*. Like *The Killing*, *Paths of Glory* failed to turn a profit.

Just when his finances were in a deep hole, the twenty-nine-year-old Kubrick attracted the notice of one of Hollywood's top moneymaking stars, Marlon Brando. At the time Brando was under contract with Paramount for a western written by the young Sam Peckinpah, who had adapted Charles Neider's novel about Billy the Kid and Pat Garrett. Brando would play Billy, of course. Now he just needed actors and a director. Brando had liked *The Killing*, and early in 1958, after *Paths of Glory*, he pitched the western to Kubrick, who was quickly sold on the idea.

Kirk Douglas generously agreed to let Kubrick work with Brando, despite the director's deal with Bryna. The risk for Kubrick was that, Brando being Brando, the star rather than the director would be running the show. But Brando's box office magic would make it worthwhile, or so Kubrick thought.

Unfortunately, *One-Eyed Jacks*, as Brando called his western, hit a long series of snags. Kubrick hated Peckinpah's script, and he persuaded Brando to bring in his old screenwriting partner Calder Willingham to revise it. The story conferences dragged on through the summer of 1958, moving to Brando's home on Mulholland Drive after his wife left him in September. The stone-faced Brando, who clearly wanted more sway over the script, sat cross-legged on the floor and banged an enormous Chinese gong to cut off arguments.

In a letter Willingham wrote to Kubrick the following year, he recalled the miserable boredom of poker games with Brando and added that he still resented Kubrick's playing along with the star's ideas.[20] The tedious routine of cards and talk finally ended in November, when Brando made it clear that he had no more use for Kubrick. Brando now wanted to direct *One-Eyed*

Jacks himself. Meanwhile, he had hired Karl Malden for the movie for a staggering $400,000, and his shooting budget would be even more extravagant. *One-Eyed Jacks* nearly drowned in an ocean of red ink, but it eventually came out in 1961, and put the kibosh on Brando's fledgling directorial career. Twelve years later, Peckinpah returned to his script and made what is probably his greatest movie, *Pat Garrett and Billy the Kid*.

"I was just sort of playing wingman for Brando while he directed a movie," Kubrick recalled about the *One-Eyed Jacks* script sessions.[21] Meanwhile, Kubrick hadn't made a movie in almost two years. But that was about to change. In February 1958, while he was still tangled up with Brando, Kubrick got an unexpected phone call from Kirk Douglas.

Douglas was playing the gladiator Spartacus, leader of the failed slave revolt that shook Rome. He had bought the story from Howard Fast, author of the novel *Spartacus* (1951), and he was using the blacklisted Dalton Trumbo as his scriptwriter. Universal had insisted on Anthony Mann as director, but after a week and a half on the set, it was clear to Douglas that Mann wasn't working out. Mann had made the mistake of criticizing Douglas's acting. He told Douglas he was wrong to play Spartacus at the beginning of the film as a "Neanderthal" and an "idiot."[22] So Mann had to go, and Douglas instantly thought of Kubrick as his replacement.

Douglas reached Kubrick in the middle of a weekend poker game and told him he'd have to start in twenty-four hours, early Monday morning. Fast's *Spartacus* was already one of Kubrick's favorite novels, so he didn't hesitate.[23] But directing a full-scale sword-and-sandals epic was something new for Kubrick.

After *Spartacus* came out, a journalist asked Kubrick whether it had been exciting to work with such a distinguished cast, which included, along with Douglas, Laurence Olivier, Charles Laughton, Peter Ustinov, Tony Curtis, and Jean Simmons. Kubrick gave a sardonic wince: "Oh yes, I was given a beautiful dinner and a gold plate, you know."[24] Making the film was no party. The select club of actors that Douglas had assembled feuded constantly. When the bisexual Olivier wasn't flirting with Tony Curtis, he was telling Laughton how to read his lines, and since Laughton was being paid only $41,000 to Olivier's $250,000, Olivier's advice stung.

For the first time in his career, Kubrick felt outranked by the eminences surrounding him. One day on the set he feared that his actors Olivier and Laughton were whispering together about him, only to discover that they were running their lines. Kubrick stayed in control of the picture, yet he faced more challenges to his authority on *Spartacus* than ever before.

Kubrick had trouble with the Hollywood veteran Russell Metty, his cinematographer. Metty wasn't used to a director looking over his shoulder, insisting on a particular lens or camera angle. While Kubrick gazed through the camera, Metty made fun of the youngster by crouching behind him and pretending to peer through his Zippo lighter as if it were a viewfinder. Notoriously, Metty at one point growled over his coffee cup of Jack Daniel's, "Get that little Jew-boy from the Bronx off my crane."[25] But Kubrick, just thirty years old and looking even younger, kept his cool, and continued telling Metty what to do. *Spartacus's* camerawork is rhythmic and artful, especially in the gladiatorial battles, and this is Kubrick's achievement more than Metty's.

Kubrick may have sidelined Metty, but he relied heavily on Saul Bass, who storyboarded the final battle and designed the gladiatorial school for *Spartacus*. Bass, known for his title sequences for Hitchcock movies, was a brilliant designer who favored geometric formations for the Roman armies. Bass came up with the inspired idea of having the slave armies roll burning logs at Crassus's Romans.

The stolid, wholehearted epic feel of *Spartacus* mostly rules out Kubrick's characteristic pessimism and black humor. But at times it does look like a Kubrick movie. When Crassus (Olivier) tries to seduce the slave Antoninus (Curtis) with a double entendre about liking both snails and oysters (a scene that Universal, fearing the censors' disapproval, cut from the U.S. release), Kubrick shows the two men from a distance. He told Ginna, "The whole thing is shot in a long shot through a kind of filmy curtain which covers his bathtub, and the figures are only about half the height of the screen. And by doing this, I think we achieve the effect of somebody [the viewer] sort of eavesdropping from the next room."[26]

The scene ends in a sharply pointed way. While Crassus gives a speech about the obligation to submit to eternal Rome, we realize that he is talking to himself: Antoninus has left to join the slave revolt. Kubrick's devastating ironic touch is visible here as in few other places in the movie.

Kubrick also brought out superb acting in a scene between Douglas and Woody Strode, who played the Ethiopian slave Draba. The two men are waiting to fight to the death in front of Crassus and his entourage. In a silent and excruciatingly tense sequence, the camera alternates close-ups between them, shot-reverse-shot. Draba gives Douglas a cold, threatening smile, but then spares him during their battle. Instead of telling Strode what to do in the scene, Kubrick played Prokofiev for him, and the music helped Strode conjure up the Ethiopian gladiator's monumental dignity. Kubrick sometimes liked to play music for his actors to guide them into a scene: it was, he said, "a device used, you know, by silent film actors—they all had their own violinists, who would play for them during the takes."[27]

Spartacus was "the only film I wasn't happy with," Kubrick told the interviewer Danielle Heymann. "First of all I told Kirk, when he showed me the script, what I felt was not right about it, and he said, 'Yes, yes, yes, you are so right,' but nothing ever changed." Swayed by Trumbo, Douglas didn't in the end "change any of the things that were dumb."[28] At one point Douglas took Kubrick to see his psychoanalyst so he could better understand the star's inner life. But that didn't reduce their sparring over the film.

Douglas wanted a robust, plainly heroic *Spartacus*. In a letter to Stan Margulies, then a Bryna production aide, Douglas worried that Spartacus suffered too much in the script as it stood: his "joylessness" was a problem. "I think perhaps we err when we make Spartacus almost too-human with his doubts and fears," Douglas added. Spartacus was doing too much "counterpunch[ing]," Douglas thought, and he worried that the hero wouldn't "bring the crowd to its feet with a roar." Douglas summed up: "Spartacus, I am trying to say, must personally convince the audience that this rebellion is good. . . . Merely to start the ball rolling, and to roll it as far as one man has power to roll it, is resounding, stimulating and joyful."[29]

Douglas didn't get his way entirely. Kubrick's own downbeat sense of Spartacus as headed for failure is a key element in the movie. Spartacus is not really a joyful rebel. Though he glows with genial satisfaction when he gazes at the men and women he is leading, he is more often grim than exuberant. The slaves celebrate no victories, instead losing all their battles against Rome, and the revolt is continually shadowed by the defeat we know will happen in the end.[30]

Kubrick wanted Spartacus to be plagued by misgivings about the human costs of revolt, as he is in Arthur Koestler's novel *The Gladiators* (1939), which he read during production. Ustinov supported Kubrick's idea of a complex, doubt-stricken Spartacus. In a letter he wrote to Kubrick sometime during the production, Ustinov bluntly disagreed with Douglas's plan to simplify the movie's hero. He complained that Spartacus's "doubts, his bewilderments have been sacrificed [*sic*] for the sake of activity, of crisp decision. Nothing is more boring theatrically than the man who knows what he wants and gets it."[31] Ustinov's letter surely reminded the director that in a Kubrick movie the hero is nearly always confused, whereas Spartacus seems unusually clear-minded.

Ustinov also told Kubrick that the film should focus on the corrupt, labyrinthine nature of Roman politics, instead of portraying Rome as "proud . . . majestic and intractable." (Kubrick, who was reading Sallust and Plutarch during shooting, must have agreed.) The film's picture of political intrigue wasn't working, Ustinov argued, because the Roman factions were "plot[ting] in platitudes." Crassus was a disappointment to Ustinov because "his desire to understand Spartacus seems to have become fretful and constipated rather than mysterious and troubling, as it once was."

The corruption that Ustinov attributes to Rome often appears when Kubrick depicts the world of the powerful, as in *Paths of Glory*, *Dr. Strangelove*, *A Clockwork Orange*, *Barry Lyndon*, and *Full Metal Jacket*. So Kubrick must have been sympathetic to Ustinov's point of view. But *Spartacus* turned out much simpler than Ustinov wanted. The hero is not plagued by doubts, and his chief Roman antagonist, Crassus, instead of being an intriguing and repellent man of power like Broulard in *Paths of Glory*, merely spouts shallow conservative clichés about Rome's eternal greatness. In a misplaced topical twist, Trumbo made Crassus at the end into a McCarthy-like figure, hunting "enemies of the state" and crowing, "Lists of the disloyal have been compiled."

Kubrick, an adept handler of actors, was put to the test on the *Spartacus* set. In addition to battling with Douglas, he also had to soothe a very discontented Olivier. In June, Kubrick wrote to Olivier apologizing for not being able to come by for a farewell drink after the end of shooting. "I hope that when you see the finished film," Kubrick wrote, "you will be less disturbed about certain things than [you] are now. In any case, I should like to thank you for the decent way you behaved about the things with which you were in such disagreement."[32]

Spartacus at times displays a wholesome, populist tinge utterly uncharacteristic of Kubrick. Pauline Kael described *Spartacus*'s slaves as "a giant kibbutz on the move," and so they are, with toddlers playing, men roasting meat, women weaving, and all caring for each other, a heartfelt antidote to Roman cruelty and decadence.[33] This antihistorical hokum, supplied by Trumbo and Douglas, could not have been pleasing to Kubrick's gimlet eye.

Kubrick could not subtly express irony at the hero's expense in *Spartacus* as he had done in *Paths of Glory*. But he did bristle at one key crowd-pleaser. Kubrick disliked the movie's most famous moment, the "I am Spartacus" scene, when Spartacus's fellow slaves conceal his identity from the Romans by each declaring himself the man sought.

The movie's final scene does look like genuine Kubrick. Spartacus and his rebellious slaves hang from crucifixes as far the eye can see. Varinia (Jean Simmons) shows her husband their baby and tells him, "This is your son. He is free, Spartacus, he is free, he is free." Now comes what might be the film's best moment: the tortured Spartacus, nailed to his cross, says nothing. Spartacus refuses the Hollywood ending that Varinia asks for. Rather than agreeing that his quest for freedom lives on in his child, he remains locked in the pain of defeat.

Kubrick had just become a father when he filmed this scene. Anya, Stanley's first child with Christiane, was born on April 1, 1959 (another daughter, Vivian, arrived the following August, a few months before *Spartacus* was released). Kubrick remembered standing outside the hospital room wondering, "'What am I doing here?' and then you go in and look down at the face of your child and—zap!—the most ancient programming takes over and your response is one of wonder and joy and pride."[34] The dying Spartacus, another new father, has a despairing response instead. Kubrick was careful to cordon off his personal feeling about paternity from the finale of his movie.

While editing *Spartacus*, Kubrick, relieved that shooting was over, let off steam by making mild mischief. "Stanley used to draw all kinds of porno pictures on my shoes," said editor Robert Lawrence.[35] During breaks he played stickball in the Universal New York Street stage set, and in the editing room he liked to bounce a tennis ball against the wall, like Jack in *The Shining*.

Kubrick and his crew spent nine months of postproduction work on the sound for *Spartacus*. Kubrick was meticulous about the sound effects, demanding that each sound be "panned," or placed, precisely right. Recording engineer Don Rogers remembered, "Every footstep, every bang, every crash . . . it took hundreds of hours to pan that stuff—it was incredible."[36] The work took place during the wee hours of the night, starting at 7 PM, with Kubrick arriving about 11 PM and the sound team breaking for lunch at 2 AM.

When *Spartacus* premiered in October 1960, the gossip columnist Hedda Hopper complained that the movie was "written by a Commie," but she had little effect on ticket sales. One night President Kennedy even snuck out of the White House in the middle of a snowstorm to see it, as part of a pitch for keeping movie productions in the United States.

Spartacus was made in Technirama, a widescreen process that involved running 35mm film horizontally through the camera. The panoramic visual splendor of the film, along with its blockbuster-style emotional cheesiness, spelled box office success. The movie trotted out many of the well-worn Hollywood tropes: righteous indignation (a Kirk Douglas specialty), solidarity with the underdog, the tenderness of budding romance.

Spartacus made a mint for Universal. But Hollywood spectacular would never again be Kubrick's brand. His next project was by contrast a bold taboo breaker: Vladimir Nabokov's *Lolita*.

"How did they ever make a movie of *Lolita*?" the film's trailer asked when it came out in June 1962. It was a good question. Nabokov's shocking novel showcases a louche European, middle-aged Humbert Humbert, who preys on delectable prepubescent girls. Transplanted from Paris to Ramsdale, an American suburb, Humbert boards in the house of a chattering, self-absorbed widow named Charlotte Haze. Twelve-year-old Lolita, Charlotte's daughter, proves to be the perfect nymphet, and helpless Humbert targets her avidly. Charlotte falls in love with Humbert, marries him, and quickly dies in a freak accident, leaving Humbert free to have his affair with Lolita. After she disappears and leaves him crushed, Humbert tracks down his nemesis Clare Quilty, who stole Lolita from him. The novel ends (and Kubrick's film begins, in a flashback) when Humbert shoots Quilty.

Lolita was a succès de scandale in Paris and then in America, where it appeared in 1958. But it seemed far too controversial for Hollywood. It was, after all, a book full of sexual details, narrated by a charming antihero who glories in his affair with a twelve-year-old girl.

Harris and Kubrick bought the rights to *Lolita* in the fall of 1958 from Nabokov's agent, Irving "Swifty" Lazar. It wasn't cheap: Harris-Kubrick shelled out seventy-five thousand dollars for the first-year option on the book, and promised another seventy-five thousand for screen rights. To finance this purchase, Harris and Kubrick sold the rights to *The Killing* to United Artists. Meanwhile, Nabokov's novel had hit the *New York Times* best-seller list: it was number one by the end of September.

When Douglas heard that Harris and Kubrick were planning to film Nabokov's novel, he shrugged off their obligation to Bryna. Douglas was sure that *Lolita* would never get made because censors would stand in the way, so he let the two men buy out their end of the contract in exchange for Kubrick agreeing to direct *Spartacus*.

Nabokov turned down the offer to write the *Lolita* screenplay, so Kubrick enlisted Calder Willingham, who had first told him about the book. Unhappy with the result, Kubrick wrote cuttingly to his old scriptwriting partner, "I hate to sound like old Marlon but you seem entrenched in your style of having the actors say what the scene is about": Willingham, Kubrick charged, was "explain[ing] in dialog what should be acted out and left to the audience to discover."[37] Like every great film director, Kubrick wanted to tell stories in pictures rather than words, and he wanted his dialogue spare, even from the florid and eloquent Humbert. Willingham's response was lacerating. Reminding Kubrick that he had brought *Lolita* to his attention in the first place, an idea, he said, that would make the director a rich man for life, Willingham called him vengeful and ungrateful.[38]

With Willingham gone, Kubrick was relieved to learn that Nabokov had changed his mind and agreed to write the script But the producer Martin Russ was not so sure, asking Kubrick, "Has Nabokov written for films? Does he have a knowledge of films and cinematic construction? . . . Do you intend to teach Nabokov this cinematic outlook yourself? Will he be taught?"[39] Russ's doubts were well-founded: Nabokov's script reads more like a long, drawn-out riff on his novel than a conventional screenplay.

By the first day of March 1960 the novelist was already in Hollywood and at work on the screenplay, hunting butterflies in the morning and scribbling on his notecards in the afternoons. Meanwhile, Swifty Lazar introduced Nabokov and his wife, Vera, to some shining stars, including Marilyn Monroe and John Wayne. When Nabokov innocently asked Wayne, "And what do you do?" he answered humbly, "I'm in pictures."[40] "You couldn't make it. You couldn't *lift* it," Jimmy Harris said years later about the four hundred–page screenplay that Nabokov completed in June.[41] Kubrick warned the novelist that his script would make a seven-hour movie, so Nabokov delivered a shortened version in September.

In the end Kubrick so heavily revised Nabokov's script that it was hardly recognizable. This was a good thing. Nabokov's screenplay for *Lolita* begins with Humbert's dead mother ("picnic, lightning") rising into the clouds like Mary Poppins, holding a parasol. This kind of sardonic whimsy did not appeal to Kubrick. But he preferred not to tussle with the eminent author, so he kept his distance during Nabokov's stint in LA. In the end Kubrick gave Nabokov sole screenwriting credit for the picture, reasoning that reviewers would be less likely to accuse him of mutilating a modern classic if they thought that Nabokov himself was responsible for the gaps between novel and film.

When Nabokov saw *Lolita* a few days before its official release at the end of May 1962, he "discovered that Kubrick was a great director, that his *Lolita* was a first-rate film with magnificent actors, and that only ragged odds and ends of my script had been used." Still, Nabokov was delighted by some of the movie's inspirations, like the ping-pong match between Humbert and Quilty. But he watched the film with only "reluctant pleasure," annoyed by Kubrick's considerable departures from his screenplay.[42]

Casting *Lolita* took some time. David Niven wanted to play Humbert, but his agent vetoed the idea as too risqué. Another candidate was Laurence Olivier, who wrote to Kubrick in December 1959 that he couldn't see how Nabokov's "brilliant, original and witty descriptive powers" could be transferred to the screen.[43] But he still asked for a first look at any script. Then Olivier's agent, like Niven's, said no: playing Humbert would hurt his client's image. Finally, James Mason, who admired Nabokov's novel, agreed to take the part. Mason had a few years earlier given a heartbreaking performance in *A Star Is Born*, as a fading middle-aged man who ends up playing second fiddle to the young starlet he loves—not unlike the Lolita story as Kubrick tells it.

With Mason cast, Harris and Kubrick had no trouble finding a distributor: Associated Artists, headed by an old school pal, Kenneth Hyman, and Hyman's father, Eliot. (Warner Bros had wanted the film, but the studio demanded final say on creative decisions, which was too much for Kubrick to swallow.)

Harris and Kubrick decided to make the movie in England, where they could write off a substantial amount of the cost if 80 percent of the workers on *Lolita* were U.K. subjects. This was the start of Kubrick's artistic exile to Britain, where it was so much cheaper to make movies than LA or New York.

Now Kubrick had to find his Lolita. Harris had told Kubrick they might be able to get Brigitte Bardot for the role, but her over-the-top sexiness was not what the director ordered. Kubrick presented Tuesday Weld to Nabokov, who nixed her (he had enlisted Nabokov's help in casting the film). Then, in June 1960, Kubrick noticed a fourteen-year-old actress named Sue Lyon, who had appeared on TV and in commercials. "She was cool and non-giggly. . . . She was enigmatic without being dull," Kubrick remembered about Lyon's screen test. As for Nabokov, he was instantly convinced when he saw Lyon's picture: "No doubt about it; she is the one," he said.[44] Nabokov also gave the nod to Shelley Winters, Kubrick's choice for Charlotte Haze.

Lyon, who was accompanied by her mother to Elstree Studios, had a snappy wit both on and off the set. The Kubrick archives contain a funny letter from Lyon, who called herself

KEEP DOING IT UNTIL IT IS RIGHT

"Head Pupil" and offered Jimmy Harris the job of "superinten-
dent of Elstree School for Girls": "Your salary will be ten (10)
pieces of gum per week so you can cope with our excellent student body."[45]

Kubrick molded Lyon's performance. In some early notes
he wrote, "Lolita—moods of naivete and deception, charm and
vulgarity, blue sulks and rosy mirth, disorganized boredom,
intense, sprawling, droopy, dopey-eyed, goofing off—diffused
dreaming in a boyish hoodlum way." Later on he added that she
should have "a certain quality of hardness," "sulky, tentative and
cagey." She was to be "a willowy, angular, ballet school type,"
"enigmatic, intriguing, indifferent and American."[46] Under Kubrick's guidance, Lyon came to embody the multifaceted, sour-
sweet American Lolita that the director envisioned in his notes.

Kubrick's most brilliant stroke was picking Peter Sellers to
play Quilty, turning Humbert's nemesis into a major presence
in the film. Kubrick was a fan of Sellers, then a rising comedian
and film star, as well as a British citizen, which made him ideal
for the movie because of the United Kingdom's 80 percent
rule. Egged on by Kubrick, Sellers injected a manic nervous
energy into his role to counterpoint the rather slow-moving
Humbert.

Kubrick saw Quilty as a mystery. Quilty's presence in the
story "should give us a kind of 'Maltese Falcon,' what's-going-
on type of suspense," Kubrick wrote to Peter Ustinov, who had
become friends with the director during *Spartacus*. "Every time
we catch a glimpse of Quilty we can imagine anything, police,
pervert or parent."[47]

Kubrick started Sellers rolling by scripting much of the
movie's first scene, the flashback in which Humbert kills Quilty.
"I am Spartacus," Quilty, togaed in a bedsheet, tells Humbert.
"Hey, you come to free the slaves or somethin' "? Elsewhere he
relied heavily on Sellers's miraculous gift for improvisation.
"He was the only actor I knew who could really improvise,"

Kubrick said later, adding that Sellers "is receptive to comic ideas most of his contemporaries would think unfunny and meaningless."[48]

When we meet Quilty at the beginning of *Lolita*, Humbert has tracked the villain to his baroque lair and is about to shoot him. This is the end of Humbert's story: Jimmy Harris claimed it was his idea to put it at the start of the movie, for a noirish touch. In this opening scene, Humbert stares down Quilty's madcap performance. He gives him a cold appraising look, the look, he thinks, of judgment, as he tells Quilty he's going to die very soon. But Humbert, unlike Lolita, cannot master a withering stare, and Quilty continues bopping through his nutty shtick. The doomed Quilty has Humbert's number, allying him with his own perversion (he makes arty porno movies, we learn in the novel): "To attend executions, how would you like that?" he asks Humbert. "Just you there, nobody else. Just watching, watching. You like watching, Captain?"

The enigmatic Quilty that Kubrick and Sellers invented is cool as a cucumber, and hipper than anyone in the room. At the parents and teens dance with his dead cool beatnik sidekick, Vivian Darkbloom, Quilty steals a glance at his watch, and melds this gesture of chic boredom into his dance moves.

Kubrick wrote to Ustinov that "we shall treat psychiatrists with the same irreverence that Mr. Nabokov does in the book," though Kubrick appreciated Freud, unlike Nabokov, who liked to launch jibes at the "Viennese quack."[49] The director spurred Sellers's turn as the fussy, Teutonic Dr. Zempf (actually Quilty in disguise), who sits in shadow in Humbert's house and expresses his therapeutic concern for Lolita. "Acute repression of the libido, of the natural instincts," is his diagnosis. Sellers's hand gestures describe an invisible melon (Lolita should be developing a well-rounded personality) as he emits a stiff man-of-the-world chuckle.

Kubrick and Sellers found a model for Quilty's speech patterns in the jazz impresario Norman Granz; Kubrick even asked Granz to record parts of the *Lolita* script for Sellers to study. But Quilty also sounds like Kubrick himself, with his skittering, Bronx-inflected style of talk. As the critic Richard Corliss notes, there is a touch of Lenny Bruce too in Quilty. Sellers seems sweaty under the collar, nervous, quick, and defensive, caroming from one prickly verbal stunt to another.[50]

While working with Sellers on *Lolita*, Kubrick began his habit of writing down actors' improvisations and making them part of the next day's script. (In a Kubrick shoot the script was always being revised day to day.) "If a scene didn't seem quite right," Sellers remembered, "we'd read it from the script and pick out the parts which went best. Then we'd sit around a table with a tape recorder and ad-lib on the lines of the passages we'd chosen; in that way we'd get perfectly natural dialogue which could then be scripted and used."[51] In his later movies, too, most notably with Lee Ermey in *Full Metal Jacket*, Kubrick would make actors' improvisations part of the script, rather than using improvised scenes in his final cut.

Encouraged by Kubrick, Sellers seems to be scrawling scurrilous graffiti across the tender love story of Humbert and Lo. Quilty is "always trying something on," like Sellers himself, says the actor's biographer Roger Lewis. "His endless re-creations also implicitly criticize the rest of us for being rigid and conventional, for being stuck with who we are."[52]

In contrast to the boundary-busting Quilty, Humbert is a square standing in the way of Lo's teenybopper fun. Kubrick's Humbert, unlike Nabokov's, is not a schemer. He doesn't plot to ensnare Lolita. Instead Kubrick gives us Humbert the squirming sufferer. Mason plays the role with a wincing, put-upon look. His manner, like that of a man who has misplaced his glasses, is sometimes too detached to be truly affecting. But Mason signals genuine pain beneath his stylish, mildly disoriented exterior. Humbert's cruelty, on abundant display in Nabokov, appears only briefly in the movie, when he reads aloud Charlotte's help-lessly ardent love letter. Here the chortling Mason, unable to stifle himself, lets loose with a guffaw, then a full-throttle whoop. Mason, happy as a cat, shines wickedly too in the bathtub scene that comes on the heels of Charlotte's death. (Nabokov loved seeing Humbert in the bath with a glass of scotch balanced on his hairy chest.)

The novel's Humbert is a godlike master of the higher sar-casm, a charming devil eager to get on our good side, like any conniving convict, by showing remorse for his sins. We need to beware of Nabokov's hero most when he is humble Hum, ex-pressing poignant regret for wrecking Lolita's childhood. But the barbed tour de force that is Nabokov's Humbert, with suave acrobatics walking the tightrope of his crimes, remains absent from the movie. Kubrick uses Humbert's voice-over sparingly, and it is devoid of verbal pirouettes. Whereas the novel makes us revel in Humbert's prowess with words, in Kubrick's movie he is often tongue-tied.

Kubrick nearly omits what Nabokov stresses: this is a child rapist we're dealing with. For the movie's latter half Humbert is the desperate loser, pinioned by orderlies in a hospital, in a starkly lit, noirish scene, and raving about the disappearance of his stepdaughter. Humbert's madcap rival Quilty steals the show, courtesy of Sellers's comic genius—something that doesn't happen in the novel, where Quilty almost seems a figment of Humbert's imagination.

If Humbert is Quilty's straight man, Charlotte Haze, Lo-lita's mother, is Humbert's. Shelley Winters's Charlotte is juice-lessly zaftig. Whiny even when she cha-chas, puffy around the eyes, and vulgar in her pretension to culture, Charlotte seems an unstoppable kitsch express. We dislike this cloying, stupid woman who is so mean-minded toward her daughter, and are relieved when she gets killed.

Winters remarked that she felt lonely on the set, and guessed that Kubrick wanted this response from her, to reinforce Charlotte's hopelessly pathetic stature. In fact, he was frustrated by her mulish obstinacy on the set. "I think the lady's gonna have to go," he mused at one point, but in the end didn't fire Winters.[53] This was the right decision: no one else could have played the Kubrickized Charlotte.

Kubrick reimagined Charlotte just as he did the rest of Nabokov's characters. In the novel she is a Marlene Dietrich wannabe, less helpless than predatory, unlike Kubrick's sodden hausfrau. In Kubrick's movie, Charlotte's motherly intrusiveness saps any possible sex appeal. Contrast Christiane Harlan Kubrick, who in her song at the end of *Paths of Glory* is both sexy and kind, fragile and nurturing.

Kubrick, even more than Nabokov, makes Charlotte unbearably clingy. Imagining Charlotte, he must have remembered Ruth the suction cup, the wife who fastened herself to him relentlessly in her effort to become essential to her husband's work. In *Lolita*, Humbert gets to discard the burdensome, too-present wife in favor of a young girl, the ideal of his romantic imagination.

The choice between wife and daughter (or quasi-daughter) haunts Kubrick's work. For decades Kubrick was possessed by but afraid to make Arthur Schnitzler's *Dream Story* (1926), in part because it depicts a husband who strays from his spouse and is drawn to younger women, including several Lolitaesque nymphets. Christiane Kubrick turned out to be less of a creative partner for Kubrick than his youngest daughter, Vivian, his protégée. Vivian, who appeared briefly as a toddler in *2001*, became a director at seventeen, with a documentary about the making of *The Shining*, and her father urged her to film a novel by Colette, a writer he much admired.[54] But by the mid-nineties Vivian had fled from the pressure of her father's ambitions for her. The *Lolita* story oddly foreshadows the relation between Kubrick and Vivian—granting, of course, the contrast between Kubrick's proper paternal love and Humbert's sexual abuse of Lolita. Lolita finally escapes Humbert and transforms herself into a grown-up he could never have imagined, just as Vivian fled from her father's love in the 1990s and transplanted herself to Los Angeles and Scientology.

Long before Vivian, Sue Lyon was Kubrick's daughterly disciple. Adept at following his direction, she delivers a wonder of a Lolita, insolent and insouciant. Her Lo is snooty, a little grubby, absentminded, and self-pleased: her majesty the teen. The ravenous Lo devouring a sandwich, prepared by a pampering Humbert, presages *Clockwork*'s Alex, another adolescent with a healthy appetite. During the tense argument between father and stepdaughter after the school play, Lyon is a bratty virtuoso of gum-chewing, her eyes shooting darts of disdain.

Lyon can be steely too. (Kubrick wanted his Lolita hard.) When Humbert visits the older Lolita, now pregnant and married, she bluntly rejects him. Here Lyon is coldhearted, nearly oblivious. In the novel Lolita also dismisses Humbert's last-minute plea for her love, but still calls him "honey," throwing him a scrap of feeling that is absent from Kubrick's scene.

The toughness of the pregnant Lolita becomes, four decades later in *Eyes Wide Shut*, Alice Harford's knowing confidence at facing down a man. Both films show the man's fear of the woman, and in both, his blind insistence shows he doesn't want to know her, but instead to have her. We don't usually realize how Kubrick grasps the subtleties of male insecurity, because he is most often flamboyantly heavy-handed when he depicts men behaving badly. But in *Lolita*, as in *Eyes Wide Shut*, he is more finely shaded.

The first emergence of Lolita is one of Kubrick's, and Lyon's, finest inspirations. The flustered Humbert glimpses her sunbathing and recognizes his mythic nymphet, and then a smile ever-so-slowly dawns on Lolita's face, not a smile of happiness or excitement, but instead a little cat and mouse, as if she has just dreamed up a winning move. A smile of prediction, really. Sue Lyon plays her first scene perfectly.

With that first sight of Lolita, Kubrick gives her the edge over Humbert, and she keeps it for most of the movie. We don't often see in Kubrick the desperate, lonely Lolita, shuttled through motels across America in an existence as artificial as a drug addict's. In the movie Lolita, not Humbert, has the upper hand, as she attracts, manipulates, and finally flees from him.

Kubrick feared depicting Lolita as a victim, probably because our sympathy for Humbert would have drained away. When Humbert tells Lolita about her mother's death, the screen fades before we see this perplexed twelve-year-old take the news in. Yet Lyon implies her suffering with subtlety: she appears superbly blank and unreadable at times, hinting at what Humbert in the novel calls "that look I cannot exactly describe . . . an expression of helplessness so perfect that it seemed to grade into one of rather comfortable inanity."[55] Somewhere beneath the surface of Lyon's performance lurks Lolita the trapped animal, her feelings deliberately dead.

Kubrick's *Lolita* is a symphony of emotions, swinging between Humbert's possessive love and Lolita's wish to escape him. "Lolita is really like a piece of music, a series of attitudes and emotions that sort of sweep you through the story," Kubrick told Terry Southern. He used recorded music to get his actors in the right mood on the set, just as he had with *Spartacus*. Songs from *West Side Story* sparked Winters's tears before Humbert, "and she would cry, very quickly, great authentic tears," Kubrick said to Southern. "And let's see, yeah, Irma la Douce, that would always floor Mason," he added.[56]

Kubrick's musical choices for Winters and Mason tell us something: his *Lolita* is less satire than sentiment. The movie mocks American suburban mores, but more significant, it celebrates the myth of romantic love. Kubrick's *Lolita* is in fact

James Mason and Sue Lyon in *Lolita*
(Courtesy of Photofest/Warner Bros)

about love rather than sex. There is nothing particularly sexy about Lyon's Lolita, attired in a grown-up's shlumpy night-gown. Instead, Kubrick delivers a straight-ahead love story, with Humbert the jilted party.

In a letter to Ustinov, Kubrick referred to Lionel Trilling's essay on the novel, and remarked in Trilling's vein that "Humbert's love" is "in the tradition of courtly love: a love that is at once scandalous, masochistic and tortured." He added that "the story will be told in the subtle style of realistic comedy. But it is a comedy in the way 'La Ronde' is a comedy; as 'Le Plaisir'; as 'I Vitelloni' are comedies."[57] Ophüls and Fellini have a free hand with pathos, but their touch is delicate too, and Kubrick follows after them. *Lolita* is in the end a mélange of comedy, heartbreak, and suspense. It is, too, an American road movie: Kubrick sent a production crew to America to scour the landscape for suitable motels.

Kubrick wasn't entirely happy with *Lolita*. He told an interviewer, Jeremy Bernstein, that the movie's "total lack of eroticism spoiled some of the pleasure of it"—but if it had been erotic, he added, "the film could not have been made."[58] With a sexier Lolita the love story that Trilling saw in the novel would have been more exciting, and the sense of the forbidden pleasurably heightened.

It was a shrewd move for Kubrick to keep eroticism out of *Lolita*, and so avoid risking the furor ignited by Elia Kazan's *Baby Doll* (1956), with the magnetically sexy Carroll Baker beatifically sucking her thumb. Kubrick, who greatly admired Kazan, no doubt had this precedent in mind. Even the unsexy *Lolita* ran the risk of being condemned as sinful. In May 1961 John Collins of Christian Action expressed his fear that the movie "could lead to rape or even murder."[59] In the end the movie got a C rating—Condemned—from the Catholic Legion of Decency, which meant that Catholics who saw it would be committing a sin. Eliot Hyman of Seven Arts tried to sway the Legion's Monsignor Little with a hefty contribution, but his morals remained intact.

Nabokov played with sex and morals in a way that Kubrick couldn't. Nabokov's novel is erotic only for about a hundred pages, the first third of the book. After that Humbert's devastation of Lolita's childhood stains any sexual delight the reader might take in the story. We gradually realize that Nabokov the magician has tricked us by promising the salacious but instead delivering a prolonged moral verdict against Humbert. When Nabokov said that Lolita was purely aesthetic and had "no moral in tow," he misled us. The novel's risk-taking pirouettes are half the story. The other is its lethal finger-pointing at Humbert the criminal.

Kubrick couldn't trap the viewer the way Nabokov trapped the reader, by mixing moral responses with sensual and aesthetic ones. Alex's antics in *A Clockwork Orange* excite and disgust the audience at once, but the censorship of 1962 made this kind of double edge impossible for *Lolita*. Geoffrey Shurlock, who oversaw the Motion Pictures Association's Production Code, was particularly concerned about the scene where Lolita whispers to Humbert about a game she played with a boy at camp. Kubrick agreed to fade out on her whisper, cutting her next line, "This is how we start."

Seven Arts made a deal with MGM to distribute *Lolita*. The film, which cost about two million dollars, grossed four and a half million in its opening run. Because Harris and Kubrick financed the film through a tax-sheltered Swiss company they had set up, Anya Productions (named after Kubrick's daughter), they reaped a windfall.

The critics liked *Lolita*. Pauline Kael even said it was the first truly new American comedy since Preston Sturges. Kael had a point. Kubrick makes the mismatch between Sue Lyon and Mason as funny as that between Barbara Stanwyck and Henry Fonda in Sturges's *The Lady Eve*, with Fonda the unworldly nerd felled by Stanwyck's goddesslike charms. Like Stanwyck's Eve, Lolita barely has to lift a finger, or a leg, for Humbert to lose his head.

But the reviews missed the movie's key question about whether a man falls in love with an imagined or a real woman, a concern that will come to maturity nearly forty years later in

Eyes Wide Shut. Lolita's enigmatic, elusive, and illusory nature sneaks up on us gradually. Sitting on the Haze lawn, peering sardonically over her sunglasses, Lolita seems to us nothing more than a slightly plump, sardonic teen, as she gives this boring, obtuse grown-up a dose of her flirtatious contempt. Really, though, she is the cruel fair of courtly poetry, and every bit as unreal. If *Lolita* is a love story, then, it is also a portrait of delusion, that crucial Kubrick theme.

A week after their daughter Vivian was born in August 1960, the Kubricks went to England for the filming of *Lolita*, "with two babies and Katharina," Christiane remembered. "We played rich people on the ship. There were posh cabins, a lot of old ladies using up their pensions."[60] After the shooting ended in March 1961, Kubrick and Christiane went on vacation: a five-day tour of the Normandy battlefields, clearly his idea rather than hers.

In 1962 the Kubricks were back in New York, on Central Park West at 84th Street, with Christiane taking painting and drawing classes every day at the Art Students League. "We went back to New York because we felt we had to," Christiane said. But she found the city "a lousy place for small children." She saw "police taking the children to schools. In the shops, roughs would slouch and sprawl across the doorways. . . . The women were harsh too. You just got elbowed out of the way by them."[61]

What New York did have was a circle of friends including the madcap satirist Terry Southern and jazz clarinetist Artie Shaw, who had given up music to produce movies and write short stories. Kubrick would develop his next two films, *Dr. Strangelove* and *2001: A Space Odyssey*, among the freewheeling writers and artists of 1960s New York.

3

Total Final Annihilating Artistic Control: Dr. Strangelove

"I WAS INTERESTED in whether or not I was going to get blown up by an H Bomb prior to *Lolita*," Kubrick told Jeremy Bernstein.[1] His interest got more intense during *Lolita*'s shooting in the summer of 1961. The Cold War was heating up, with JFK and Khrushchev in a nerve-racking standoff over Berlin, and the threat of a war between superpowers gripped the world. After his return to New York, the now-obsessed Kubrick read a long list of books about nuclear apocalypse. Among them was the Welsh author Peter George's *Red Alert* (1958), a novel about a rogue air force general who orders a nuclear attack on the Soviet Union. In 1961, Kubrick decided that *Red Alert* would be his next movie. He started work on the project with Jimmy Harris, but soon Harris was on his way to Hollywood to become a director himself.

Kubrick thought that nuclear war was a horrible absurdity, so he wanted make *Red Alert* a comedy. He and Harris had come up with some broad comic touches during their story conferences, imagining, for example, the Joint Chiefs of Staff ordering from a deli during the atomic crisis. But now Harris was getting worried. A feature-length comedy about the Bomb just wasn't feasible, he thought: the subject was simply too dreadful. Harris remembers thinking, "'I leave him alone for ten minutes and he's going to blow his whole career.'"

Harris was wrong. *Dr. Strangelove or: How I Learned to Stop Worrying and Love the Bomb,* turned out to be Kubrick's best work so far: his first truly pathbreaking film, ghastly and hilarious at once in a way never seen before in Hollywood. After watching it for the first time, Kubrick's high school friend Alex Singer wrote to him, "I laughed so hard and so often that I thought I'd be asked to leave the theatre."[2] Along with many *Strangelove* fans, I've had the same thought.

Harris's split with Kubrick during the *Strangelove* scriptwriting was an amicable one. Kubrick had been feeding Harris's filmmaking ambitions, telling him, "You'll never know complete satisfaction until you've tried your hand at directing." "Kubrick invited enormous input from me on *Lolita*," Harris remembered. "Stanley had a very open mind," he added. "He admired anybody who thought enough about something to have an idea."[3]

On *Lolita*, Harris had been inspired by Kubrick's assured manner. "You've got to supervise everybody, and answer all the questions," Harris told an interviewer. "It seemed so easy for Stanley." But Kubrick confessed to Harris that the hardest time for a director was "the moment when you arrive on the set each morning." As Harris put it,

> You've got a city block filled with equipment, trucks, extras in costume, honeywagons. There you are pulling up, and dozens if not hundreds of people are looking straight at you. They've all got questions, and they need them answered right away. Everybody likes the idea of being a director—of being

that guy that everybody looks to—but the reality is a whole other ballgame. You've got to be ready to answer, but you've got to keep your nerve and not answer too fast.[4]

When Harris went off to LA, he remembered, Kubrick "wrote down things for me like I was a kid he was sending to school. 'Don't get bullied into making a shot-list' was key advice. He said, 'A lot of magic happens on the set; it's no disgrace to not know what you want to do.' ... If you're not careful, people will bully you into thinking there's something wrong with you if you don't have a clear image of where every shot is, and where you're going to put the camera. Stanley said, 'It's much better to discover your strategy with dialogue scenes. You want the actors to make a contribution. Don't put them in a position where they're told what to do.' "[5]

Harris went on to direct a series of odd, intriguing movies, including a Cold War thriller that ends with an atomic blast, *The Bedford Incident* (1965), the unclassifiable erotic fairy tale *Some Call It Loving* (1973), and *Cop* (1988), a white-knuckle James Ellroy adaptation starring James Woods.

Strangelove grew out of Kubrick's deep research about nuclear war. His favorite prophet of radioactive Armageddon, and the chief model for Dr. Strangelove himself, was Herman Kahn, a theorist at the RAND Corporation, the think tank where scientists loosened their ties and lolled on the floor as they pondered the unthinkable. Kahn, who spoke frequently to military and civilian groups, warned that "nuclear war is an immediate peril," and he added, "prepare to be struck, fight back, and survive." *On Thermonuclear War* (1960), which Kubrick read at least three times, featured spookily calm postapocalyptic summaries like "Table 3, Tragic but Distinguishable Postwar States": "2 million dead=economic recuperation 1 year; 10 million= 5 years; 20 million=10 years; 80 million=fifty years; 160 million=100 years." Even if the fifty major cities in the United States were struck by Soviet bombs, Kahn stressed, the country could rebuild them in ten years, "complete with slums, and some extra ones," he joshed.[6] The cheeriness was deceptive, since Kahn failed to mention the devastating long-term effects of radiation.

Kahn was, by any standard, a true character. Sharon Ghamari-Tabrizi, his biographer, says he was "buoyant and ingratiating. He was appealingly eccentric: grossly fat, a stammerer and a wheezer, nearly narcoleptic at times, but, when awake, insatiably chatty." Kahn, who would talk to anybody, wanted to figure out what made the peace movement tick. He said to a reporter in 1968, "I like the hippies. I've been to Esalen. I've had LSD a couple of times. In some ways I'd like to join them."[7]

He also wasn't afraid to sound crazy. "At the Hudson Institute" (another think tank where Kahn worked) "we're proud to say we stand halfway between chutzpah and megalomania," he jested. Kahn thought "frivolity [was] a permissible approach to intolerably catastrophic ideas," writes Ghamari-Tabrizi[8]—and so did Kubrick. The Kubricks had dinner with Kahn a few times, and they were highly impressed by the rotund, wisecracking theorist.

After Kubrick's movie came out, the *Daily Mail* called Kahn "the real Dr. Strangelove," and they weren't far wrong. Strangelove, like Kahn, plays around with the line between passionate idiocy and shrewd strategic gamesmanship. And Strangelove echoes Kahn nearly word for word when he asks, "Will the survivors envy the dead?" after the Doomsday Machine goes kaboom. Kahn, for his part, when he heard that Strangelove was based on him, badgered the director for royalties. ("It doesn't work that way," Kubrick told him.)[9]

Kahn spoke to one of Kubrick's key obsessions, the blurry line between mastery and insanity. Without meaning to, Kahn illustrates a key theme of the eighteenth-century Enlightenment, that reason can run amok. He sounds like a character in Swift whose dream of rational control starts to look like madness. Yet he was on to something, since his thinking mirrored the paranoid Cold War reality. The Soviets might feel compelled to attack us, Kahn said, out of fear that our strategic vulnerability would tempt us to strike them first. But if we said that we were considering a first strike, and thought we could survive a nuclear war, we would look strong rather than weak, so war would be less likely. Such were the labyrinthine twists of Kahn's logic. The Kennedy administration did in fact draw up plans for a first strike, and Strategic Air Command chief General Tommy Powers glowered, "If a general atomic war is inevitable, the US should strike first."[10]

Kahn's daredevil paradoxical thinking both entranced and scared Kubrick. Life is not a war game, he knew. "The people who make up these war scenarios are not really as inventive as a great writer, or as reality," Kubrick told Bernstein. "Herman Kahn is a genius, but the scenarios don't read like the work of a master novelist."[11]

In *On Thermonuclear War*, Kahn argued against a Doomsday Machine, which was supposed to deter a nuclear first strike by ensuring worldwide destruction. (That's right, the Doomsday Machine was a serious idea, not merely a Kubrickian fantasy: in February 1950 nuclear physicist Leo Szilard publicly warned that Soviet or American scientists might build a cobalt-coated H-bomb that could destroy all life on earth.)[12] But Kahn did not see the special danger of the Doomsday Machine highlighted in *Dr. Strangelove*, that craziness combined with human error might bring about the end of the world.

Here Kubrick was a better theorist than Kahn. *Dr. Strangelove*'s plot is not nearly so absurd as it might seem: in a *New Yorker* article from 2014, Eric Schlosser argued that such nuclear mishaps had come close to happening.[13] And in 1983, the Soviet general Stanislav Petrov saved the world by disobeying orders and disregarding a satellite warning that American nuclear missiles were heading for Russia. Terrifyingly, a technical glitch had made the satellite malfunction.

For most of 1962 Kubrick worked with Peter George on what would become the *Strangelove* screenplay. Kubrick liked George, who had flown night missions for the RAF during World War II, and Christiane found him "a lovely man."[14] George had a dark side, though: depressed and alcoholic, he killed himself a few years later, in 1966.

Kubrick and George soaked their script in black humor, influenced by *MAD* magazine and Paul Krassner's scabrous underground magazine the *Realist*, a Kubrick favorite. In mid-November 1962 Terry Southern came in as a third screenwriter. Southern had written a wild satire called *The Magic Christian* (1959) that Peter Sellers liked to give as a birthday present. Southern is not "the writer" of *Dr. Strangelove*, as he has sometimes been called, but his pitch-perfect black comedy proved essential to the movie.

Southern would arrive at Kubrick's house in Knightsbridge, London, at 5 in the morning, and sit down with him in the back seat of Kubrick's Bentley. While they were driven to Shepperton Studios, Kubrick and Southern wrote side by side on two small tables in the back of the car. Their work on the script continued until the end of 1962.

At home, too, Kubrick and Southern fixated on the nuclear peril. "Stanley and Terry Southern talked and talked about it and whipped themselves into a frenzy of fears," Christiane says. "People were really afraid and there were long conversations about 'when is it going to happen, and don't think it's not going to happen.'"[15]

Kubrick even decided to move to Australia, out of the likely range of the coming nuclear destruction. "Stanley had this fantasy," Christiane recalls:

> We'd go on a ship to Australia. He said, "The Jews always made jokes, 'Oh it's not dangerous, they can't kill us all,' we have to learn a lesson and go to Australia." I said, "Okay, let's go." Weeks later he still hadn't bought the tickets. He said, "Well they don't have a bathroom, we'd have to share a bathroom."
>
> I said "Go, I'm all for it, I've got suitcases." It became a very weird joke—other people teased him and he teased himself. "No, I haven't done anything yet but next week we have to do something," [he said]. "Well go ahead, I can go as I am" [I said]. My readiness drove him crazy. If his typewriter was on a different desk he was upset. I said it's not so bad if we have to go on a ship where we share a sink. "You're just very destructive now," he said. "I'm not joking. I don't appreciate it, it's not funny. Your not saying anything is another way of being horrible."
>
> [We had] the most asinine conversations—"When are you going? Have you booked on the ship? Okay, I'm ready to go, I'm so packed. . . . I can leave everything else behind, can you?" This went on until it became an absolute family joke, everyone pounced on him.[16]

Kubrick was too wedded to home to consider taking off for the ends of the earth, even to save himself and his family from the apocalypse.

All his life Kubrick wanted well-defended stasis, which went along with his wish to exert control and minimize risk. But in a world on the brink of nuclear war such security seemed impossible. War games were the order of the day, and their twisted plots had the earth hanging in the balance. The nuclear planners hinted at a macabre upside-down reality: the most secure state of all was universal annihilation, apocalypse being the surest way to control fate.

Dr. Strangelove argues that a single crazed individual with access to the Bomb might decide to go out with a bang, taking down the whole of the human race along with him. Exhibit A is the openly wacko General Jack D. Ripper, a cigar-chewing macho monolith muttering darkly about Commie conspiracy. Kubrick matches Ripper with the more strategic minded but equally bananas General Buck Turgidson, jockish, pigheaded, and snorting disdain, who clamors for a first strike against the Russkies.

Dr. Strangelove's plot is ignited by Ripper's mad decision to start a nuclear war with the Russians. The movie cross-cuts between the American War Room, with the president trying to recall Ripper's bombers, and a B-52 bomber crew headed by Major King Kong. The Soviets, we learn, have a Doomsday device that will detonate a series of world-destroying explosions if even one atomic bomb strikes Russia. Meanwhile, the black-gloved ex-Nazi Strangelove is clearly excited by the prospect of global ruin. The world ends with a bang, or rather lots of them, when Major Kong's plane makes it through and triggers the Doomsday Machine.

Kubrick's movie makes its terrific impact because instead of just mocking the military industrial complex, it has an awe-struck appreciation of the power-mad generals Ripper and Turgidson, as well as the doom-hungry Strangelove. Strangelove is a perverted savior promising rebirth through violence. Ripper and Turgidson are manly colossi, unafraid to welcome the death of millions as the way to victory. They are Achilles, Ahab, all the mad warriors from the canon, made ridiculous, yes, but with their warlike integrity front and center. Kubrick was an enthusiastic reader of Rabelais, and his style in *Strangelove* is rich and savage Rabelaisian satire, rather than any pinched, humanistic denunciation of militarism.

"We are simply going to have to be prepared to operate with people who are nuts," President Eisenhower said in 1956, speaking of nuclear strategy.[17] Kubrick's movie cherishes such madness. Everyone remembers Jack D. Ripper puffing his cigar in an extreme low-angle shot, his forward-jutting jaw looming like Mount Rushmore, as he tells the stiff-upper-lip British Group Captain Mandrake, "I don't avoid women, Mandrake, I just deny them my precious bodily fluids."

Kubrick enlisted Sterling Hayden, the star of *The Killing*, to play Ripper. For the previous six years Hayden had been living on a houseboat in Paris while the IRS extracted chunks of back taxes from his stateside property. He was jittery. On his first day of shooting Hayden muffed his lines. "I was utterly humiliated," he remarked, but Kubrick bucked him up, telling him that it could happen to anyone. "He was beautiful," Hayden said.[18]

Ripper was based in part on the former head of SAC, General Curtis LeMay, a spikey, testosterone-fueled troglodyte who had overseen the destruction of Tokyo, Hiroshima, and Nagasaki, and who later proposed bombing the Vietnamese "back into the Stone Age." Add a strong whiff of John Birch Society paranoia about Commies fluoridating the water supply, and you get Ripper.

For his General Turgidson, Kubrick picked George C. Scott, who had most recently appeared in John Huston's *The List of Adrian Messenger* (1963). Scott's Turgidson is the gum-chewing, belly-slapping, whooping male ego, a thirteen-year-old boy grown to monstrous size. He clutches his briefing book to his chest, and we notice the title: "World Targets in Mega-deaths." Scott, like Hayden, was an ex-Marine, and expert at conveying the bluff macho stance that shoos away doubts like pesky flies. For Turgidson war is a matter of breaking some eggs. He predicts that the bombs the Russians drop on America will kill "ten or twenty million tops, depending on the breaks."

"Apocalyptic warnings arouse passion and militancy" since

"nothing but complete victory will do," Richard Hofstadter noted in his classic essay "The Paranoid Style in American Politics."[19] Victory starts to seem a little silly when you think of the mountains of smoking corpses involved, but Turgidson wants us to look on the bright side: winning is what matters. You can deal with megadeaths like a fan at a football game, rooting hard for the home team.

In an early script Kubrick called the Turgidson character General Schmuck, "a gruff, tough, folksy Air Force Chief" who "keeps in top physical shape, and is proud of it."[20] In order to turn Shmuck into Turgidson, Kubrick needed to inflate the character to grandiose size. During shooting Kubrick urged Scott to play Turgidson with broad strokes and make his character larger than life. The coaching worked: sublimely unaware of his idiocy, Turgidson is a giant figure in Kubrick's satire.

While directing Scott, Kubrick relied on his usual calm, reassuring manner with his actors. Scott later said that "Kubrick most certainly is in command . . . but he's so self-effacing. It is impossible to be offended by him. No pomposity, no vanity." He added that Kubrick "has a brilliant eye; he sees more than the camera [does]."[21] Kubrick saw more at the chessboard too, where he invariably beat Scott at their games on the set.

Kubrick relished Scott's splashes of buffoonery, however he could get them. At one point Scott trips as he points to "the big board," which he's afraid the "Russkies" will see if their ambassador enters the War Room. This was an actual mishap, but Kubrick decided to keep the shot in the movie. Scott recovers acrobatically, laughing a little at himself, and never breaks his stride.

When the shooting was over Scott was convinced he had given a terrible performance, since Kubrick had coaxed him into big, bold, hyperbolic acting. Kubrick wrote to Scott, "I hope you will at least be somewhat assuaged knowing that if, in fact, this is the worst performance you have ever given, everyone will think it is the best":

> The opinion of approximately 1000 people who have seen the film is that your performance is one of the most brilliant, penetrating and hilarious they have ever seen. This includes directors, producers, writers, actors, critics, editors, publishers, disc jokeys [*sic*], secretaries, executives, lawyers, housewives, hairdressers and psychiatrists.[22]

Columbia Pictures appears to have insisted that Peter Sellers star in *Dr. Strangelove*, convinced that his comic zest as Quilty had made *Lolita* a success. According to Terry Southern, Kubrick groused about this decree.[23] But Sellers was crucial to the movie, as Kubrick must have quickly realized. In a tour de force, Sellers played three characters: the nuclear theorist Strangelove, the American President Merkin Muffley, and British officer Lieutenant Mandrake. Mandrake, stiff upper lip and oh-so-British, and Muffley, a liberal egghead modeled on Adlai Stevenson, are the movie's straight men. At first Sellers played Muffley with a bad cold, blowing his nose and sniffling incessantly, but Kubrick reined him in. Muffley blandly embodies humanist normality, his plainness spectacularly overshadowed by the loonies crowding around him.

Dr. Strangelove is probably Sellers's most memorable film role. It's certainly his most frightening. Strangelove speaks in a herky-jerky rhythm that shifts between serpentlike cooing and impulsive shouts forced out through gritted teeth. His hand itches to make the Heil Hitler salute, so he twists and pounds it into submission, struggling furiously. Strangelove's rogue hand is a stupendous repurposing of Rotwang's aggressively gloved fist in Fritz Lang's *Metropolis* (1927), and his wheelchaired body, first seen in ominous shadow, shows how the leather-and-steel glint of fascism has migrated into the American military think tank.

Despite Kubrick's repeated denials, Strangelove seems clearly modeled on Henry Kissinger, author of a best seller about "limited" nuclear war, as well as on Kahn and nuclear physicist Edward Teller. These men were all Jewish, but Strangelove is a Nazi through and through, one-man proof that Hitler's excited devotion to mass slaughter as a cleansing force lives on. "It's a German name, Merkwürdigliebe," someone tells Turgidson (a goofy literal-minded translation: the actual German title for *Dr. Strangelove* was the less bizarre-sounding *Dr. Seltsam*).

Kubrick's Strangelove has a peculiar love for death on a vast scale, an old Nazi's ecstasy over being the master who remains exempt from destruction. Facing the endless spectacle of the dead, he feels immortal. Who can watch the exhilarated Strangelove crowing "Mein Führer, I can walk" without feeling chills down the spine at this macabre rebirth? It could be the most penetrating moment in any movie, ever, summing up as it does our twentieth century's heartless excitement at the mass death of other people.

Along with Strangelove, Muffley, and Mandrake, Sellers was supposed to play Major King Kong, commander of the B-52 bomber. Sellers was having trouble with Kong's Texas accent, but he was in the role for a day. It would have been his fourth in the movie, but he sprained his ankle (or claimed that he had), and so could not climb the plane's ladders. Kubrick turned to Slim Pickens, a former rodeo clown and stunt rider who had appeared in a number of westerns, including Brando's *One-Eyed Jacks*. Pickens arrived in London in his Stetson hat and cowboy boots. When Southern asked him how he liked his hotel, Pickens replied, "It's like this ole friend of mine from Oklahoma says: jest gimme a pair of loose-fittin' shoes, some tight pussy, and a warm place to shit, an' ah'll be all right."[24]

As Kong, Pickens relishes the prospect of "nucular combat, toe to toe with the Russkies." Dogged and ingenious, he gets his bomber to swoop through to its destination, and so single-handedly destroys the world. The killer ape rides again.

Kubrick came up with the genius idea of having Pickens ride a nuclear missile to world annihilation. Bronco-busting his bomb as it plummets, Major Kong feels the biggest thrill on earth, a wargasm to end all wargasms. (A Herman Kahn coinage: he once joked that people don't have war plans but wargasms.) Here *Dr. Strangelove* is again close to real history. One of the *Enola Gay*'s bombs had a picture of Rita Hayworth on it: mass destruction as the ultimate fuck.

Kubrick knew that *Strangelove* needed to have a sleek modern look, fitting for the atomic age. He chose Ken Adam, a German Jew from Berlin who was an RAF pilot during World War II, to design the movie. Kubrick had liked Adam's futuristic-looking work on the James Bond flick *Dr. No* (1962). "I think I fell in love with him," Adam said of Kubrick. "It was like a marriage."[25] Adam was, like Kubrick, Southern, and Sellers, dry, low-key and ironic. The four men, quizzical cynics all, fit well together.

In *Dr. Strangelove*, Adam created one of the most distinctive sets in movie history, a masterstroke of military modernism: the cavelike, triangular War Room with its vast round table in the middle. The table was covered with green baize, to suggest that the politicians and generals were playing poker with the fate of the world (a detail lost in the film's exquisitely stark black-and-white photography). The set's floor was black and shiny, as if to suggest the abyss. In later years Adam loved to tell the story that when Ronald Reagan became president he asked to see the War Room, having confused *Dr. Strangelove*'s set with reality.[26]

Dr. Strangelove cost just under two million dollars. The critics' screening, scheduled for November 22, 1963, was canceled when President Kennedy was shot that day. "A fella could have a pretty good weekend in Dallas" with the flight crew's emergency kit (condoms, stockings, pep pills), Slim Pickens remarks. After November 22, "Dallas" became "Vegas."

An exultant George C. Scott in *Dr. Strangelove*
(Courtesy of Photofest/Warner Bros)

Kubrick made another, bigger change to *Dr. Strangelove* before its general release. He had spent two weeks filming a pie fight in the War Room, the intended conclusion of the picture. (The pie fight exists in a set of still photos taken by Weegee, the production's still photographer, but I don't know anyone who has seen the actual footage.) Kubrick decided that this was farce rather than satire, and inappropriate for the ending of *Strangelove*. Instead, after Strangelove rises from his wheelchair, the movie ends with a series of mushroom clouds and Vera Lynn singing "We'll Meet Again," a World War II era classic for British soldiers heading off to the front.

When *Strangelove* was first screened at Columbia, Kubrick was consumed with worry that the studio had no idea how to promote the movie and was planning to shrug it off as a wacky novelty flick. "I have the feeling distribution is totally fucked," he gloomily confided to Southern. But the next day, Southern says, Kubrick was full of cheer, trumpeting, "I have learned . . . that Mo Rothman is a highly serious *golfer*." (Rothman was one of the film's producers.) He had an expensive electric golf cart delivered to Rothman's Westchester Country Club, but much to Kubrick's disappointment, Rothman refused to accept the gift. "The son of a bitch . . . said it would be 'bad form,'" Kubrick reported to Southern. "Can you imagine *Mo Rothman* saying that? His secretary must have taught him that phrase!"[27]

"I think that the film will be grotesquely successful everywhere," James Mason wrote to Kubrick from Malibu about *Dr. Strangelove*. "In the US of course much bile will be secreted & many will die frothing," Mason added. To an extent this was true. The public relations firm that handled *Strangelove* remarked, "Among the Hollywood opinion-makers, there are at least three who are like the psychotic Air Force General of the film. They feel the film is a tool of the devil which plays into the hands of the Commies."[28]

As Mason predicted, *Strangelove* was a huge hit, eventually grossing more than nine million dollars. Elvis Presley, who screened *Strangelove* at Graceland, was a big fan. The movie was nominated for four Academy Awards: best screenplay, best director, best actor (Sellers), and best picture—none of which it won. But Kubrick did pick up an award for best director from the New York Film Critics, the last time he would get such acclaim from New York's critical establishment. *Strangelove* was his own favorite among his movies, Kubrick said at the time, followed by *Lolita* and *Paths of Glory*, in that order.[29]

Robert Brustein wrote the best review of *Dr. Strangelove*, responding to critics who saw it as just a gag, an irresponsible way to treat the end of the world. Brustein said that "Kubrick has managed to explode the right-wing position without making a single left-wing affirmation: the odor of the Thirties, which clung to even the best work of Chaplin, Welles, and Huston, has finally been disinfected here. Disinfected, in fact, is the stink of all ideological thinking. . . . Its only politics is outrage against the malevolence of officialdom." "Humanitarians will find it inhuman," Brustein added—but they're wrong. *Dr. Strangelove* "releases, through comic poetry, those feelings of impotence and frustration that are consuming us all; and I can't think of anything more important for an imaginative work to do." Kubrick himself said that Brustein's review of *Strangelove* was "the most perceptive and well-written one I have read."[30]

In the wake of *Strangelove*'s success Kubrick got many speaking requests, but he nearly always declined. "I can't do TV or radio without getting tongue-tied," he told Herbert Mitgang of CBS News. He said to Gilbert Seldes in April 1964, "I never make speeches or write articles. I like to think I do this out of humility, but it is probably a form of the most supreme egotism. Seriously, I always feel there is something not quite right about film makers or writers who decide to become critics or lecturers." "I am a lousy lecturer, I avoid all speaking engagements, TV shows, etc.," he wrote to the Actors Studio, turning down an invitation to do a workshop for young film directors.[31]

Kubrick also slighted the New Left, ignoring a request from Todd Gitlin of SDS to appear at their conference. The antinuclear war organization SANE offered Kubrick its Eleanor Roosevelt Peace Award, which he refused. Kubrick didn't want *Dr. Strangelove* to be labeled "a peace group effort," though he "obviously share[d] most of [SANE's] views and objectives," he said. Kubrick did enjoy seeing a *Toronto Daily Star* cartoon of Barry Goldwater as Dr. Strangelove, and he asked for a copy of Lyndon Johnson's anti-Goldwater campaign commercial with a child picking daisies.[32]

Since the beginning of the sixties, Kubrick had been turning down offers to write bylined pieces for the press. In a letter to Thomas Fryer from August 1964, he explained, "It's really not possible to say what you think about critics, distributors, actors, etc., etc. with any honesty, without sounding far too misanthropic for the sensitive feelings of one's fellow human beings."[33]

A taste of what Kubrick meant is the rough draft of an undated piece called "Focus + Sound," in which he complains that "the movie industry is still at the mercy of a projectionist" who can't tell from where he sits that the movie is out of focus. Kubrick describes going to the movies and asking to see the theater manager about a badly out-of-focus projection. The manager, he writes, is normally "locked into an office, which requires a complicated series of buzzers. . . . After a lot of buzzing, phoning and waiting a little door usually opens and a very suspicious looking man looks up from a very small desk covered with papers." The manager would then tell Kubrick, "It can't be out of focus, it's pre-focused," or "It's a bad print."[34]

Kubrick's mantra when dealing with theater managers in later years, Warner Bros producer Julian Senior remembered, was "It's as easy to do it right as it is to do it wrong." He would have better success in controlling the screening of his films after *A Clockwork Orange*, when he insisted that European theaters use the correct 1.66 lenses to project the movie. His assistants got used to calling up and visiting movie theaters to make sure that there were no catastrophic glitches when a Kubrick film was shown. Senior recalls that "Stanley would say [to the theaters], 'Don't you understand? This is not just for my movie, but for everybody's movie.' "[35]

In the spring of 1964, basking in *Strangelove*'s success, the Kubricks moved to a Lexington Avenue double penthouse at East 84th Street. Stanley was enjoying family life. In a letter to Martin Russ from August 1964, he described a talk with his five-year-old daughter Anya, who insisted to her father that she be allowed to go to lunch with a seven-year-old boy at a restaurant across the street. Kubrick had to argue with her for forty-five minutes, he reported to Russ, but he won. These are the rules of the game, he jokingly added: if he didn't stop her from going to lunch at five she might be dating at nine.[36] Like her father, Anya was, it seems, a steady, determined arguer who knew what she wanted.

Looking for a project to follow *Dr. Strangelove*, Kubrick read voraciously. A list of his books compiled in the early sixties includes *The Voice of the Dolphins* by Leo Szilard, Ivan Goncharov's *Oblomov*, the Kama Sutra, Kingsley Amis's *New Maps of Hell*, *The Fire Next Time* by James Baldwin, *The Book of Meat Cooking*, *How to Succeed with Women* by Shepherd Mead, Simone de Beauvoir's *The Second Sex*, *Deterrent or Defense* by B. H. Liddell Hart, J. G. Ballard's *The Drowned World*, and *Now It Can Be Told* by Leslie Groves. There are books by Rabelais, Italo Svevo, Colette, "Philip Wroth" (*Letting Go*), and, of course, Herman Kahn.[37]

One oddball book on Kubrick's reading list was *The Prospect of Immortality* by Robert Ettinger. In the summer of 1964 Kubrick initiated a lengthy correspondence with Ettinger, writing to him in August that "95% of the people" he told about the book had a "blocked-up" response to Ettinger's scheme for making humans immortal by freezing and eventually reanimating them. "I suppose that in order to consider immortality [t]he[y] must first admit death," Kubrick continued, "and this is something which is apparently not often accomplished." He added, "Incidentally, did you know that John Paul Jones was buried in a lead casket filled with alcohol? I wonder if he had some scheme in mind."[38]

Kubrick was intrigued by but skeptical about Ettinger's immortality plan. "I think you tend to gloss over the banal difficulties. It's almost impossible to get a sink repaired," he wrote to Ettinger.[39] Kubrick's interest in immortality would develop into *2001*, where a man is finally transfigured into a godlike infant with powers far beyond Strangelove's.

In June 1964, Kubrick turned down Columbia Pictures'

offer of a two-film contract. Among the twenty-three pages of notes he took on the contract is this one: "I must have complete total final annihilating artistic control over the picture." The studio would be allowed sway only over the budget and the choice of the two principal actors. He also wrote, "I do not agree under any circumstances to be required to make any changes or revisions of the script, the picture or my style of combing my hair when ordered by Columbia."[40] His next movie would be Kubrick's greatest demonstration so far of total artistic control. In *Strangelove* he blew up the world. In *2001*, he would create a cosmos unlike any seen before in film, sublime and exhilarating beyond our moviegoing dreams.

4

The Tower of Babel Was the
Start of the Space Age:
2001: A Space Odyssey

IN HAIGHT-ASHBURY it was the Summer of Love, and the new Adams and Eves, barefoot and bedraggled, were spawning cosmic peace. But during the summer of 1967 at Borehamwood Studios, England, Stanley Kubrick's man-apes ran screaming, jabbering, and fiercely exulting in prehistory's first act of bloodshed. Kubrick was filming the Dawn of Man, the opening section of *2001: A Space Odyssey*.

A few minutes into *2001*, a mysterious, matte-black monolith touches down among the apes. This object hums and buzzes with the agitated spiritual strains of György Ligeti's music. Ready for liftoff: now the apes, on the cusp of humanness, start to kill animals for meat. They kill each other, too. The entire wordless prehistoric sequence lasts sixteen minutes, a dare to the audience and an audacious leap into moviemaking history. Finally one ape, Moonwatcher, flings his bone into the air and lo, as every schoolchild knows, it morphs into a spaceship, serenely gliding through the void. So crude prehistoric violence rockets forward into the space age, subtly infecting *2001*'s supermodern, clean, computer-driven rationality. With the Dawn of Man, Kubrick echoed the writer Robert Ardrey, who argued that lethal violence first made us human.[1] The "territorial imperative" meant capturing space for one's tribe and fending off rivals with a rock to the head or, as in *2001*, a dead tapir's bone.

Was the monolith a Mosaic tablet designed by Mies van der Rohe, as one critic suggested? Or a Golden Calf, with the apes dancing and chattering around it? Make of the monolith what you will. (For *MAD* magazine's bewildered cartoon apes it was a prehistoric handball court.) This faceless alien god—or is it an idol?—jolts the apes into new knowledge. For the fierce anti-Rousseauian Kubrick, the monolith is the Tablet of our first Law: thou shalt kill.

The Dawn of Man's monolith was only the first of the film's many puzzles. The wide-open quality of *2001*, the way it demanded that viewers speculate rather than simply being absorbed by what they saw on screen, was something new in Hollywood movies. *2001* contained little dialogue, and much space for imagination.

2001 was one of a kind, and it still looks shockingly new more than five decades later. After the apes we find ourselves beamed into space, where everything turns, slowly and magnificently, to the tune of a Strauss waltz. At the end, more than two hours later, we are left to wander with the astronaut Dave Bowman (Keir Dullea), everyman and blank slate, through a Louis XVI bedroom, until the Starchild turns his gaze on us—no more innocently, perhaps, than the rapist and murderer Alex does in the first shot of Kubrick's next movie, *A Clockwork Orange*, which like Altamont sounded the death knell to a decade's hopes for peace and love. There is the clarion music of a different Strauss (Richard), a Nietzschean dare for us to brave metamorphosis, and the sublime overload of the avant-garde

Stargate sequence, where Bowman sees and feels new thresholds, new anatomies (per Hart Crane), and during which one early audience member—who was tripping of course, like most everyone in the theater—ran through the screen shouting, "It's God!"

"Not even heroin or the supernatural ever went this far," said the critic David Thomson about what cinema does to us, its superreal spell-casting power. No movie has ever gone as far as *2001*, soaring before and beyond the human, showing us the silence of infinite space. More than any of his other movies, this one fits Martin Scorsese's comment: "Watching a Kubrick film is like gazing up at a mountaintop. You look up and wonder, How could anyone have climbed up that high?"[2]

The seed for *2001* was planted in 1964, when Kubrick first heard about Arthur C. Clarke. That spring Kubrick was in New York, enjoying the growing success of *Dr. Strangelove*, which had opened in January. Stanley and Christiane's friends included Terry Southern, Artie Shaw, and their wives. Shaw, who hadn't played clarinet for years, was trying his hand at writing fiction and distributing films. He was a champion marksman, and like Kubrick he had a big gun collection. He and Kubrick bonded over their shared love of jazz, weaponry, and movies. Shaw knew that Kubrick wanted to make a science fiction film and was looking for a co-screenwriter, so he told him to look into a novel called *Childhood's End* by Arthur C. Clarke. Clarke, who was also a science writer and amateur astronomer, lived in Ceylon, and he was chronically short of money, mostly as a result of funding the projects of his filmmaker boyfriend.

Kubrick got Clarke's novel and read it eagerly with Christiane by the bedside of four-year-old Vivian, who had a dangerous case of the croup. Listening anxiously to Vivian's breathing, Kubrick tore the paperback into chunks, handing the pages to Christiane when he had finished them. "Arthur, we thought, was the ultimate," Christiane remembered. Kubrick's friend

Roger Caras sent a telex to Ceylon, and Clarke cabled back, "Frightfully interested in working with enfant terrible."[3]

Kubrick treasured Clarke's ability to give a human response to the expanses of cosmic space. He said to Jeremy Bernstein that Clarke "captures the hopeless but admirable human desire to know these things that they can never really know . . . the sense of sadness, the poetic sense of time passing, the loneliness of worlds." Clarke, Kubrick told Bernstein, "has a way of writing about mountains and planets and worlds with the same poignance that people write about children and love affairs."[4]

It was clear that *2001*, with its vast sense of scale, was going to be a different kind of science fiction movie. Kubrick told Danielle Heymann that "every single company turned it down except for MGM: what they said at the time was 'what, science fiction pictures never gross more than two million dollars,' because up until that point all science fiction had been kind of cheap, stupid."[5]

"He had a night person pallor," Clarke remembered about Kubrick when the two first met in New York over dinner at Trader Vic's. In the mid-sixties Kubrick was clean-shaven and he had, Bernstein remarked, "the somewhat bohemian look of a riverboat gambler or a Romanian poet."[6] Before long Clarke was ensconced in the Chelsea Hotel, where he ate a lot of liver paté on crackers, pursued a love affair with an Irish merchant seaman who lived down the hall, and rubbed elbows with fellow Chelsea residents William Burroughs and Allen Ginsberg. Clarke was writing several thousand words a day of the script, and he met with Kubrick constantly to hash out the details of what would become the most innovative science fiction movie ever.

"Science-fiction films have always meant monsters and sex," Clarke said later, but his and Kubrick's was going to be different, a serious glimpse into the destiny of the human.[7] In an early version of the script, spindly Giacometti-inspired aliens welcome the surviving astronaut: a Spielberg touch avant la lettre.

Kubrick and Clarke eventually came upon the idea to end with the Starchild, who spurs fright and bliss at once. In a revolutionary twist, the aliens themselves remain invisible and unspeaking, like a philosopher's idea of the divine.

It's possible that Napoleon's march to Moscow involved more practical challenges than the making of *2001*. Then again, maybe not. (Michael Benson tells the whole story of the production superbly in his book *Space Odyssey*.) Filming began with the sequence in which the scientists, posing for a selfie around the monolith they discover on the moon, reel from the ear-piercing sound it emits. As on *Strangelove*, Kubrick was his own cinematographer for these handheld shots. Production ended with the Dawn of Man, the most difficult part of *2001*, since the right costumes and gestures had to be invented so that men could realistically play apes.

Live action production for most of *2001*, with the exception of its prehistoric prelude, occurred in the eight months between December 1965 and July 1966. Then came nearly two years of postproduction. Kubrick was a fiend about asking for one more take, and the crew slowly got used to his mantra "do it again." *2001* was at the time, and may still be, the most technically daunting movie ever made. It demanded Kubrick's constant attention, and even more constant inventiveness. The movie required more than two hundred process shots: the original negative was stored as a "held take," and then foreground and background elements were painstakingly added—for example, the stars or the earth through a spaceship window. After many months of trial and error, the outer space scenes started to look right.

Kubrick's groundbreaking filmic inventions in *2001* demanded careful decision making. Christiane said that Kubrick was "very much a chess player" when he made movies: "He said, 'Don't relax too soon. That's when you make mistakes.'" Kubrick once commented that "chess teaches you . . . to control the initial excitement you feel when you see something that looks good," and to "think just as objectively when you're in trouble."[8]

During early work on the script Clarke noted in his diary, "Stanley has invented the wild idea of slightly fag robots." The robots eventually became the HAL 9000 computer. Kubrick chose the Canadian actor Douglas Rain to play HAL because, he said, Rain's voice had a "patronizing, asexual" quality.[9] HAL is both strangely soothing and malevolent, a blend that seems just right for today's technological inroads into your life. You can now even order an Alexa terminal that looks and sounds like HAL, though, as someone joked, you might not want to give him control over your garage door opener.

2001, that halcyon and disquieting film, has at its center the strangely human pathos of its computer, the main character of the film's middle section, along with the astronauts Dave Bowman and Frank Poole (Gary Lockwood), who have been sent to Jupiter to investigate the source of the signal given off by the monolith found on the moon. HAL is both the movie's bad guy, when he decides to kill off the astronauts to ensure the success of the mission, and its sacrificial victim, when Bowman disconnects him. The movie's point-of-view shots are mostly from HAL's perspective: that nervously pulsating red eye, beating softly like a heart.

HAL can read lips—this is how he finds out about the astronauts' plan to pull the plug on him—and he can read emotions. He is also something of a philosopher. Here is HAL's cool definition of the good life, which sounds straight from a techie-minded self-help book: "I am putting myself to the fullest possible use, which is all I think that any conscious entity can ever hope to do." "Whether or not he has real feelings is something that I don't think anyone can truthfully answer": Dave says this in HAL's hearing to a BBC interviewer.

HAL's ego is based on his reputation for faultlessness. He

encapsulates reason, that god of the future. But he also has a very human feature built into him: when he lies and gets caught, he feels guilty. HAL can't figure out what ought to come first, his guilt over tricking his human colleagues or his duty to his NASA bosses, which causes him to lie.

Here is the lie that trips HAL up. This pivotal moment of *2001* occurs when HAL tells Dave he has doubts about the mission. Bowman shrewdly replies, "You're working up your crew psychology report," correctly intuiting that HAL is only pretending to be doubtful in order to test the reliability of his human colleagues. HAL admits to Dave that he has indeed been investigating the crew's psychology, and he seems relieved at being found out. But HAL then nervously changes the subject, reporting an equipment malfunction that doesn't actually exist. This is a mirror-neuron response that suggests HAL's own guilty similarity to the fallible humans. The computer feels guilty because he has been given the job of spying on the very creatures in whose image he is made, and this job requires him to speak falsely. At this moment HAL finds himself transformed from a faithful AI assistant to a person who is, like us, capable of betraying his friends. He has eaten the fruit of knowledge, and his eye is now open. Panicked, he invents the failing equipment shield because he instinctively wants to show himself at fault, and so prove his sympathetic likeness to the humans he shepherds.

When Bowman and his fellow crew member Frank Poole discover HAL's mistake, they decide to disconnect him, so HAL, fighting to survive, begins to kill the crew, starting with Frank and the three hibernating astronauts who were meant to be awakened when the ship neared Jupiter. The computer tells himself he must terminate his colleagues not because he wants to live but for the sake of the mission, which is too important to be jeopardized by humans. He is now lying to himself, and so becomes even more like us.

These moments of *2001*'s plot make clear the decisive contrast between Moonwatcher's leap into a primitive lethal humanity and HAL's leap into a more advanced, equally deadly one. Kubrick suggests that these two transformations are fatefully linked, but their difference turns out to be more significant than their likeness. When Moonwatcher crushes his rival's skull, this act prompts no rationalization and no feelings of denial, both of which HAL displays.

Kubrick's computer becomes a person by knowing, and then fiercely reacting against, his own closeness to humanity. With the apes, killing was freedom, the key to a bold new era. But HAL, a high-tech, twenty-first-century mind, kills in a shrewd, underhanded fashion, by first setting Frank adrift in space and then locking Dave out of the spaceship by refusing to open the pod bay doors.

Dave in *2001*, confronted with the murderous HAL, is a chess player. This is Keir Dullea's great scene, accomplished with the smallest, most subtle facial gestures.

"Open the pod bay doors, please, HAL. Do you read me, HAL?"

When HAL answers Dave we hear something new in his voice. He has erased from himself all sympathy, in the disturbingly human way adopted by every *Schreibtischmörder*, every bureaucratic killer, in the twentieth century. "Affirmative, Dave. I read you," HAL says. And then: "I'm sorry, Dave. I'm afraid I can't do that." The computer sounds dreamy, remote.

We read Dave: every emotion is in him now. Fury, resolve, frustration, fear, hesitation ripple across Dullea's usually impassive face when HAL refuses to open the pod bay doors. But the man, brave and ingenious, beats the computer, and becomes a futuristic Odysseus propelled through the emergency airlock.

Kubrick makes us ask a crucial question: would the unseen aliens who are behind the monolith want to adopt a troubled hybrid creature like HAL, or do they prefer the purely human

Bowman? *2001* implies that just as Homer prefers Odysseus over his divine and semidivine rivals, Kubrick and Clarke, in their Odyssey, favor Bowman, who is finally reborn as the Starchild.

Kubrick's hero Bowman, unlike Homer's, seems half-alien himself in his deadpan competence. Though his voice cracks and he feels a pang of sympathy when the discombobulated HAL, recalling his own birth in the lab in Urbana, Illinois, sings a wobbly version of "Daisy Bell (Bicycle Built for Two)," Dave keeps on unplugging the computer's circuits. The song, like "Der treue Hussar," sung by Christiane to the French troops in *Paths of Glory*, is a tearjerker, but Dave stays focused. During editing Kubrick pared down Dave's dialogue so that he says only two short sentences in the whole scene: "Yes, I'd like to hear it, HAL. Sing it for me."[10]

It's fair to suppose that the superior intelligence behind the monolith must itself be, like Dave, rather machinelike. Spielberg's aliens, attracted by human pathos, want and offer acknowledgment, but Kubrick's monolith stays forever remote from us.

The Hebrew Bible, rather than Homer, contains the closest analogue to Kubrick's alien, untouchable god. In his copy of Kafka's *Paradoxes and Problems* Kubrick wrote, "The Tower of Babel was the start of the space age."[11] *2001* presents a new kind of Babel, a gate to the divine made by humans to take them beyond the human, to the sleek and sublime nonverbal future.

Dr. Strangelove and *2001* share a theme with the biblical Tower of Babel: the wish to build a foolproof system that can eliminate human error, a seamless web that will make humans godlike, the Doomsday machine in *Strangelove*, the space-age computer savant in *2001*. Such hubris has its price. The rabbis say that if one of Babel's workmen fell to his death, his corpse would be ignored. The Babel builders end in jabbering confusion and descend into more war.

Kubrick loves this hubris theme. *Strangelove* is full of human error, since nothing is more looney than being rational about nuclear war. In *2001*, by contrast, reason has become dully monotonous, a ground bass humming along beneath the steady state of our existence. (The movie's opening line, welcoming us to the future, is as threadbare as you could wish, a space station stewardess announcing, "Here you are, sir, main level please.") HAL is the figure of hubris in *2001*, with his insistence that eliminating human error means getting rid of humans themselves.

Despite the clichéd joke that HAL is the most human character in *2001*, it's not the computer but the people who provide reminders of humanity, usually through resonant gestures or, as in the case of Dave ordering HAL to open the pod bay doors, facial subtleties. Hints of our mortal nature peek out through the slow banal pace of space travel in *2001*. Kubrick passes directly from Moonwatcher's bone weapon to the floating pen of Heywood Floyd (Richard Sylvester), snoozing aboard the flight from earth to the space station. When the stewardess retrieves the pen, stepping with awkward grace in her zero-gravity slippers, we see Floyd's hand curled like that of Rodin's Adam. The great art critic Leo Steinberg argued that for Rodin this hand signifies mortality, the tragic weight borne by Adam hunched and stricken after the fall. That curled hand is the opposite of Adam's finger reaching out to God on Michelangelo's Sistine Chapel ceiling, which we will see echoed at the end of *2001*, when the dying Dave Bowman extends his hand to the monolith and gets reborn as the wondering, ominous Starchild.[12] Another echo of art history in *2001* is subtle but strong. Kubrick will recall Michelangelo's Pietà with Frank Poole's body clumsily grappled by the space pod's metal claws. Dave, his brother astronaut, is forced to discard that body so that he can return to the ship *Discovery:* it swirls off into empty space, turning slowly with the inert leisure of any object in the void. Apes, empty of history, didn't bury the dead; neither does space-age man. But Dave's quest to retrieve Frank's body testifies to the persistence of humane gestures even in the thinned-out realm of space.

The supercontrolled astronauts, the men in their business suits and space outfits, give us an antidote to the wild apes who act out primal emotions, shrieking with anger and fear. "I'm sure we all want to cooperate with Dr. Floyd as fully as possible," Floyd's colleague blandly says on the space station: a far cry from beating your fellow primates to death. But there is also a deadly continuity between prehistory and the future. In space murder will happen too, but it will need control and calculation, both from HAL and from Dave.

Earlier, at the international space station, there is a small dance of calculation, with Floyd's shrewd response to the Russian scientist Smyslov (Leonard Rossiter), named after the uncannily accurate Russian chess champion Vasily Smyslov, who was called "the hand." Floyd denies that there's an epidemic on Clavius, the American moon base, so that Smyslov will believe there is one. Instead of an epidemic, of course, Clavius's scientists are wrestling with a stunning enigma, the buried monolith left by aliens millions of years ago.

2001 features many design triumphs. In space Kubrick's humans inhabit a white, gleaming world where style and function are mated. When Frank Poole jogs and shadowboxes on his wheel-shaped path past the coffinlike hibernacula of his fellow astronauts, Kubrick brilliantly gives viewers the feel of a zero-gravity environment, a "Möbius strip . . . WTF quality," as Benson notes.[13] Frank, softly punching the air for exercise, never lands a blow, unlike the murderous apes: in the future aggression seems only form, not substance. Here too design rules.

The revolutionary slit-screen technique used for *2001*'s trippy Stargate sequence was devised mostly by Doug Trumbull, though Kubrick rather than Trumbull would get the special effects Oscar. Watching the scene in an IMAX presentation of *2001*, as I recently did, frightens and enraptures. First we see time moving at superspeed, with dashes of radiance slipping past, and then a viral sublimity, as if from an electron microscope. Suddenly there's a gaping maw out of Francis Bacon, then a glowing blood-red embryo-like shape, bursting volcanoes of light with cascading lava, desert ravines, and mountains, all in febrile, supersaturated colors. We are truly beyond the human. The lights flickering on Dave's face in the Stargate scene replace the range of emotions we observed during his duel with HAL. Dave, like Alex later in *A Clockwork Orange*, is being splayed open, operated on through the optic nerve. And so are we: Kubrick's avant-garde invasion of our sight is no mere display, as so often in sixties experimental cinema; instead, it seizes the viewer. We are swallowed up, taken over by this new cinematic divinity.

I first saw *2001* at about age twelve, a few years after its premiere. From the beginning, the movie possessed me completely. I pored over Jerome Agel's book *The Making of 2001*, which was full of curiosities (the zero-gravity toilet instructions, HAL's deathbed monologue printed in full). My twelve-year-old self also wore out an eight-track tape of the movie's soundtrack, one of the most famous in movie history.

Kubrick commissioned a full soundtrack from Alex North, who had scored *Spartacus*, before deciding on using already existing classical music. The riskiest choice was the Blue Danube waltz (because, in space, everything turns, Christiane noted). In the version Kubrick used, Karajan conducting the Berliner Philharmoniker, the piece has majestic, massive serenity, and a poignant diminuendo too. Conjuring up the elegance of a ballroom was exactly fitting for space travel: such a daring metaphor on Kubrick's part.

Then there was the piece by the Hungarian Jewish avantgardist György Ligeti, which Christiane heard on the radio and brought to her husband's attention: Ligeti's hymnlike haunted chorale attends the apes' dance around the monolith, and Aram

Khachaturian's plangent Adagio accompanies Frank's jog around the *Discovery* as the Jupiter mission begins. The timpani beats of Richard Strauss at the movie's end, heralding the Starchild, take us back to the apes' bone banging, bluntly invading our head and opening us up to a strange future.

Kubrick employed some colorful characters on *2001*. The sleek space helmet, based on men's Ascot riding hats, was invented by Harry Lange, a German scientist who had followed Wernher von Braun to NASA's base in Huntsville, Alabama. Lange had a confederate flag and a model of a V-2 rocket in his office, until the British crew threatened a walkout and Kubrick made Lange remove the flag and the rocket.

Another memorable personality was Dan Richter. Kubrick hired Richter, a professional mime, for the production's climactic adventure, figuring out how to turn human actors into Stone Age apes. One of Richter's big hits was the Pinball Machine, in which, scuttling and rolling around with his knees up to his chest, he played four balls with distinct personalities. Richter and his girlfriend were drug addicts under legal supervision in Britain, and the doctor who gave them heroin, he recalled, was "an aristocratic lady in tweed suits and a gold lorgnette."[14]

Like Kubrick himself, Richter was a fanatic about getting things right. He remembered that as a child he once spent all afternoon trying to jump over a large box in his backyard. Finally, after hours of trying, he put together all he had learned that day and cleared the box. Kubrick had found the man for the job.

Richter spent many weeks studying primates at the zoo before he figured out how to become Moonwatcher, the ape who propels his cohort into murder and meat eating. Stuart Freeborn, who devised the ape costumes, was as tireless as Richter. Making the apes look real required letting them bare their teeth, snarl and grimace, which seemed impossible to do while wearing rubber masks. After long trial and error, Freeborn found his answer to the dilemma: seven tiny, tilted field magnets behind the actors' teeth, along with powerful elastic bands, gave the apes a full range of expression.

Richter as Moonwatcher is a superb actor. He touches the monolith gingerly, like a hot stove. This is his delicate, electric moment of initiation. A little later he plays with a tapir's bone, banging and flipping the animal's skeleton. Then the world historical lightbulb flashes on, celebrated by a montage of the raised paw gripping the bone, then a falling tapir (Kubrick echoes a famous shot of a cow being slaughtered in Eisenstein's *Strike* [1925]).

Here is Richter on Moonwatcher's crucial moment of problem solving:

> I let Moonwatcher play with the bones. He gets the feel of a bone in his hand. He has never held a bone in his hand before; he has never used a weapon. This is not only the first time for him, but it is the first time any creature has ever picked up a weapon. He feels it, smells it, and lets it fall against the other bones. He begins to sense the weight in his hand, the power, the release from an eternity of fear and groveling in the dirt for food.
> "Action."
> I give it all I have as I move forward into film history.[15]

The question is, what comes after Moonwatcher's exultant claim to violence as creation, what new human phase?

Man in the beginning fought for his tribe, like the apes or like Spartacus. Then he became a passenger, a role that sums us up, Kubrick implies: anywhere you look, in the modern urban age, you see passengers. *2001* is full of passengers, from Floyd to Bowman, who finally passes through existence and is transformed into the iconic Starchild.

Dave moves from being a passenger, then, to becoming a god. There is no telling what the Starchild will do. ("But he would think of something," reads the final line of Kubrick and Clarke's novelization of *2001*, rather ominously.)[16] What looks like playfulness and splendor to the Starchild might be untold suffering for us. Kubrick implies that violence and creativity are twinned in a double-edged, potentially lethal way: for us, for Moonwatcher, for the Starchild.

2001 answers *Dr. Strangelove* not with optimism but with a rich ambiguity that surpasses the earlier movie's nihilistic flair. The destiny of humankind is now open to Nietzschean specu-lation, and the film's ending spurs wonder rather than *Strange-love*'s pitch-black ecstasy.

Kubrick's spectacular vision of the future was costly. When the shooting was done, he had spent more than two times *2001*'s projected budget of five million dollars. The future of MGM was balanced on the fortunes of *2001*, since the studio was still hurting from a series of big-budget flops in the early sixties. When Kubrick unveiled his masterpiece, studio executives, bored to tears by the movie, were sure they were doomed. Droves of MGM suits walked out during the first New York screening in April 1968.

A disheartened Stanley retreated with Christiane to a hotel room, where, she remembered, he "couldn't sleep and couldn't speak and couldn't do anything." She told him that the movie would find its audience, even though the middle-aged Holly-wood brigade didn't get it.[17]

Christiane was right. By the next afternoon reports started to stream in: audiences under thirty were flocking to *2001*. Word of mouth spread like a fever, and soon an advertising team devised a new slogan for the film: "the Ultimate Trip." People were watching *2001* over and over, and always, it seemed, in an altered state. Before long John Lennon remarked, "*2001*, I see it every week."[18]

2001 premiered in 70mm Super Panavision with a 2.21:1 aspect ratio at a series of theaters that had a special curved screen with five stereo speakers hidden behind it. The best approximation to this experience is seeing the film in IMAX: you will feel you are hanging off the edge of space with the stranded Frank Poole. An IMAX viewing of Christopher Nolan's restored *2001* reminds us how Kubrick's outer space vistas combined the ideas of harmony and abandonment, like no other movie before or since. Grand and eerie, the planets turn, their movements precisely calculated like fine watchworks.

2001 also opened in regular 70mm and, later on, in 35mm. It became one of MGM's five top-grossing films, joining *Dr. Zhivago*, *Lawrence of Arabia*, *Gone with the Wind*, and *The Wizard of Oz*. Four years after its opening, the movie was still in release, playing every day across the country. In the seventies, MGM rereleased *2001* five times.

With *2001* Kubrick became against his will a prophet for sixties youth culture, though a rather wary and skeptical one. As usual, he refused to appear on television, make speeches, or otherwise pronounce on the Zeitgeist.

The New York critics were not nearly as impressed by *2001* as its youthful audiences who saw it again and again. Kael savaged the movie remorselessly, and Andrew Sarris was also doubtful about the merits of *2001*, though after seeing the movie a second time "under the influence of a smoked substance," he wrote that he had started to appreciate Kubrick's vision.[19]

Stanley Kubrick's "mythological documentary," as he called *2001*,[20] will probably live on as long as movies are made and watched. It's one of those achievements that Ardrey talks about in Kubrick's favorite passage of *African Genesis*:

> We were born of risen apes, not fallen angels, and the apes were armed killers besides. And so what shall we wonder at? Our murders and massacres and missiles and irreconcilable regiments? Or our treaties, whatever they may be worth; our

symphonies, however seldom they may be played; our peaceful acres, however frequently they may be converted into battlefields; our dreams, however rarely they may be accomplished. The miracle of man is not how far he has sunk but how magnificently he has risen.[21]

2001: A Space Odyssey is evidence of that brief transcendent elevation.

5

Let's Open with a Sicilian Defence:
A Clockwork Orange

IN SEPTEMBER 1968, the Kubricks were living in Abbots Mead, near Borehamwood Studios outside London. Kubrick had decided to take on the most famous hero in European history: he wanted to make a movie about Napoleon. *Paths of Glory* and *Spartacus* were historical movies with large set piece battles. Now Kubrick was moving on to another vast subject, Napoleon's wartime career. He had been reading deeply for years in military history, and he was particularly obsessed with Napoleon.

Kubrick had been thinking more than ever about how to show war on film. A few years earlier, in August 1964, he wrote to MGM's Ron Lubin to turn down a film about Simón Bolívar that the studio wanted him to make ("My only problem is I have no real interest in the old boy," he said). Kubrick remarked to Lubin that "representing a broad panorama of history has always proved to be the undoing of film makers." He recommended that the movie, whoever was to direct it, have voice-over narration, not too much dialogue, and a "documentary visual style." Kubrick added that "costume war scenes tend to look like so many extras thoughtlessly dressed on a beautiful hill. . . . The thing that usually makes movie battles idiotic is that the terrain is senseless. Almost all battles are shaped and finally decided by the terrain itself."[1]

While planning his epic *Napoleon*, Kubrick brooded over the terrain he could use for the film. Most of the actual Napoleonic battlefields had been turned into suburbs or industrial parks, so Kubrick looked elsewhere, to Romania and Yugoslavia. His dreams for the movie were gigantic: he planned on "fifty thousand extras" supplied by the Romanian military. He wanted cinematic diagrams of the battles, showing with maps and voice-over narration how Napoleon cut the Austrian forces in two at Austerlitz. The "sheer visual and organizational beauty" of the battles was important to Kubrick, but also, he told the interviewer Joseph Gelmis, the clash between these rational patterns and the dismal human reality of war.[2] Kubrick was once again on to one of his basic themes, the split between reason's all-controlling plans and the blunders and chaos that mark actual life.

Kubrick had a scholarly interlocutor for the Napoleon project, Felix Markham, the Oxford historian. In addition to reading a small mountain of books about Napoleon, Kubrick hired Markham's graduate students to provide notes on hundreds more sources.

Kubrick's interviews with Markham on Napoleon make fascinating reading. At one point he tells Markham about the "in-between" move (*Entzwischenzug*) used by chess players, and asks him whether Napoleon's Achilles' heel was his inability to make such a move: Napoleon was comfortable attacking or defending, but remained at a loss when he was prevented from doing either. (Kubrick's description of the *Entzwischenzug* is rather misleading: in chess it is part of a tactical sequence, not a delaying maneuver.) Markham agrees with Kubrick that Napoleon had a hard time standing still.[3]

Kubrick's script begins with Napoleon the alienated child who suddenly grows up and plunges into action. (Many Kubrick movies and unfilmed screenplays, from *The Burning Secret* to *Lolita* to *The Shining*, share this pattern.) Kubrick begins with a scene of the four-year-old Napoleon "dreamily suck[ing] his thumb."[4] Then we glimpse Napoleon at boarding school in France insisting that someone has put glass in his pitcher of water: the Corsican boy had never seen ice before. A few quick scenes later, after the storming of the Bastille, Napoleon coolly shoots in the head a leader of the revolt, one "Citizen Varlac"— a thoroughly fictional incident.

In Kubrick's retelling Napoleon makes his way effortlessly to the top, and soon he is giving Tsar Alexander military tips as they sit naked together in a sauna. The script ends with Napoleon's death, and then a maudlin shot of his grieving mother surrounded by her son's childhood wooden soldiers and teddy bear. Earlier, Kubrick described the four-year-old king of Rome, Napoleon's son, sitting alone and playing with his soldiers, never to see his father again. The Napoleon screenplay is haunted by childhood, and perhaps suggests that Napoleon's conquering of Europe was a boyish fantasy come true. After Napoleon lost his empire, Kubrick implies, he once again became a mere boy, bereft of power. He proved to be not a godlike Starchild but instead an all-too-human figure whose life expands grandly and then shrinks back to its minor-scale origins.

Napoleon's "sex life was worthy of Arthur Schnitzler," Kubrick said to Gelmis.[5] (Schnitzler wrote thousands of pages recording each of his sexual encounters.) In the screenplay Napoleon meets Josephine at an orgy, though Kubrick refrains from depicting explicit sex. Kubrick verified with Markham that such an event was historically possible: Josephine, the lover of the rakish politician Paul Barras, traveled in fast circles.

But Napoleon's rapturous desire for Josephine never seems quite real in Kubrick's script, and he treats their infidelities with clumsy prurience. Despite several sex scenes in mirrored bedrooms, nothing here sizzles. Kubrick's heart is instead with Napoleon the brilliantly innovative general, a personality rather like Stanley Kubrick the film director. "There is nothing vague in it. It is all common sense," the Corsican says about the art of war. "Theory does not enter into it. The simplest moves are always the best."[6] This Napoleon is an elegant, cold-blooded calculator. His disastrous Russian campaign is depicted, briefly, but left unexplained: if Napoleon was such a genius, how could he have erred so mightily?

Kubrick completed his *Napoleon* script in September 1969. The next month, he estimated the budget for the movie at four and a half million dollars if it was filmed in Romania.

Christiane remembered that during the negotiations over Napoleon "the studios told Stanley that Americans don't like films where people write with feathers." This line, originally the complaint of a movie exhibitor in the mid-thirties who was saddled with yet another costume epic drawn from a classic European novel, had been kicking around Hollywood for decades.[7]

MGM was wary of the Napoleon project because Sergei Bondarchuk's *Waterloo* (1970), starring a somewhat weaselly looking Rod Steiger, had bombed at the box office. (During the making of *Waterloo* the Romanians received warnings not to work with Kubrick, but they carried on doing so anyway.) United Artists was interested for a time, but negotiations ended in November 1969. After this point Kubrick still wanted to make the movie. He was dreaming of Audrey Hepburn as Josephine, and for his hero he had in mind Jack Nicholson, also a Napoleon buff. If Nicholson said no, David Hemmings or Oskar Werner would do, Kubrick thought.[8]

"Napoleon is a character unfinished, like Hamlet; and like Hamlet, a puzzle—full of contradictions, sublime and vulgar," writes his biographer Steven Englund. In Kubrickian terms, the contradictory Napoleon has something of both Starchild and ape, as James Naremore suggests. Napoleon's life gives us "the awe-evoking sense of human *possibility*, which is a different thing from hope," Englund judges.[9]

Just as Napoleon pushed the world to extremes, so Kubrick expands cinema. It's possible Kubrick's film would have been more equal to its subject than any earlier movie about Napoleon, because Kubrick, as he showed in *2001*, knew how to approach a giant enigma. Yet his script, which glosses over the catastrophic aspects of the retreat from Moscow, doesn't inspire confidence. Masses of freezing, starving men could not be harmonized with Napoleon's heroic image in Kubrick's mind.

As his chances to make *Napoleon* waned, Kubrick realized he needed a new project. Terry Southern and Bob Gaffney, Kubrick's right-hand man with the Romanians on the Napoleon deal, had both turned Kubrick on to the novels of Anthony Burgess. When Kubrick read Burgess's *A Clockwork Orange*, he knew right away that this was his next movie.

A Clockwork Orange was published in 1962. "I was very drunk when I wrote it," Burgess said. "It was the only way I could cope with the violence." Burgess added, "I was trying to exorcize the memory of what happened to my first wife, who was savagely attacked in London during the Second World War by four American deserters. . . . I detest that damn book now."[10]

Kubrick closely followed Burgess's plot in his movie. Alex, Burgess's teen thug antihero, terrorizes London by night with his gang, and is sent to prison for murder. Scientists then give him the innovative Ludovico Treatment, which manipulates his responses, causing him to feel nausea when he sees violence, which had thrilled him before. Alex is now harmless, but, Burgess implies, the Ludovico Treatment has sidestepped the question of good and evil, ignoring the human soul and opting for rigid social control instead.

Burgess invented a new lingo for *A Clockwork Orange:* Nadsat, which incorporates smirking, coiled-syntax eighteenth-century inflections ("to what do I owe the extreme pleasure?") as well as a passel of transmuted Russian words. Alex narrates the book in raw and electric fashion. Listening to classical music, he dreams up a rapturous bout of violence:

> As I slooshied, my glazzies shut to shut in the bliss that was better than any synthemesc Bog or God, I knew such lovely pictures. There were vecks and ptitsas, both young and starry, lying on the ground screaming for mercy, and I was smecking all over my rot and grinding my boot in their litsos. And there were devotchkas ripped and creeching against walls and I plunging like a shlaga into them.[11]

Kubrick echoes this page when Alex, playing with his pet snake in his bedroom, listens to his favorite Ludwig van's Ninth Symphony. In both book and movie, the scene ends with our hero masturbating to orgasm. Here once more is the solitary transport felt by Strangelove rising from his wheelchair, by Major Kong riding his missile, by Moonwatcher excitedly pounding a carcass with his bone weapon. All these characters are boys at heart, autistically sheathed in their ecstasy. Kubrick loves these passionate rocketings. Frightened like the rest of us, he makes clear the cost of such savage masculine exultation, but his attraction to it is always there.

Kubrick was drawn to Burgess's Alex. He "wins you over somehow, like Richard III despite his wickedness because of his intelligence and wit and total honesty," Kubrick said.[12] Kubrick's Alex is a '70s Candide as well, a vicious innocent making his progress. *Clockwork* is an Enlightenment movie if ever there was one, with its meditation on using science to reshape human nature.

Finding the right Alex was crucial to *Clockwork*'s success. Kubrick selected Malcolm McDowell, the twenty-eight-year-old hero of Lindsay Anderson's *If . . .* (1968). There was really no other choice, Kubrick later said. McDowell had a curled-lip insolence and a ready way of mimicking the British aristocratic accent (as Kubrick biographer John Baxter describes it, "always too quick and too loud").[13] He could put underlings in their place, and with superiors he could lay on the smarmy obsequiousness.

"If you need a motor car, you pluck it from the trees," says Alex to his droogs. "If you need pretty polly [money], you take it." Alex is an overgrown child who delights in his easy life. Whatever he wants, he just grabs it. Living with his parents, sleeping late, he awakens yawning, scratching his buttocks, ready for a nice breakfast and a day of record shopping, drug taking, and a bit of the old ultraviolence.[14]

A Clockwork Orange is a movie about juvenile delinquency, a key Hollywood genre whose most famous instances are *The Wild One* (1953) with Marlon Brando, *Rebel Without a Cause* (1955) with James Dean, and *West Side Story* (1961). Brando and Dean were trained in the Method, and both had the soft inwardness that Lee Strasberg and Stella Adler nurtured in their pupils. Brando used delicate, distracted gestures to convey his vulnerability. Dean sometimes seemed, for obscure reasons, on the verge of tears. These rebels were tender, confused teenagers, not roughnecks. Like French existentialists, they carried the weight of the world. Though it was never very clear why the world was so intolerable, their beautiful souls were clearly suffering from it. *Rebel Without a Cause* depicts suburban existence as a quiet hell.[15] "You're tearing me apart!" Dean yells at his befuddled parents, as Nicholas Ray's canted camera angles pinion him like a Christ figure. *West Side Story*, like *Rebel*, deals in teenage tragedy, adding an amused contempt for the headshrinkers and sociologists who try to diagnose adolescent rebellion. But *West Side Story* has a split consciousness. With its freewheeling dance routines it says, "We're only in it for kicks: Take that, Officer Krupke." But it also sells poignance in typical Hollywood fashion, shedding tears over young lives wasted by violence.

Kubrick declares an epochal break from these earlier movie classics of juvenile delinquency. There is nothing tender or tearful about Malcolm McDowell's Alex. He is the natural man as hoodlum, a character that the sixties couldn't imagine. That decade was hung up on revolution and expanding consciousness, neither of which would ever occur to Alex. McDowell's superb performance is full of force but also simply matter of fact. He has killer style: jaunty and sharp in his Chaplinesque bowler, a buoyant boychik who will never realize how dumb he is. When *MAD* magazine depicted Alfred E. Neuman as Alex (in "A Crockwork Lemon"), it had Alex's number: "What, me worry?" is his credo. McDowell turns on the charm, and doesn't sweat it. We sense that, somehow or other, he will thrive in the end. Alex is not an abandoned soul like Humbert in *Lolita*, though they both have verbal talent to burn. ("You can always count on a murderer for a fancy prose style," says Nabokov's Humbert.) Instead, Alex plays our louche pal: "O my brothers," he says to us.

For Alex, like *2001*'s Moonwatcher, bloodletting has the freshness of discovery. In one of *Clockwork*'s set pieces, the flat-block marina scene, Alex, struck by "inspiration, like," rises up in the air, mouth contorted like Moonwatcher, about to teach his droogs a lesson by slashing open the hand of Dim, the most cloddish of the gang.

In *A Clockwork Orange*, Kubrick argues against the hugely popular behavioral psychologist B. F. Skinner. Kubrick told *Rolling Stone* that he thought Skinner was wrong, and his movie clearly denounces Skinner's behaviorist plans for social control.[16]

His two doctors, Dr. Brodsky and Br. Branom, are satirical portraits of Skinner-like behaviorists.

Kubrick's point wasn't just about Skinner. Behaviorism could be the movie industry ratcheted up a few notches: both of them manage our responses by doling out exciting stimuli. Significantly, Alex is rehabilitated by being forced to watch films as palpably violent as *Clockwork* itself.

Kubrick, when he read *A Clockwork Orange*, must have been drawn to Brodsky's words to Alex during his Ludovico Treatment. Brodsky has been showing Alex films of Nazi atrocities to the tune of Beethoven. "The sweetest and most heavenly of activities partake in some measure of violence," Brodsky tells Alex: "the act of love, for instance; music, for instance."[17] He is echoing Alex's own insight throughout the novel, where sublime music conjures up the joys of ultraviolence. Kubrick in many of his movies shows rapture and destruction blending together. Brodsky aims to control this dangerous combination, quashing Alex's fervor with his sterile mastery.

"In less than a fortnight now you'll be a free man," Brodsky tells Alex reassuringly, patting him on the pletcho (shoulder).[18] For Brodsky freedom is subjection to behavioral law, the trained response grilled into the body by chemical injection. As in Orwell's *1984*, freedom is slavery.

Shot in winter 1970–71, *A Clockwork Orange* cost a mere two million dollars. Except for some key scenes, it required fewer takes than usual in a Kubrick film. This was partly because "Malcolm knew his lines," as another brilliant boyish star of the day, Tom Courtenay, said, but partly also because *Clockwork* has an improvisational feel unusual in Kubrick.[19] It uses slow motion and fast forward in the rough-and-ready way of early-seventies cinema.

The film required design genius: as with *2001*, Kubrick imagined the world of the future in unforgettable fashion. He commissioned the sculptor Liz Jones, who had crafted the Star-child, to design nude female mannequin tabletops for the Korova milkbar. Drug-laced milk plus spurts from a mannequin's nipple ("'Allo Lucy, 'Ad a busy night?" asks Dim as she squirts out the liquid drug). Kubrick dressed his droogs in white pants and shirts, bloodshot eyeball wristbands, paratrooper boots, bowlers, and codpieces. *A Clockwork Orange* heavily influenced the punk movement, then still years in the future. The movie eschews the glam gender-tweaking of Bowie or Nicholas Roeg's *Performance* (1970) in favor of a tougher, quasi-military style.

A Clockwork Orange is Kubrick's most zestful movie, a joy-ride from the moment it opens with a steady backward zoom from Alex's false-eyelashed stare and hearty smirk. Many of its vignettes are pure oxygen, like the comic opera turn when Alex's boys tussle with a rival crew of hoodlums.

The dazzling, dangerous brio of *A Clockwork Orange* is nowhere better shown than in its *West Side Story*–style rumble between the two bands of young goons. Alex interrupts Billy Boy and his gang, who are about to rape a squirming, half-naked girl on an abandoned theater stage: "Just getting ready to perform something on a weepy young devotchka," as Burgess puts it. When Alex appears, the girl, grabbing her clothes, runs away unheeded. Rape takes a second place to the male-on-male showdown. Here Kubrick follows one of Ardrey's key ideas, that men want power and territory more than sex.[20]

"How art thou?" Alex sneers to Billy Boy like Prince Hal addressing Falstaff, as the soundtrack strikes up Rossini's *Thieving Magpie* overture. What follows is a balletic showdown, with the two bands of droogs rhythmically flipping and socking each other.

We next see the droogs on a hell-for-leather car ride, with their hair whipping in the wind and the road in cheap-looking back projection: shades of *Bonnie and Clyde*. Suddenly they glimpse a sign reading HOME, and, Alex reports, he gets that "vibrating feeling all through my guttywuts." (Alex's Nadsat is ear-catching: a painter I know works while listening to the *Clockwork Orange* soundtrack, including the dialogue.)

The notorious home invasion–rape scene that follows took three days of sitting around the set to figure out, with the cameras not yet rolling. After much cogitation, Kubrick asked McDowell, "Can you sing?" McDowell answered that he knew only one song, "Singin' in the Rain." So Alex does his famous routine while preparing to rape the helpless wife of the writer Mr. Alexander, played by Adrienne Corri in a red pantsuit. Alex's chipper singing, the throwaway air of the scene, the distorting fish-eye lens that targets Mr. Alexander as he is forced to watch the assault on his wife, all this throws us off balance. As Kolker says, "the whole sequence is slightly ridiculous, as well as horrifying." We feel "disgust and astonishment," rather than the thrill that violence in movies usually provides.[21] Much later in the movie, Alexander, played with vindictive glee by Patrick Magee, gets his revenge, and we are again disconcerted. We don't know how to take this simpering, twitching, red-faced nutball blasting Beethoven's Ninth at Alex, who after the Ludovico Treatment reacts with suicidal desperation. Our laughter is uneasy; we can't relax into enjoyment.

McDowell's sloppy brilliance in the "Singin' in the Rain" rape scene is to give Alex not the glossy brutality of a film noir thug but the self-satisfaction of an eleven-year-old boy. Predictably, the scene was hard to film. Corri said, "For four days I was bashed about by Malcolm and he really hit me. One scene was shot 39 times until Malcolm said 'I can't hit her anymore!' "[22]

Alex lands in jail after murdering the "cat lady," a skinny middle-aged woman in a leotard who commands him to put down a penis-and-buttocks sculpture: "That's a very important work of art!" she screeches. We can't help but root for dildo-nosed, codpieced Alex over the snobbish cat lady. Here Alex's native wit contends with a snooty bourgeois whose taste is far more vulgar than Alex's own. Alex is a primitive and, like all primitives, has integrity. But the cat lady leans toward kitsch: paintings of women in bold pornographic poses hang on her walls. When Alex brutally smashes the sculpture into the cat lady's face, Kubrick cuts to Roy Lichtenstein–like cartoons of a mouth, echoing the jump-cut extreme close-ups of Janet Leigh in *Psycho*'s shower.

Clockwork draws from Chaplin and Keaton in its artful routines of physical violence. ("I wanted to slow it to a lovely floating movement," Kubrick told Gelmis about the marina scene where Alex fights his droogs.)[23] The movie is also, like nearly every Hollywood musical, an ode to feeling good. The Ludovico treatment lowers Alex to the depths of nausea, as the crown of thorns–like apparatus that encircles his head and pries open his eyes turns him into a version of Frankenstein's monster. But at the end he is riding high once more. In *Clockwork*'s finale, joy reappears.

Naremore notes that *A Clockwork Orange* ends like *Dr. Strangelove*, "with the maimed body of a villain brought back to virile life."[24] Worldwide nuclear annihilation was Strangelove's fantasy, but this is Alex's: lying naked on snowy ground, he is having sex with a lovely, nearly naked woman who, rocking on top of him, is clearly enjoying herself greatly. Meanwhile a crowd of gentlemen and ladies in Edwardian getup applauds the couple enthusiastically, all to the strains of Beethoven's Ninth heaving toward its conclusion. Once again Alex adores the pummeling of Beethoven's rapacious sublime, the overflow of spirit, healthy and violent. Alex, in voice-over, speaks the famous last line, "I was cured, all right," and we cut to credits accompanied by Gene Kelly's "Singin' in the Rain."

McDowell reported that when he ran into Gene Kelly at a party some time after *Clockwork* opened, Kelly walked away without shaking his hand.[25] Fair enough, but McDowell and Kubrick were repurposing the tune in the way great art does. What a glorious feeling, and a disturbing one too.

"But, brothers, this biting of their toe-nails over what is the *cause* of badness is what turns me into a fine laughing malchick," Alex says in Burgess's novel. "What I do I do because I like to do." He gives us his sermon: "Badness is of the self, the one, the you or me on our oddy knockies, and that self is made by old Bog or God. . . . They of the government and the judges and the schools cannot allow the bad because they cannot allow the self."[26]

"Old Bog or God" (Bog is Russian for God) keeps coming up in *Clockwork*. The behaviorist doctors recite a parody of Pauline Christianity, where knowing your miserable sinfulness puts you on the road to Jesus. Dr. Branom tells Alex, "You are getting well," and explains that this is why he feels sick. The doctors only manipulate Alex's physical reactions, instead of making him see that his crimes are wrong. The minister in Alex's jail similarly misses the point. Alex need only respond properly to his cues for piety and obedience to be thought well on the road to redemption. But really Alex relishes the Bible for the sex and violence done by "those old Yehudis," not for its moral fiber. The prison minister naïvely thinks Alex's good manners signify sincere repentance, while the Ludovico treatment instills knee-jerk responses so that we no longer have to worry about anyone's sincerity. Rehabilitation becomes a matter of outward behavior only. "Kill the criminal reflex, that's all," as Burgess's novel puts it.[27]

Kubrick shows how the Ludovico treatment fails when Alex's unruly libido bursts out again at the end of the film. But he doesn't celebrate this liberation so much as ask us why we find it so exhilarating. The choice between behaviorist repression and raging desire is, Kubrick knows, too neat a dichotomy. Though he imagines himself a free man, Alex's banquet of pleasures is just as predictable as the behaviorists' nausea-inducing program. Libido too can be a form of bondage. And some regimes, like the Nazis, combined behavioral manipulation of the masses with the unleashing of violent desires.

In Burgess's *A Clockwork Orange*, Alex watches wartime atrocities, including Nazis murdering Jews, during his rehabilitation. Kubrick merely shows a snippet from *Triumph of the Will*, along with German newsreel footage of tanks and planes, all set to a Moog synthesizer version of the Ode to Joy. Kubrick mentioned to one interviewer "the enigma of Nazis who listened to Beethoven and sent millions off to the gas chambers."[28] But he decided not to juxtapose death camps and Beethoven. Instead he cuts from Riefenstahl's banal propaganda to a few Nazis kicking in a door. We are reminded, though, of the central place of Beethoven's Ninth in Hitler's Germany: though the words of the Ode celebrate peace and brotherhood, the victorious surge of chords suggests triumphant aggression.

Kubrick's anti-Rousseauian animus, richly apparent in *A Clockwork Orange* and already forecast in *2001*'s Dawn of Man, put him at odds with sixties dreams of peace and love. In a February 27, 1972, letter to the *New York Times* he condemned "Rousseau's romantic fallacy that it is society which corrupts man, not man who corrupts society," adding that this was a "self-inflating illusion leading to despair."[29]

In *Clockwork*, the party of Rousseau loses. When Alex stumbles back to HOME late in film, Mr. Alexander, Rousseau-like, welcomes him as "a victim of the modern age."[30] Alexander, Alex's namesake, hates government repression, and with Rousseau he is convinced that human impulses are benign. The joke is on him: when he realizes that Alex is the man who raped his wife and crippled him, he tortures him with vindictive glee by playing Beethoven. Alexander is no longer a good-hearted believer in humanity.

A Clockwork Orange was released a few years before Jane

Goodall discovered that chimpanzees enjoy murdering and tor-turing their fellow chimps. No movie has ever been a better il-lustration of Freud's declaration that in our unconscious we are all rapists and murderers. It still has the force of scandal, after all these years. Along with Mel Gibson's *The Passion of the Christ* (2004), it is one of the most controversial films ever made. The film originally got an X rating in the United States, where the Motion Picture Association of America had recently instituted ratings (censors were much concerned about the speeded-up scene where Alex has a threesome with two teen girls). Kubrick trimmed less than a minute to secure an R rating.

In Britain the press crowed that Kubrick's film had led to a wave of copycat crimes. Young British hoodlums, the reporters said, were being inspired by Alex, and even dressing like him, with his bowler hat, long underwear, false eyelash, and codpiece. Kubrick had given them a taste of ultraviolence, and they wanted more. The movie, so the charge went, made raping and killing look like fun. Though in fact there is slight evidence for copycat crimes inspired by *Clockwork*, the furor that the news-papers aimed at Kubrick had its effect. Because of threats to him and his family over the movie, Kubrick in 1973 withdrew *Clockwork* from circulation in the United Kingdom.

Not only British tabloids but the New York film critics felt their bile rising in response to *A Clockwork Orange*. Pauline Kael, who had hated *2001*, lashed out in disgust at the movie. It was "an abhorrent viewing experience," she wrote in the *New Yorker*, with a "leering, portentous style." Kubrick, she said, was "sucking up to the thugs in the audience," and she worried about "the possible cumulative effects of movie brutality."[31]

Kael's unspoken complaint in her review of *A Clockwork Orange* is that if only the movie were not so arch and forced, "literal-minded in its sex and brutality, Teutonic in its humor," we might enjoy some of this bad behavior.[32] The same month she panned *Clockwork*, January 1972, Kael thrilled to Sam Peckinpah's *Straw Dogs*, a movie that exults in ultraviolence far more straightforwardly than does Kubrick's. The two films were released the same week, causing a minor panic among moralists. Andrew Sarris was just as negative as Kael. "See *A Clockwork Orange* . . . and suffer the damnation of boredom," he wrote in the *Village Voice:* "What we have here is simply a pretentious fake."³³ Audiences disagreed, in Europe as well as America: they rushed to see Kubrick's scandalous bombshell of a movie.

Before Kubrick came along, Burgess had unluckily sold the screen rights for *Clockwork* for a few hundred dollars, so he never profited directly from the film's success. But sales of his novel skyrocketed, and Burgess defended Kubrick's version of his work in a series of newspaper and television interviews. Burgess made the case that the film was a serious statement about human freedom, not a thrill ride for wannabe teen gangsters.

A Clockwork Orange deals with freedom by depicting its opposite: the compulsive nature of both Alex's enjoyment and the behaviorists' programming. Kubrick also provides a hidden commentary on the lack of freedom in the cathartic release that most Hollywood movies provide. After its release the *Hollywood Reporter* enlisted a psychiatrist named Emanuel Schwartz to comment on *A Clockwork Orange*. "It is the recurrence of peak experiences in clockwork, mechanical fashion that makes this particular film instructive," Schwartz said. "The pursuit of the peak experience is the manic search for omnipotence."³⁴

Hollywood movies are all about repeating peak experiences to feed the audience's fantasy. Kubrick was intent on troubling that fantasy. He said to *Rolling Stone*, "We have seen so many times that the body of a film serves merely as an excuse for motivating a final blood-crazed slaughter by the hero of his enemies, and at the same time to relieve the audience's guilt of enjoying this mayhem."³⁵ *A Clockwork Orange*, unlike most Hollywood products, made the audience feel guilty about enjoying it—a key point that Kael failed to catch. The guilt gets mixed with the pleasure, so that neither feeling controls our viewing experience. A failure of mastery, then, to remind us what radically imperfect creatures we are.

When it came to showing the movie, though, Kubrick exercised all his mastery. With *A Clockwork Orange*, Kubrick became more concerned than ever before that his films be screened properly. Julian Senior remembers that after the first print of *Clockwork* had gone out for the press screening at Cinema Five in Manhattan, Kubrick discovered that the wall around the screen was glossy white. "That's going to be terrible. There'll be reflections," Kubrick said. "We have to repaint the theatre."[36] Kubrick then pored through the Manhattan phone directory for two hours to find painters who could redo the wall in matte black.

Kubrick was hands-on with the European distribution of *Clockwork* as well. "Ask the managers if they know what lenses are being used," Kubrick told Senior. "I want everything projected in 1.66." The theaters didn't have 1.66 lenses. "Well let's get them some lenses," Kubrick said. "He bought 283 lenses," Senior remembers, "gave them to Andros [Epaminondas, his assistant], gave him the Mercedes and a map."[37] Kubrick got his way: *A Clockwork Orange* was projected in Europe with 1.66 lenses.

"Let's open with a Sicilian defence," Kubrick would tell Senior, who didn't play chess and so missed the point (be aggressive), before beginning one of his campaigns to ensure correct distribution and publicity. "I've been measuring the ads in the Frankfurt newspaper, they're screwing us," he might say.[38] With publicity as with screening everything had to be right: this was Kubrick's gift to the moviemakers who came after him, as well as his audience and himself.

A Clockwork Orange has always done brisk business, and has remained the notorious must-see item among Kubrick's oeuvre. Christiane, whose paintings appear in Mr. Alexander's home, detested it for its violence. In the wake of *Clockwork*'s bloody mayhem, Kubrick would return to the slow, contemplative mode of *2001* with a grandly poised movie set in the eighteenth century, when people wrote with feathers, as far away from Alex and his droogs as could be imagined: *Barry Lyndon*.

6

◆┃◆┃◆

You Can Talk for Hours about a Thing with Stanley:
Barry Lyndon

AT ABBOTS MEAD, Kubrick's driver and courier Emilio D'Alessandro took the director's daughters to school each day. In 1971, Anya was twelve and the rambunctious Vivian eleven. "Because of her wild character, Vivian needed constant attention," D'Alessandro remembered. "She never meant any harm, but it was hard going." Anya, by contrast, was "very calm and contemplative." Katharina, Kubrick's stepdaughter, was eighteen and an avid horseback rider, while Vivian studied piano and Anya took voice lessons. D'Alessandro drove them everywhere. "Stanley's children spent more time with me than with him, and I spent more time with his children than with my own," D'Alessandro said.[1]

The Kubrick family had frequent dinner parties. "Socially, he was very much an American in Europe and did astonishing things that were very endearing," Christiane said. Stanley liked to play chef. Christiane remembered, "Stanley had a secret fan-

tasy of being a short-order cook. He was very good. The kitchen
was a bit full of blue smoke and too many dirty pans, but he was
very good at that. He did a sort of American food that Europe-
ans find so astonishing—hamburgers, and then, later on, he
was king of sandwiches. He would pile up high things. He was
a good host and was trying desperately to tidy everything up so
people didn't say we're sloppy."[2]

Kubrick was looking for another project to follow *A Clockwork Orange*. He wanted something from the Napoleonic era
or the eighteenth century, radically different from the futuristic mise-en-scène of *2001* and *Clockwork*. William Makepeace
Thackeray's *Vanity Fair* (1848) was one of Kubrick's favorite
novels, with a wonderful scene of a party the night before the
battle of Waterloo. But the story of Becky Sharp had been
filmed several times already. Kubrick settled instead on Thackeray's *The Luck of Barry Lyndon* (1844), a rollicking picaresque
zinger.

Fleeing the squalid council flats of *Clockwork*, in *Barry Lyndon* Kubrick takes refuge in the eighteenth century. Yet Thackeray's novel has some similarities to Burgess's. Thackeray's Barry
is an Alex type, a scurrilous charmer and a brute. Like Alex,
Barry tells his own story. He is rough, disdainful, and hilarious,
with a strong taste for violence. Kubrick's screenplay alters the
hero radically. Kubrick transforms the scabrous swaggerer of
Thackeray's novel into an innocent, a cynical innocent at that.
He takes a hero with a defiant screw-the-world smirk and re-
places him with someone who seems embarrassed even at his
most confident moments.

With *Barry Lyndon*, Kubrick could have made a tumultu-
ous film full of gusto like Tony Richardson's *Tom Jones* (1963),
but he went in the opposite direction, creating a work of great
poised beauty. *Barry Lyndon* is a gorgeous, painterly film, with
strong echoes of Gainsborough, Constable, and Stubbs. A few
times the light seems like Vermeer's. These effects are espe-

cially stunning in the Blu-ray restoration of the film supervised by Leon Vitali, who played Bullingdon and later became Kubrick's intensely hardworking factotum. (Tony Zierra's documentary *Filmworker* [2017] gives a striking portrait of Vitali's career with Kubrick.)

The movie tells the tale of Barry's rise and fall. A country boy from Ireland, he becomes a loyal servant to several masters and then sets his sights on a wealthy marriage and a title: society is his new master. He succeeds in part, achieving (and squandering) wealth, and hobnobbing with the aristocracy. Yet a fugitive sense of not belonging always haunts Barry. He leads a vicarious existence, and like *Lolita*'s Humbert, he never gets over the loss of a beloved, in Barry's case his young son Bryan.

Ryan O'Neal's Barry is somewhat waiflike, though physically sturdy. He shares little with Thackeray's vividly disdainful hero. Jack Nicholson would have made a delicious Thackerayan Barry, but would be hopelessly miscast in Kubrick's movie. Marisa Berenson's Lady Lyndon is nearly inert, reprising the disaffected, melancholy beauty she played in Visconti's films. "There is a sort of tragic sense about her," Kubrick said of Berenson.[3]

Kubrick wanted the stolid, plain O'Neal and the languid Berenson not just for their contrast but for their similarity, since they both remain distant from every possible flamboyance. Like the astronauts in *2001*, O'Neal and Berenson don't seem to be doing much acting as Barry and Lady Lyndon. Yet O'Neal especially is solid, steady, and perfectly apt.

O'Neal, fresh from success in *Love Story* (1970) and *Paper Moon* (1973), was a big box office draw. On the set Kubrick and O'Neal, a former boxer, bonded over their love of the sport: together they watched films of heavyweight matches. Berenson, granddaughter of the fashion designer Elsa Schiaparelli, seemed haughty and standoffish to O'Neal, but Kubrick was happy with her performance.

Barry is a quietly troubling Kubrick hero, since we can't be sure of him. Against our better judgment, we tend to see him as a naïve youthful romantic rather than a mature conniver, even at his most selfish and shallow. When Barry first glimpses Lady Lyndon, he appears just as lovelorn as when he earlier looked at Nora, his first love, over the dinner table. We know he is out for Lady Lyndon's money, not her love, yet we are swayed by his melancholy looks, and by the fact that he never *seems* wily or calculating.

The status that Barry aims for remains artificial and unreal. He can never truly possess the gentlemanly stature he yearns after, so his aspiration has an air of the tragic. "I never saw a lad more game in all me life," his lively friend Grogan tells Barry, yet Kubrick's hero is not at all gamesome. While Thackeray's Barry happily drinks, whores, and swindles his way across Europe, Kubrick's dwells in a limbo of unfulfillable hope.

As Geoffrey O'Brien notes, Kubrick's *Barry Lyndon* is far richer and more ambiguous than Thackeray's novel. Kubrick's film, O'Brien comments, is "almost an exemplary catalog of life experiences, with all their variety and all their oppressive limitations." Yet for all the movie's range the world it shows still feels as far off as the noble rank that Barry sets his sights on. O'Brien writes that "the more intimately present [*Barry Lyndon's*] reality becomes, the more ephemeral and ghostly the people in it seem. The past never stops being the past; the images freeze and recede into a frame, beyond our reach."[4] The camera specializes in slow backward zooms, enforcing our detachment from what we see. Meanwhile, Michael Hordern's superbly restrained voice-over offers a continual dose of irony at Barry's expense, and so keeps the hero at a distance.

Kubrick carefully planned *Barry Lyndon*'s preproduction. The film's elaborate sets, he thought, required the man he saw as the best art director in the business, Ken Adam. One day in 1972 Adam, who had last worked with Kubrick on *Dr. Strangelove*,

Kubrick directing *Barry Lyndon*
(Courtesy of Photofest/Warner Bros)

got a phone call from the director asking him to design the sets
for *Barry Lyndon:*

> Stanley said he's got this film for me and he can't afford my
> money. So I said, "Stanley, it's not a good way to start talking
> to me, you know." So we had an argument. . . . Five weeks
> later, I got another phone call from him saying . . . money is
> no problem and will I do the picture? Our relationship was
> almost like a marriage in a way, a love-hate relationship. I
> felt to go through another film, you know, life is too short.
> But I was stuck.[5]

So at the beginning of 1973 Ken Adam began work on *Barry Lyndon*. He went scouting for eighteenth-century houses with Kubrick, who was determined that the movie be shot entirely on location. Adam wanted quite reasonably to use sets instead. He was worried about the smoke damage that might be done to the houses by the many candles that Kubrick wanted to use in the film. But Kubrick insisted, and as usual prevailed.

Kubrick was fanatical about relying on clusters of candles in *Barry Lyndon* because he had found a revolutionary lens made by Zeiss that could photograph candlelight. The disadvantage for his art director Adam was that repeated takes had to show the candles burned down to exactly the same level each time.

"Eventually I became very ill," Adam remembered. "Utterly exhausted—because he used to run dailies with me late at night. Stanley could really get away with four hours' sleep. Obviously, I couldn't. So I went back to London, and he was unbelievably concerned. His letters to me at the time were really quite touching." Roy Walker replaced Adam, who, as Julian Senior put it, was "taken off the set by men in white coats."[6]

During preproduction Kubrick decimated a pile of eighteenth-century art books, cutting out and studying their images. It took a year and a half to make the costumes: thirty-eight for O'Neal and twenty for Berenson. Kubrick had liked two Swedish films, Jan Troell's *The Emigrants* (1971) and *The New Land* (1972), in which the costumes looked like actual clothes, properly weathered rather than freshly sent from wardrobe. So he hired Troell's costume designer, Ulla-Britt Söderlund, who worked on the clothes for *Barry Lyndon* along with Milena Canonero, the designer for *A Clockwork Orange*.

Kubrick's perfectionism with the costumes extended to every other aspect of his movie's mise-en-scène. The look of *Barry Lyndon* is unique, full of artifice and décor, yet somehow still open to the freshness of the landscape. Though the actors wear heavy makeup, their flesh shines through, and you can see the wickedness in their faces. Class-based cruelty comes naturally to these vain aristocrats in their shark tank, as the nobles first siphon off Barry's riches and then swiftly discard him after his cataclysmic tussle with Bullingdon.

Barry Lyndon's shooting ran nearly nine months: with each movie Kubrick was taking longer to get what he wanted on film. During 1973 Kubrick and his crew shot for seven months, mostly in Ireland, then abruptly suspended production in January 1974 because of IRA bomb threats. The next month production resumed in Wiltshire, England, a hundred miles southwest of London. Kubrick filmed at Wilton House, then at Longleat House and Petworth House, both near Bath.

At Petworth House, D'Alessandro remembered, Kubrick hired the magician David Berglas to teach O'Neal and Patrick Magee, who played the Chevalier de Balibari, how to cheat at cards. Kubrick was fascinated by Berglas's card tricks and tried to unlock their secrets. He made Berglas do the tricks over and over and questioned him at length. D'Alessandro said to Berglas, "When something new comes along, first [Stanley] wants to know *if* it works, then when it works, he wants to know *how* it works. And when he knows how it works, he wants to know *when* it might not work. You can talk for hours about a thing with Stanley."[7]

The crucial arena for seeing how things work was, as always, in front of the camera. Kubrick on *Barry Lyndon* demanded many takes from his actors, typically saying something like "Let's go again" instead of telling them what he wanted. Murray Melvin, who played the diminutive, wormlike Reverend Runt in the film, explained Kubrick's shrewd practice of simply asking for repeated takes. "If someone tells you you've done a good bit," Melvin told Richard Schickel, "then you know it and put it in parentheses and kill it."[8]

Kubrick was running an experiment on his actors, waiting to see where more and more takes might lead them. "I had a funny feeling that Stanley liked to see the actor break a little bit perhaps because he would see them reveal something else," Steven Berkoff (Lord Ludd) remembered. "I said to myself, 'I will never break down—never!' . . . I started to relish each take. After about twenty-five takes, Stanley said, 'Okay, we've got it.' I said, 'Oh, is that all?' "⁹

Barry Lyndon is a subtle, deliberately paced movie, and initially it didn't inspire great box office enthusiasm. *Time* magazine journalist Lawrence Malkin remembers flying to England in the middle of a raging snowstorm with colleagues Martha Duffy and Richard Schickel to see a screening of *Barry Lyndon*, which Malkin had championed as a *Time* cover story. "About half an hour into the movie," Malkin recalls, "we turned to each other and said, this is beautiful, but this is not the kind of movie that usually winds up on the cover of *Time*."¹⁰ Marisa Berenson stared hauntingly out from *Time*'s cover on December 15, 1975, and it was one of the magazine's worst-selling issues.

Barry Lyndon premiered in New York on December 18, 1975. The picture cost eleven million dollars and, though it lost money at the American box office, it eventually broke even worldwide. Slowly but surely, it started doing well with European audiences. The film won four Oscars, for Ken Adam's production design and John Alcott's cinematography, as well as for the adapted score and the costumes. European showings made up for the shortfall in the United States, and the movie turned a profit for Warner Bros. But *MAD* magazine's parody "Boring Lyndon" hit a nerve. Kubrick's movie demanded a kind of patient attention that the American masses weren't quite ready for. *Barry Lyndon* lacked the far-out futuristic appeal of *2001*. Instead it was an ornate journey into eighteenth-century

Europe with an aura of the art house, including an allusion to Resnais's *Last Year at Marienbad* (1961) when Lady Lyndon performs a slow moonlit pavane before Barry.

The sheer slow poise of *Barry Lyndon*, the serene pacing of it, the perfection, never finicky, of each shot, marks it as the mighty opposite of seventies filmmaking, with its ragged, shoot-from-the-hip verve. It is an anti-Zeitgeist movie, harking back to the eighteenth century with its rage for order. Kubrick insists on careful battlefield design in a flat-out absurd yet historically real skirmish, with the British, including Barry, marching steadily to fife and drum toward a group of kneeling French soldiers, and getting just as steadily mowed down, since they cannot reload their muskets while marching. As in many of Kubrick's war scenarios, utter irrationality unites with regimented control.

Kubrick makes *Barry Lyndon* poised and sumptuous, but it also harbors sudden scenes of violence, just as *2001* combined the stability of space flight with the killing thrusts of the prehistoric Moonwatcher. The steady decorum gets ripped apart by sudden tumults like the brawl between Barry and his stepson Lord Bullingdon, who fight like the apes of *2001*, as Kubrick scholar Michel Ciment remarks—a jolting sequence with Kubrick himself manning the handheld camera.[11] There is a rough energy in *Barry Lyndon* lurking behind its tableaux.

There's more to *Barry Lyndon* than there is to most movies, more to every painterly frame. Kubrick often nods to the era's artists. Like Hogarth, he arranges groups of characters so that they tell a story. One shot, of a drunken, sleeping Barry surrounded by hangers-on, stylishly cites *The Rake's Progress*. Marisa Berenson's Lady Lyndon evokes the languid beauties depicted by Reynolds. Barry and his young son Bryan sit beneath a monumental van Dyck family portrait in Wilton House, the setting for Castle Hackton, the home that Barry acquires when he marries Lady Lyndon. The van Dyck dwarfs Barry and his son, art historian Adam Eaker notes: Barry is still the lonely Irish upstart out of place in this vast aristocratic home.

The detailed pattern that Kubrick weaves in *Barry Lyndon* is best explored step by step, by retracing the narrative. The film's story begins when Barry, a romantic youth, falls in love with his cousin Nora. But Nora's family matches her with the wealthy, cowardly Englishman Captain Quin, played with delightful strutting relish by Leonard Rossiter. Forced to leave Ireland in disgrace after dueling with Quin, Barry is briefly dragooned into the Prussian army (the Seven Years' War is on), then finds a patron in the crafty Chevalier de Balibari, a cardsharp and con man who preys on the aristocracy. Barry, who has become Balibari's right-hand man, helping him cheat at cards and fighting his duels for him, looks innocent as ever, but like Alex in *A Clockwork Orange*, another boyish charmer, he'll stop at nothing.

Like the self-satisfied Alex in the first half of *Clockwork*, Barry seems to get what he wants when he marries the immensely wealthy Lady Lyndon, whose decrepit husband has expired while fiercely mocking Barry, his uproarious guffawing metamorphosing into a choking fit. (The scene is played to the hilt with a rich comic tang, one of the antic disruptions to the film's slow pace.) But there is a nemesis ready to spoil Barry's plan to become an aristocrat: as usual in a Kubrick movie, the hero's scheme will fail. Barry inherits not only Lady Lyndon's money but also her troublesome, snobbish son, Lord Bullingdon, very finely played by Leon Vitali. Barry whips the unfortunate Bully, who gasps and tearfully vows that Barry will never beat him again. The battle between Barry and his stepson stands at the center of the movie, much more than the rather lifeless relationship between Barry and Lady Lyndon.

Kubrick provides a spectacular climax to the Barry-Bullingdon quarrel when Barry throttles his stepson at a concert, in a nasty knockdown, drag-out tussle. Various onlookers pile on rugby-style while Kubrick operates his shaky handheld camera. "I know I hurt him. I didn't want to hurt him, but I hurt him," Ryan O'Neal remembered about the fight scene.[12]

Kubrick sets off the raucous chaos of the Barry-Bullingdon fight with the most sentimental scene by far in his work, the death of little Bryan, apple of his father's eye (the pampered young boy falls from a horse). Kubrick no doubt wanted this Dickensian weepiness as a counter to the irony exhibited through most of *Barry Lyndon*, but I have never been able to reconcile myself to it. Here Kubrick wholly surrenders to the Hollywood tearjerker mode that he scorned everywhere else in his work. I much prefer the film's sinuous, asexual Reverend Runt, perfectly played by Murray Melvin as a thoroughly nauseating figure of virtue, to Bryan the doomed innocent, who seems so out of place here. Bryan's demise, complete with deathbed instructions to his parents about their forthcoming meeting in heaven, is too direct in its pathos to fit properly in the movie, and in the end he is more a Spielberg boy than a Kubrick one (though Spielberg would doubtless have suspensefully resuscitated him). I like better Barry's amiable uncle Jack Grogan, expiring after a skirmish, who tells Barry, "Kiss me, me boy, for we'll never meet again."

The death of his son is a blow of fate from which Barry never recovers. Bryan, while he lived, provided Barry's only real delight in the movie. Teaching the boy to fence, he discovers a lightly competitive playfulness he never knew before. The father-son bond is too easy and too winning in this hidebound aristocratic world, and so Bryan must die, Kubrick's sacrifice to enforce Barry's tragic loneliness.

Barry, utterly abandoned to sorrow after Bryan's death, agrees a duel with the vile Bullingdon, who has returned to assert his filial rights over Lady Lyndon's estate. What follows is one of Kubrick's masterpieces: a slow-moving, perfectly paced faceoff between Barry, attired like Gainsborough's blue boy, and Bullingdon, who proves both cowardly and despicably vengeful. The duel is Barry's finest moment, consisting not in what he does but what he doesn't do. Granted the first shot by the coin toss, he refuses to fire at Bullingdon, and declares he has received satisfaction.

Barry's grief-induced insensibility gives him an advantage in the duel. With his beloved son Bryan dead, what has he left to live for? And so he behaves nobly, throwing away his shot rather than aiming at Bullingdon. The dreadful Bullingdon, who vomits from fear when he thinks he has to face Barry's shot, now aims hard at his stepfather. When Barry falls, he yelps in childish joy. (Trying to get Vitali to vomit, Kubrick first tried semiraw chicken and then—this did the trick—raw egg.)

Kubrick began the movie with an extreme long shot of Barry's father being killed in a duel, beautifully echoing the final scene of Max Ophüls's masterpiece *The Earrings of Madame de* . . . That opening was comic: we see the father plop down abruptly in a stunning Gainsborough landscape, with the faraway death cosseted by Hordern's exceedingly polite, refined voice-over. The climactic duel between Barry and Bullingdon, by contrast, is deadly serious, confronting Bullingdon's petty vengeance with the nobility of spirit that desperation has brought out in Barry.

The duel revolves around the grimly conventional phrase "to receive satisfaction." Barry has never received satisfaction. Instead of truly existing, he has led a vicarious life as a pretend aristocrat. Like Alex in *A Clockwork Orange*, Barry is a sexual hedonist, and he spends money like water, but actual enjoyment remains out of reach for him except when playing with Bryan, who is now lost forever. Barry rises in the world as the hapless Johnny Clay of *The Killing* could not. Unlike Johnny, he has an idea of belonging. But it remains only an idea, and finally, a broken man, he belongs only to his mother, who succors him after he loses his leg in the duel. Like Humbert, he ends a damned, wretched figure.

Kubrick cannily generates suspense as well as ceremonial stasis during the duel, which is accompanied by what sounds like an Ennio Morricone version of the Handel Sarabande we hear so often in *Barry Lyndon*. The duel scene crawls along at a stately pace, while birds flutter in the nave of the church where Barry and Bullingdon face off. The play of light and shadow, like the rustle of the birds, ravishes the viewer, reminding us that digital technology cannot yet approach the fine gradations available to Kubrick's camera. As Adam Eaker notes, a single ray of light contains various tones of the same color, and different levels of shade, and Kubrick plays on this variety.[13] Vitali's 4K restoration of *Barry Lyndon* burnishes the film and adds 5.1 surround sound, a feature that Kubrick would surely have wished for just as Bach would have wanted a piano instead of his harpsichord. (From *Clockwork Orange* on, Kubrick insisted on monaural sound for his films because it was safer than stereo: movie theaters often had broken speakers.)

Tony Lawson, *Barry Lyndon*'s editor, remembered that the duel scene took six weeks to edit. Kubrick painstakingly matched shots from various takes, just as Glenn Gould, late in his career, patched together his recordings from short segments of different performances.

After the duel we observe the crippled Barry lying in bed playing cards with his mother, "utterly baffled and beaten," as the narrator remarks. The least painterly shot in *Barry Lyndon* is the last we see of him, a nouvelle vague freeze frame as he stoops into the carriage with his mother, his shrewdest and most loyal companion.

Kubrick follows Barry's exit with a gorgeous sterile tableau, the wordless shot-reverse-shot between Bullingdon and Lady Lyndon that ends the movie. As she signs over living expenses to her ex-husband Redmond Barry, we glimpse the date above her signature: 1789. A revolution is coming that will sweep away the stagnant hierarchy that triumphs in the movie. Yet mother and son, Bullingdon and Lady Lyndon, now reunited with no Barry between them, live forever in this moment. (When Spielberg realized Kubrick's plan for his final film, *A.I.*, he likewise ended with a perfect union between mother and son.) The brief intimacy between father and son, Barry and Bryan, has been shattered by fate, but there is an unbreakable bond between mother and son. This difference echoes Kubrick's own relation to his parents: from his mother he received open-ended approval, from his father the ambition to be a doctor, which Kubrick the son frustrated by nearly flunking out of high school. Tension and disappointment animate father-son relations in *Barry Lyndon* as they did in the teenage Kubrick's life.

Kubrick's parents visited him during *Barry Lyndon* postproduction in late 1974. Jack and Gert Kubrick came from Los Angeles to visit their son at Abbots Mead, since Kubrick had long ago decided never to fly again, and his last trip back to America, by ship, had been for the release of *2001*. (Kubrick as a young man had learned to fly a small plane and been traumatized by what he said was the uncertainty of air traffic signals: all his life Kubrick had a fear of factors beyond his control.).

The family matrix was on Kubrick's mind. *Barry Lyndon*, like its successor *The Shining*, is a notably Oedipal movie. Critic Julian Rice describes the love scene between Barry and Lischen, a young mother who gives him shelter during his early travels: "As they embrace, the child looks up at them with large, solemn eyes."[14] Later on, when Lady Lyndon says to Bullingdon, "Lord Bullingdon, you have insulted your father," he responds like Hamlet: "Mother, you have insulted my father."

Balibari is a father figure to Barry, but a more powerful father, George III, fails to grant him the lordship that he craves. He remains Mr. Redmond Barry, and never becomes Lord Lyndon. Telling a bedtime story to Bryan in which he boasts of cutting off heads in battle, Barry admits to Bryan that he didn't get to keep the heads: "The heads always remain the property of the king."

Barry never gets to exercise fatherly authority. Like *Clockwork*'s Alex, he is in the end a grown-up boy, but unlike that happy-go-lucky ruffian, he is conscious of being dwarfed in a world much bigger than he is. Finally he remains a minor figure framed in a faraway scene, thwarted in every possible way. Kubrick's next hero, Jack Torrance of *The Shining*, will be another such case.

7

—◆◦◆◦◆—

Something Inherently Wrong
with the Human Personality:
The Shining

IN EARLY 1977 Warners executive John Calley sent Kubrick the galleys of a new novel by a young horror writer. The novel was *The Shining* and its author, Stephen King, was already well known for *Carrie* (1974) and *Salem's Lot* (1975). Kubrick had been thinking of making a horror movie, but most books in the genre left him cold. King's book was different. Despite its flawed, baggy style, it had a mythic punch. The book was all about a father going to pieces and terrorizing his wife and son. *A Clockwork Orange* and *Barry Lyndon* featured two sons, Alex and Bullingdon, whose angry energy triumphed over an older generation. *The Shining*'s son, Danny, is much younger—a boy of about six—and the contest between him and his father is a matter of life and death: bloodthirsty Jack chases Danny with his axe.

The Shining is the story of Jack Torrance, a schoolteacher from Vermont and an aspiring writer. Looking for seclusion that will allow him to write, he takes a job as winter caretaker of the Overlook, an immense, empty hotel in the Colorado mountains. The hotel turns Jack into a "thing," a monster aching to murder his wife and child. King's book is about a writer trying to escape, like King himself, from alcoholism. Kubrick cuts the novel's elaborate backstory, its flashbacks to Jack's childhood and his life in Vermont, and makes *The Shining* puzzling and spare in a way that King never could.

King's novel dealt with two themes dear to Kubrick's heart: the failure of mastery and vicarious, hollowed-out existence. Jack's violent effort to control or "correct" (kill) his wife and son falls short, and in Kubrick's film he ends up frozen to death in a snowy hedge maze. *The Shining*, which confronts family violence and male rage even more directly than *Barry Lyndon*, would turn out to be Kubrick's most personal movie so far.

In June 1977 Kubrick chose a screenwriting partner: Diane Johnson, a novelist and professor at Berkeley. Kubrick had read Johnson's adroit, spooky 1974 novel *The Shadow Knows*, told in the scared voice of a woman whom the reader can't entirely trust. Johnson got a phone call from Kubrick and went to London, where the two of them, working at Kubrick's home, produced draft after draft of *The Shining*'s screenplay. They talked about Freud, horror fiction, and Bruno Bettelheim on fairy tales.

Kubrick rather than Johnson invented the most hideous and memorable scenes in the screenplay: Room 237's bathtub nude turned into a decomposing old woman—an echo of a shocking moment in Clouzot's *Diabolique* (1955)—and the twin elevators gushing blood. The latter shot became the film's preview, omnipresent in movie theaters during Christmas season 1979. As usual, Kubrick needed to get the shot exactly right: he used so much fake blood during the many takes of the elevator scene that the villagers downstream from Borehamwood Studios were convinced a massacre had occurred.[1]

Kubrick felt a surprising affinity for the murderous Jack.

Johnson said that Jack Torrance "had to be a specially demanding verbal combination—intelligent, unpleasant, mordant, and sarcastic. What struck me was how well Stanley wrote Jack. Much better than I could. Considering the ease with which Stanley wrote Jack, you wouldn't imagine Stanley to be the pleasant, kindly husband and father he is."[2] Jack is in fact Kubrick's doppelgänger: his madness reflects the director's own work ethic. Jack the writer is more than dedicated, he is obsessive, just like Kubrick the filmmaker. Unlike Kubrick, though, he has no partners in his creative project, no sense of spontaneity or teamwork, just a will to control. And unlike Kubrick, he answers frustration with wrath. Losing control makes him a monster.

Jack is a type, an empty vessel filled by the anger that storms through the American male. No one embodied such anger with more panache than Jack Nicholson. The hopped-up Nicholson, with his big bad wolf grin and agile quotation mark eyebrows, made gonzo fury look charming.

Kubrick early on settled on Nicholson to play Jack Torrance. Nicholson had just won an Oscar for *One Flew Over the Cuckoo's Nest* (1975), in which he starred as the rebel misfit Randle McMurphy. At the time Nicholson's life was in turmoil. He was breaking up with Anjelica Huston, and he had just found out that the woman he thought was his mother was actually his grandmother, and his elder sister really his mother. Nicholson was a refugee from the coked-up LA scene, but there were drugs in London too. He modeled his mad Jack partly after Charles Manson, whose gang had murdered actress Sharon Tate, girlfriend of Roman Polanski, a good friend of Nicholson. He called his performance "sort of balletic," and he was right: Nicholson moves with grace as he jabs the air with his fists, thumping and hollering in macho release.[3]

Kubrick wanted Shelley Duvall as his Wendy. He and Johnson had earlier thought that Wendy would be a strong, defiant character, perhaps to be played by Jane Fonda or Lee Remick. But Kubrick went in the opposite direction with the gangly, twitchy Duvall, who was so high-strung as to seem almost otherworldly. A regular in Robert Altman's movies, she had just won at Cannes for her role in Altman's *Three Women* (1977). Duvall's job in the film was to be terrified, at times to the point of hysteria. To this end, Kubrick made her life miserable on set, yelling at her over her mistakes, and he warned his crew not to show her any sympathy. Duvall knew why Kubrick was making her suffer, and she acknowledged later that she learned more about acting from him than she had from Altman. But the filming was no fun for her.

Vivian Kubrick depicts her father taunting Duvall in her short documentary about the making of *The Shining*. (She shot more than 100,000 feet of film, but the movie that exists is just half an hour long.) Gordon Stainforth remarked that Kubrick wanted the scenes cut out in which "he was very warm and nice" and "what was left were the sequences of him shouting at Shelley in the snow."[4] He wanted to play the ogre, not papa bear, and align himself with the madly irate Jack.

The last two members of *The Shining*'s ensemble were both inspired choices. For Dick Hallorann, Nicholson recommended his friend Scatman Crothers, a singer and television and film actor. Crothers, then seventy years old, was a kind, genial man with a bowlegged stride. As Hallorann he played the nice guy, cautious by instinct, with a touch of severity underneath. Kubrick's practice of doing take after take—invariably saying something like "Let's go again" rather than telling his actors what they had done wrong—took its toll on Crothers. When Nicholson axed him, Crothers had to fall thirty times. Kubrick filmed more than a hundred takes of one seven-minute sequence, Hallorann's early conversation with Danny over ice cream.

Crothers sometimes had trouble remembering his lines, but that wasn't the case with the boy who played Danny. Leon

Vitali headed a crew that interviewed more than four thousand American boys before selecting five-year-old Danny Lloyd, the son of a railroad engineer. Vitali was Danny's dialogue coach and constant companion on set. Lloyd had no idea that he was making a horror movie: he saw none of the paralyzing frights of the Overlook Hotel, no blood, no ghosts.

The Shining relies on Danny Lloyd's firm and assured performance. When he crouches in his hiding place and hears his father's mad bellowing, he is a boy in a Grimms fairy tale, stark and still. We see Danny watching a Road Runner cartoon: like Chuck Jones's agile hero, he outwits his enemy. Danny finally wins by retracing his steps in the maze, tricking the ogre of a father who wants to murder him.

Along with the actors, the star of *The Shining* is the Steadicam. Kubrick's cameraman Garrett Brown had recently invented a device to produce tracking shots without tracks or a dolly. (Brown first used it in John Avildsen's *Rocky* [1976].) "It's like a magic carpet," Kubrick said.[5] A spring-jointed platform attached to the cameraman eliminated the bumps and jerks that came with handheld shots. The Steadicam created shots that were perfectly smooth, the camera gliding forward without a ripple.

Kubrick wanted the Steadicam to accompany Danny's Big Wheel as he pedaled through the halls of the Overlook. So he put Brown in a wheelchair equipped with a speedometer, his camera about fifteen inches above the ground. As Wendy wheels the hotel's room service cart to give her husband a late breakfast, Kubrick crosscuts to Danny manically driving his Big Wheel through the Overlook's corridors. Forward-driving Danny, whose play has the determination of work, will turn out to be the hero of the movie. Like the pulsating heartbeat that later invades the film when Jack goes crazy, the sound rhythm of Danny's endless rolling sets the pace: muffled when on the hotel's carpets, loud when he crosses its hardwood floors. (Kubrick is fond of sound-based timekeeping: remember Dave's heavy breathing in *2001* when he crosses the spaceship to disconnect HAL.)

"We are falling into the movie," writes David Thomson, a "cool and premeditated" plunge. *The Shining* is full of smooth, vertiginous forward motion from its first moment, an implacably level helicopter shot swooping across a rocky western landscape. The shot shows an island surrounded by blue water, fitting emblem for a movie about being marooned in a lonely stronghold called the Overlook Hotel. The island seems to be moving toward the viewer, a frequent effect in Kubrick's inexorable-seeming tracking shots (as well as the Stargate sequence in *2001*). Urged by Kubrick, two cameramen, Greg MacGillivray and Jim Freeman, had developed a new way of doing helicopter shots, from the front rather than the side door of the helicopter, to produce a forward-sweeping effect similar to the Steadicam's.[6]

The smoothness of *The Shining* hypnotizes the viewer a little. Like Jack, we space out, ready to be taken in. We feel open, empty, before this film, Kubrick's shiny monolith. In the movie's only trick shot, Jack in the Colorado Lounge, out of ideas as usual, looks down on a model of the maze and sees a tiny Wendy and Danny running through it. We then observe in medium shot a menacing, vacant-headed Jack, mouth slightly open, eyes tilting upward, ready to submit to some invisible power. Having failed as an author, poor Jack waits to be possessed.

When we think of *The Shining* we remember Nicholson venting his world-consuming rage at the trembling Duvall. But the movie also relies on an equally familiar male strategy, repression. Being interviewed by Ullman (Barry Nelson), the hotel manager, early in the movie, Jack dutifully keeps his answers as dull as possible. How will his wife and son take to the isolation of the vast, deserted hotel in winter? We wait a beat while Jack composes his most compliant face, and then: "They'll love it." When Ullman, with a nervous chuckle, tells Jack the story of Charles Grady, the caretaker who a few winters earlier went mad and "killed his family with an axe," Jack responds with a leaden, impassive face. Superbly, this reaction shot of Jack is held just a few seconds too long, enough for us to get uncomfortable. Then Jack, cracking a polite, measured grin, says, "That is, uh, quite a story."

Jack at the movie's beginning has the job applicant's steady blankness, the false self you need to get ahead. Just as bland is Danny's interview with a child psychologist (Anne Jackson): Danny, like his father, is good at concealment. Jack, we have to assume, fails to tell Wendy about the Grady murders, the primal trauma in the Overlook Hotel. Instead, he says to Wendy that he just loves the place, and does a spooky, parodic *whoo-ooh*.

The Shining's scenes are replete with clichés. Wendy tells Jack, "It's just a matter of settling back into the habit of writing every day." Hallorann reminds Wendy of the dried prunes in the storeroom: "I tell you, Mrs. Torrance, you got to be regular if you want to be happy." While he drives through a snowstorm, Hallorann's car radio announces, "We have what you call your bad weather out there . . . get the cows in the barn." Such platitudes are the American way, defending us against all manner of disasters. You got to be regular if you want to be happy.

Keeping things normal and repressing trauma, via clichés if need be, is an American tradition. But then the blood starts to gush out, as in a fairy tale, and it doesn't stop. "They ate each other up?" Danny asks Jack about the Donner party, with a little boy's winning accent. "They had to," Jack confirms with satisfaction. This family will eat itself up when its ferocious energies come out, coaxed by the Overlook. Jack and Wendy are a perfect pair, her cringing submissiveness and his masculine torrent echoing against each other forever and ever.

Jack's real target, though, is his son, not his wife. Danny is Jack's competition: he has the creative gift that the hollow Jack lacks. This kid would be eager, curious, and innocent in a Spielberg movie, his senses wide open and wondering. Kubrick's universe is far darker. In *The Shining*, Danny glimpses blood and disorder, a confused image of what lies beyond childhood.

Danny tells himself that the Overlook's flood of gore and the Grady twins, now holding hands like Diane Arbus's famous pair and now lying hatcheted in a hallway, are like pictures in a book. And Jack pretends the hotel's frights are safely fictional, like a horror movie designed to thrill and chill us. In *The Shining* the vicarious becomes real, a prime fantasy of the movies. The frights Jack invoked in fun take him over: they are the only inspiration this failed writer ever finds.

Kubrick's *Shining* is a not-so-typical horror movie, but it also nods toward the western. Jack, Wendy, and Danny are a pioneer family assaulted by horrors, the VW bug their covered wagon, as they talk about the Donner party. The Overlook, Ullman tells Jack, was built "on an old Indian burial ground," a reminder of the old West's clash between white and Indian (and a perfunctory tip of the hat to a favorite Stephen King topos). The western often pits the man's intransigent need to do his duty against stereotypical female concerns like the health of a child. "Let's talk about Danny. . . . You believe his *health* might be at stake," Jack sneers at Wendy in the cataclysmic staircase scene, the peak of their battle. His masculine obligation, the deal with the devilish Overlook Hotel, overrules her maternal instinct. "I have *signed* a letter of agreement, a *contract*," Jack tells her, his hand whipping through the air. Like HAL, Jack takes on the white man's burden, responsibility for the mission.[7]

"There's something inherently wrong with the human personality," Kubrick said to interviewer Jack Kroll, explaining what drew him to King's novel. "There's an evil side to it."[8] It was just like Kubrick to describe evil as something "wrong with" humans, a kind of misfiring. In many Kubrick movies characters stumble over a malfunction, a design flaw, from Johnny Clay in *The Killing* to HAL in *2001*. "What is your major malfunction?" *Full Metal Jacket*'s Drill Instructor Hartman shouts at Private Pyle, who promptly shoots him in the chest. Jack's breakdown in *The Shining* is a catastrophic design flaw that comments on the American wish to live large, to express oneself with terrific power.

In horror movies the monster is not angry; it is merely an overriding, demonic force. In *The Shining*, as in no other horror film I can think of, male anger itself is monstrous. Kubrick's movie joins the mainstream of great American movies about masculine rage, from Nicholas Ray's *In a Lonely Place* (1951) to Ford's *The Searchers* (1956) to Scorsese's *Taxi Driver* (1976).

Jack is shouting and moaning in his sleep, head slumped on his desk in a puddle of drool. When Wendy shakes him awake he stammers out his nightmare: he murdered her and Danny, chopped them to bits. Then a frozen-looking Danny appears with a wound on his neck. Wendy, suspended between father and son, accuses Jack. This is her one moment of indignant rage: "You did this to him . . . you son of a bitch," she yells. The next scene begins with Jack dancing furiously down the hallway to the Gold Ballroom. Jack's walk, which required many takes to get right, shows Nicholson at his balletic height, pummeling the air as he stalks along.

Jack approaches the ballroom's bar, sits downs and claps his hands over his eyes, just like Danny blocking out the sight of the blood-filled elevators. "I'd give my goddamn soul for just a glass of beer."

And so Jack rubs his eyes open to the magic of one of Kubrick's greatest scenes, one that required eighty-plus takes. Jack sees none other than Lloyd the Bartender, played with robotic finesse by veteran Kubrick actor Joe Turkel. A slow grin dawns on Nicholson's face. Turkel's jaw appears wired to a grim un-dead levity. The clichés that *The Shining* loves now come to vicious life. "Women, can't live with 'em, can't live without 'em," Lloyd recites. In Jack's mouth such platitudes gather a vast satiric energy: "Words of wisdom, Lloyd . . . words . . . of . . . wisdom." Jack's eyes gleam with manic delight. Suddenly there's nothing more hilarious than sustaining oneself with lines like these, and Jack and the audience are in on the joke together. "A momentary loss of muscular coordination": that's how he dislocated Danny's arm when he came home drunk. Just a minor malfunction: and he mimes the snapping of the arm in a way that only Jack Nicholson can, with manic barbed-wire delight. The more we exult in Jack's declaration of inde-pendence from "the old sperm bank upstairs," as he names Wendy, the more we fear him.

Jack sells his soul for the intoxicating flavor of rebellion, cutting himself loose from the wife who keeps him down. (We can't help but remember Kubrick's script ideas of the 1950s, when he fantasized about walking away from the clingy Ruth Sobotka.) Yet what he gets is not freedom but "orders from the house," as Lloyd tells him later on: he is a servant to the hotel's endless cycle of death. The shots of bourbon that Lloyd gives Jack will convey him to the underbelly of the Overlook, Room 237: the place where trauma dwells, like the fruit cellar in *Psycho* (1960).

Danny goes to Room 237 before Jack does. We see Danny responding to what he thinks is his mother's voice inside the room. Some Freudian legend seems aprowl here. The strange woman lurking in Room 237 is the polar opposite of Wendy, with her girlish, unerotic naïveté. Instead of a mother with her comforting banalities, Danny finds a female devourer. A sign of adult sexuality run amok may have traumatized Danny, giving him the guilty mark on his neck.

When Jack investigates, he finds in Room 237 a sallow and

impassive naked young woman rising from the bathtub. This wan succubus, who has the alien sheen of a mannequin, embraces the slack-jawed, vacantly lustful Jack. She then turns into a decomposing old hag who cackles madly as Jack flees. He locks the door of 237 and backs away fearfully. (Kubrick will shrewdly rhyme this moment with Danny retracing his steps in the snowy labyrinth at the end of the movie.)

The two women in 237 are an emblem of Vanitas, who promises fair but conceals the mortal decay that lies beneath the surface of youth. Jack, while kissing his naked muse in 237, may think he is being anointed by immortal beauty, but the hotel plays a joke on him: he finds himself "chained to a corpse" (a phrase that King repeatedly used to describe Jack's marriage to Wendy).

Schopenhauer supplies the best comment on the two women in Room 237. Discussing "the vanity of all endeavor," the German philosopher gives as his example the conversion of Raymond Lull, a medieval "adventurer" who became a monk and philosopher: "Raymond Lull, who had long wooed a beautiful woman, was at last admitted to her chamber, and was looking forward to the fulfillment of all his desires, when, opening her dress, she showed him her bosom terribly eaten away with cancer. From that moment, as if he had looked into hell, he was converted."[9]

Here's one more passage from Schopenhauer: "Most of us carry in our hearts the Jocasta, who begs Oedipus for God's sake not to inquire further; and we give way to her, and that is the reason why philosophy stands where it does."[10] Sure enough, an inscrutable-looking Jack reports to Wendy that there was "nothing at all" in Room 237. Earlier, Dick Hallorann said the same to Danny. Both men have given way to their internal Jocasta: and so repression wins again.

Ironically, Penderecki's "The Awakening of Jacob" plays while Jack is in 237—"Truly the Lord is in this place, and I did not know it," Jacob says when he rises from his dream in Genesis. Kubrick's pitch-black humor is at work again.

Later on in *The Shining* we hear Penderecki's *Polymorphia*, the sound, according to the scholar Roger Luckhurst, of "a horde of insects eating their way out of the string section."[11] The film's soundtrack is subtly layered, with heartbeats, ambient sound, and at times several music tracks at once. Penderecki and Ligeti would later be horror film staples, but Kubrick pioneered the use of these avant-gardists.

Room 237 is the core of *The Shining*'s horror. Now Danny, dribbling spittle and shaking like an epileptic, feels the shock waves from what Jack sees in Room 237. So does Hallorann, transfixed on his bed in Miami like Dave Bowman in the Stargate. Lying on his bed after Jack visits 237, Danny sees REDRUM for the first time: the red room, the room of blood that ties sex to death, the place where a father tries to kill a mother and a son.

The Shining's tension escalates further as Kubrick gives us another unforgettable sequence. Here is Wendy rifling through Jack's manuscript, which, she sees to her horror, contains the same sentence thousands of times over: "All work and no play makes Jack a dull boy." (Like Sobotka, she is a "suction cup" who aggravatingly tries to help Jack with his work.) The edge of Jack's typewriter looms like *2001*'s monolith, perfectly centered in the frame beneath Shelley Duvall's panicked face. Wendy's husband has, indeed, been hard at work, and now, while we gaze from a distance, from Jack's distance, at her back, the man himself enters the Colorado Lounge. Drily, softly, he says, "What are you doing down here?" Wendy jumps like a jerked marionette, and so do we. *The Shining*'s greatest scene has begun with an electrifying jolt.

Earlier, Jack warned Wendy to "stay the fuck away" from his desk, in response to her chipper offer to read his writing. "That's the one scene in the movie I wrote myself," Nicholson said. Years earlier, when he was a young man with a wife and daughter, Nicholson was acting in a movie during the day and writing a screenplay at night. Once while he was writing, he said, "my beloved wife, Sandra, walked in on what was unbeknownst to her, this *maniac*."[12] That performance ended Nicholson's marriage. But in *The Shining*, Wendy meekly retreats, saving her fire for the "all work and no play" sequence.

The wife has uncovered the husband's secret: not a concealed love affair but instead hopeless, endless *writing*. Jack is a mere drudge chained to this hell, the Overlook, bereft of a creative spark. Empty repetition shows the hotel's power. Like a minor-league demon in Dante or Spenser, Jack does the same thing over and over, locked into his pact with the hotel. Here the joke is about the American male's reliance on steady routine for his self-definition. What happens when your job gets you down, when you become a dull boy, when things get "all balled up at the head office," as Charlie (John Goodman) puts it in the Coen brothers' parabolic masterpiece *Barton Fink* (1991)? What happens is the floodgates burst: "Look upon me, I'll show you the life of the mind," Goodman chants, jogging murderously through his inferno, a burning hotel with rows of separate fires, one for each room.

The Coens' Charlie Weathers (aka Mad Man Mundt) derives from Flannery O'Connor's Misfit, but also from Jack Torrance. These killers are masters of American lingo, expert polishers of the glad-handing phrase. We saw Jack's average Joe routine with Lloyd, at the bar. Now, with Wendy in the all-work-and-no-play scene, he lunges into snide, vicious parody: "You're *confused*," he sneers, aping her shrinking manner. Wendy is now a quivering, sobbing wreck. "You need *to think things over*. . . . You've had your whole fucking *life* to think things over!" he shouts, as if he were vitality incarnate, and she the ball and chain of bourgeois stupidity. Then, rather lightly, with a little smile, now savagely savoring the words: "What good's a few more minutes gonna do you?" Poor Wendy has only a few more minutes of life left, of this Jack is sure. He is all set to whack her with that baseball bat. But—and here comes the scene's high, impish joke—first he has to convince her to give him the bat. And she won't. "Wendy. Light . . . of . . . my . . . life," Jack says. (A line from *Lolita!*) Just for the fun of it, Jack plays the psychotic he has become: "I'm not gonna hurt you Wendy. I'm just gonna bash your brains in. Bash them right . . . the fuck . . . in."

"Give me the bat." Nicholson says it straight, gazing direct, like a hypnotist willing control over his patient. Then comes his tongue flick, a small stroke of genius: "Give me the bat. Wendy. Give me. The bat." But now the tables turn. Shaking like crazy, she lands two solid blows, first to his hand—she'll get him again there, with her knife in the bathroom—and then to his neck, right where Danny was wounded. Swatted powerfully by his frail, jumpy wife, Jack tumbles down the staircase. Wendy proves to be no basket case but rather, as Grady (Philip Stone) notes later, surprisingly "resourceful."

The baseball bat scene on the Colorado Room's staircase works in part because Kubrick enlists us on Jack's side. A small part of us wants, with Jack, to bash the irritating Wendy's brains in. When she bashes Jack instead, we are not so much exultant as nervous about what comes next. Her bright idea, to drag Jack to the pantry and lock him in, ought to put him out of commission. But Grady intervenes to free Jack from his prison. Jack rampages through the hotel with his axe and, with one blow, kills Halloran, who has just arrived in the Sno-Cat.

When he had Jack axe-murder Halloran, Kubrick was thinking of the killing of Arbogast in *Psycho*, a rapid shock to the viewer's system that, when Hitchcock's film first opened, caused more screams than the shower murder. Kubrick filmed Jack landing three vicious blows to Halloran's chest, but the next day decided that this was too brutal, too much of a play for audience reaction. In the final cut Jack axes Halloran once, then glides up slowly like Murnau's Nosferatu from the dead

The Shining's staircase scene, with Jack Nicholson and Shelley Duvall
in the foreground (Courtesy of Photofest/Warner Bros)

body. Kubrick's parents, Jack and Gert, were on the set the day
the death of Hallorann was filmed, and Kubrick was afraid that
they would be traumatized by it. Kubrick's worry replays the
theme of the movie: a son's concern about what will become of
his parents. As it turned out, the Kubricks, not at all distressed,
enjoyed the scene greatly.[13]

Even more terrifying than Jack's murder of Hallorann is his
attack on Wendy, who cowers in the bathroom, her upraised
knife shaking wildly. Jack Torrance swings his axe like a pro,
with expert well-muscled heft. (Nicholson was for a time a vol-
unteer fireman.) Heaving that axe into the bathroom door, grinning "Heeere's Johnny," Jack is at his most big-bad-wolfish.
But the fairy tale shrewdness of his wife and son gets the better
of him.

Kubrick and Johnson struggled over the end of *The Shining.*
At one point they pictured Hallorann becoming "murderous,"
"an appalling figure of savagery" who kills the entire Torrance

family and then shoots himself. Another "Ending idea: Danny and maybe cook left alone," or Danny "saved by cook."[14] But Hallorann turned out to be expendable. By contrast, King makes him Wendy's new boyfriend, and a kindly father substitute for Danny, after Jack's death.

Both *Psycho* and *The Shining* tease us with their endings. Frozen Jack in the labyrinth, like grinning Jack in the 1921 photo that concludes the movie, reminds us of Hitchcock's final close-up of Norman, with Mother's skeletal teeth shining through his smile. In both views the men are possessed by something that America loves: mother, work. But the two men are quite different. Norman is just a dutiful son, with no particular ambition. Jack by contrast imagines he is a writer who needs his solitude, but in fact he creates nothing. By freezing Jack, Kubrick thwarts the romantic selfhood so basic to American fantasies.

The maze's "snow" was fine, powdery dairy salt; the lights were bright orange, later passed through a blue filter. As in the ballroom scene, oil smoke was used to cloud the air. The temperatures neared a hundred degrees. The crew got lost in the maze, the smoky "orange hell," as Brown called it. "It wasn't much use to call out 'Stanley!'" Brown said, "as his laughter seemed to come from everywhere."[15] Kubrick was the absent sarcastic god ruling over the labyrinth, this big boy's play set. Kubrick repeatedly measured the height of the fake snow, making sure it was between eight and ten inches high—essential if the footprints were to look real. Like a fairy tale ogre, Jack chases his son with an axe, itching to commit bloody murder. He howls like a beast into the snowy void. "Danny, I'm coming for you," Jack bellows, a pathetic wounded animal.

Even though Jack the monster has frozen to death in the Overlook's maze, he lurks forever in the photograph from 1921.

The movie's magical Borges-like ending was originally followed by a sequence shown when *The Shining* premiered in May 1980 in New York and Los Angeles. Leon Vitali described the added scene to an interviewer:

> [Wendy is] in bed, and Danny's in the corridor in his dressing gown reading comic books. Then Ullman, the manager that we saw at the beginning, turns up coming in all the way from Florida to see if they're okay. He says to her you mustn't worry, these things . . . What'll be great is I'll invite you to my house, and it's warm, there's fresh air, and the sea. Danny can run around. Then she breaks down and cries in gratitude and relief. And he walks out into the corridor and sees Danny there on his way out, and he says, "oh Danny, I've got something for you." Then he throws out a yellow tennis ball which he had in his pocket, which Danny catches.

In the final shot of this scene we realize that the hotel manager was clued into the Overlook's diabolic power all along. "There was a Hitchcockian side to this resolution, and you know that Kubrick was crazy about Hitchcock," said Shelley Duvall, who liked this first ending.[16] In his final movie, *Eyes Wide Shut*, Kubrick would use Victor Ziegler (Sydney Pollack) as such a Hitchcockian figure of mastery. But in *The Shining* he preferred something more perplexing. The epilogue, Kubrick must have realized, was too shadowy-conspiratorial, with its hint that Ullman was the master of the sinister hotel that waited like a spider for its next victim.

Julian Senior remembers that Kubrick asked him "Whadda ya think?" about this first version of *The Shining*'s end:

> I said, you know Stanley, for me the most extraordinary shot of the whole movie is the track into the photograph—that's it. The stuff at the hospital room, the tennis ball, the kid . . .
> He stopped fifteen paces behind with a face like thunder. And Stanley had dark brown eyes with no pupils, it was

like looking into an abyss. And there was a pause and he said "Don't you ever tell me how to direct a movie."[17]

But Kubrick agreed with Senior, as it turned out, and cut the hospital room scene. Like the *Dr. Strangelove* pie fight, the sequence seems to have disappeared: no one I know has seen it since *The Shining*'s 1980 opening.

In the end Kubrick let the forces that inhabit Jack remain invisible. The finished movie ends with a slow zoom in on Jack in black tie, dapper and ready, at the Overlook's July 4 party, 1921.[18] Kubrick insisted on July 4 because Jack began with a declaration of independence, his ferocious plea that he is a writer, and therefore bound to go it alone. Jack chained to the typewriter, tapping out the same awful sentence hour after hour, was desperate to be released from work. Play was what Jack so badly needed, and the high-stepping 1920s is a supreme American image of play. But the twenties Jack Torrance, like most of the self-invented Gatsbys that pepper American history, is really just an image, not a lived reality. In Jack's end is his beginning: he will happen again and again, an empty shell coming round for his latest incarnation. We'll meet again, Jack Torrance, the next time we watch the movie. Cinema, like the Overlook, promises a ghostly immortality.

Yet Danny rather than Jack might be the real center of *The Shining*. The embattled child, who, like the boy Kubrick, perseveres into self-reliant strength despite the threats coming from authority (whether the father's or, in Stanley's case, the school's), again offers a key to his work. Here's a Freudian fable, submitted for your approval. Imagine Danny coming up with the plot of *The Shining*. He has been left alone with a placating mother and a sometimes violently moody, abstracted father. He's getting tired of the dull game he witnesses every day, in which one parent deflects the other's frustration and disappointment. So the child turns his father into a wild man, and he makes his mother bear the brunt of the father's bloodthirsty rampage. In the end, the father gets killed off by his own fury. By bringing out the rampant chaos within the father, Danny survives and becomes someone other than Jack, an escapee from the Oedipal bloodbath. A bit sharper-edged, no, than the Spielbergian saga of a boy trading in his parents for a gentle alien pal?

8

◆┃◆┃◆

Make Sure It's Big—Lon Chaney Big:
Full Metal Jacket

In 1980, a few months before *The Shining* opened in New York on May 23, Kubrick moved from Abbots Mead into a very large house on 172 acres in Childwickbury, just north of St. Albans, about an hour's drive from London. The sprawling grounds included a block of stables, two ponds, servants' cottages, a park, a rose garden, and a cricket pitch. The manorial setup was ideal for Kubrick's needs. The stables became offices and cutting rooms, and nearby was a gun club where he could do his target shooting.

"Childwickbury Manor wasn't so much a big house as a collection of rooms randomly added onto a narrow Georgian building," Kubrick's driver, Emilio D'Alessandro, remembered. There were 129 rooms in all, and Kubrick told D'Alessandro to make four copies of each room key. "We need one for me, one for you, one for Christiane, and a spare copy, just in case all three of us lose the same key," he said.[1]

Kubrick's office was in Childwickbury Manor's Red Room (shades of *The Shining!*). He liked to hole up there and devour books, wearing his usual household uniform: tennis shoes, baggy threadbare pants, and shirts with lots of pockets, some of them ink-stained. The pockets were for little notebooks that he bought by the dozens at W. H. Smith, the stationery store in St. Albans. Kubrick still dressed like the same messy Greenwich Village bohemian he had been in the fifties. When he was on set and it was cold enough, he liked to wear a military jacket and an anorak over his rumpled shirt and trousers.

Kubrick's beard was getting shaggier, and he had become noticeably more portly. He enjoyed being something of a Jewish Santa Claus during Christmas season, welcoming the children of St. Albans, who were allowed to pick out a Christmas tree from a heap of them he had cut and ready from his grounds. "Thank you, Mr. Kubrick," the children recited. Like many New York Jews of his generation, Kubrick loved Christmas.

Along with the Kubrick family, Childwickbury housed a collection of pet dogs and cats. Kubrick loved the animals and worried incessantly when one of them fell sick. ("If the cat was sick he would drop everything and talk to the vet and tell him 'We will do so-and-so,' and argue with him," Christiane remembered.)[2] D'Alessandro, originally hired as Kubrick's driver, became an impromptu veterinarian, as well as a handyman, technician, gardener, builder, and errand boy.

Kubrick's employees loved him, but he was taxing to work for. "Stanley kind of ate you up," Leon Vitali admitted.[3] Like D'Alessandro, Vitali worked sixteen hours a day for Kubrick, whose demands often seemed endless. Andros Epaminondas, who was Kubrick's assistant for ten years, quit in 1980, worn out by the pressure, so Vitali had to labor harder than ever. He fielded phone calls from Warner Bros, tussled with distributors, theater owners, and advertisers, and painstakingly supervised the prints of Kubrick's films. Kubrick insisted that Vitali watch as many prints as he could to make sure they were as flawless as possible. When Vitali restored some of Kubrick's movies for Blu-ray years after the director's death, he was well prepared: he had seen them hundreds of times.

Kubrick drove Vitali and D'Alessandro hard, but he cared about them, and they stayed loyal. He couldn't do without them, and he made sure they knew that. "He was always so kind to me that I couldn't say no to him," D'Alessandro said.[4] Vitali's love and appreciation for Kubrick shine through the moving documentary *Filmworker*, which covers Vitali's years as the director's assistant.

Ever the control freak, Kubrick liked to tell people both on and off the set, "Don't touch anything until you've read the instructions!" The zero-gravity toilet in *2001*, with its lengthy set of directions, is Kubrick's joke about his own penchant for writing step-by-step guidelines. At the Childwickbury house he explained what to do in case of fire, for example (two solid pages, including much detail about how to rescue the animals). On the set, Kubrick the doctor's son liked to give medical advice. "He was certain that he was a good doctor," Christiane recalled, "and would drive people crazy telling them to take pills of one kind or another. He would explain to the women who worked on the set what to do about a difficult menstrual period—'Don't eat salt, eat this and this'—and would walk away, his cigarette leaving a trail of smoke."[5]

Kubrick needed to have his wife and daughters close by at Childwickbury. He had traditional ideas about a father's role, and was at times a quizzical interrogator of his daughters' boyfriends. "You're kidding, right?" he asked his stepdaughter Katharina after talking to one of her dates. A crisis came when Katharina decided at age thirty that she wanted to leave the house and live in London. (She was getting married to a caterer named Phil Hobbs, who later worked as a producer on *Full*

Metal Jacket and *Eyes Wide Shut*.) Later, Anya, who was six years younger, decided to leave as well. "Why are they doing this to me?" Kubrick asked D'Alessandro.[6]

Surrounded by his family, his employees, and his pets, a busy hive of activity, Kubrick was the reverse of a hermit. He liked to cook for his daughters and for guests, and could even be seen doing the laundry. And he was perpetually on the phone. Kubrick loved to talk to Warner Bros executives John Calley, Terry Semel, and Julian Senior, as well as Ken Adam, Spielberg, and other Hollywood insiders. He called his sister Barbara nearly every night. The director John Milius remarked, "Stanley had no regard for time. He'd call you in the middle of the night, whenever he felt like calling. I'd say, 'Stanley, it's the middle of the night.' He'd say, 'You're awake, aren't you?' He'd never talk for less than an hour. He just had all kinds of things to discuss—everything."[7]

When he wasn't on the phone or the fax (a new favorite toy), Kubrick was trying to decide what kind of movie to make next. During the early eighties he pursued a science fiction project, an adaptation of a short story by Brian Aldiss about an android boy called "Super Toys Last All Summer Long." In the end Kubrick, after years of work with Aldiss and other writers, passed the idea on to Steven Spielberg. It became Spielberg's *A.I.: Artificial Intelligence* (2001), which came out after Kubrick's death, a unique Kubrick-Spielberg hybrid.

Kubrick had another idea brewing. Early in 1980 he started talking to the writer Michael Herr about making a war movie. The conversations with Herr would eventually come to fruition in 1987's *Full Metal Jacket*. Herr had gone to Vietnam as a freelance war correspondent and seen action during the Tet Offensive. He told his tales of combat in *Dispatches* (1977), one of the greatest books of war journalism ever written. Then Herr wrote the screenplay for Francis Ford Coppola's *Apocalypse Now*

(1979), a movie that Kubrick admired. (After making *Full Metal Jacket*, he said that he thought Coppola's movie was like Wagner and his own like Mozart, precise and classical.)[8]

Herr and Kubrick hit it off. Like Kubrick, Herr was Jewish, and he liked Kubrick's wit and wide scope of interests. He found that Kubrick's voice was "very fluent, melodious even," despite his "Bronx nasal-caustic" twang. He talked "with a pleasing and graceful Groucho-like rushing and ebbing of inflection for emphasis," Herr said.[9]

Herr got to hear plenty of the Kubrick voice. The director, he soon discovered, liked to call him up and talk for hours about everything under the sun. "I once described 1980–83 as a single phone call lasting three years, with interruptions," Herr later remarked. "Hey, Michael, didja ever read *Herodotus?* The Father of *Lies?*" Kubrick might ask, or wonder why Schopenhauer was always considered such a pessimist: "*I* never thought he was pessimistic, did *you*, Michael?"[10] They also covered opera, Balzac, Hemingway, and a full range of Hollywood gossip.

The day after their first conversation—about Jung, the Holocaust, Schnitzler's *Dream Story*, and a few other things—Kubrick had D'Alessandro deliver two books to Herr: the Schnitzler novella and Raul Hilberg's *Destruction of the European Jews* (1961). Lately he had been thinking of making a movie about the Holocaust. Kubrick bugged Herr every few weeks to read Hilberg, until finally Herr said, "I guess right now I just don't want to read a book called *The Destruction of the European Jews.*" "No, Michael," Kubrick replied, "The book you don't want to read right now is *The Destruction of the European Jews, Part Two.*"[11]

Kubrick and Herr had both read a 1979 novel by Vietnam vet Gustav Hasford called *The Short-Timers* (Vietnam slang for soldiers whose tour of duty ends soon). Hasford, a combat journalist with the First Marine Division, got caught up in the Tet

Offensive, just like Herr. While still in Vietnam he joined Vietnam Veterans Against the War. After returning stateside he moved to Washington State, where he was a desk clerk in a hotel catering to loggers who, he said, had "been in fights and they'd be dragging these scrubby, extremely ugly prostitutes with them. The job gave me a lot of opportunity to read—like Nathanael West, you know. After about 3 o'clock when all the loggers had passed out."[12]

Hasford eventually drifted to LA, where he stayed for a time in science fiction writer Harlan Ellison's house and became an editor at porno magazines. As a sideline, Hasford stole books from libraries, amassing a large collection on the American West. When Kubrick, through Jan Harlan, bought the option on *The Short-Timers*, Hasford was working as a security guard and living in his car.

Hasford, who was paunchy and tightly wound, with an Alabama accent, ended up working a little with Herr and Kubrick on the screenplay, but his gonzo aggression didn't go over well. Hasford's letters to Kubrick, scabrous and funny, make entertaining reading, as Hasford by turns taunts, cajoles and butters up the director (he signs one letter "Warm regards, Fred C. Dobbs Hasford").[13]

Kubrick began his relation with Hasford in his usual style: over the phone. Three or four times a week, he pumped Hasford relentlessly for information about Vietnam. Their longest conversation, Hasford said, lasted six hours. In a letter of January 1983, Hasford told a friend, "Stanley and I, after about a dozen long talks, are lobbing frags. I told Stanley he didn't know shit from Shinola about Vietnam." In August 1985 he was blunter: "Stanley is bullying me, threatening me." Then, in March 1986, Hasford wrote, "I finally pried a copy of the shooting script out of Stanley's famously anal-retentive fingers. It's 99% mine." Herr and Kubrick, he said, had simply "retyped" his book. Hasford demanded the return of a set of battlefield photographs he had lent Kubrick, and he also insisted on screenplay credit (which he got).[14]

No doubt a little freaked out by Hasford's outbursts, Kubrick displayed his trademark calm in a letter that feels as if it could have been written by HAL. Remarking on "the extraordinary lack of objectivity which pervades your letter," Kubrick wrote, "I cannot help but realize that you are very disappointed and unhappy, and I am genuinely sorry about that and wish it were otherwise. . . . I thought we were, at least, some sort of friends."[15]

In *The Short-Timers*, the cantankerous Hasford shows an eerie eloquence that attracted Herr and Kubrick. "To carry death in your smile, that is ugly. War is ugly because the truth can be ugly and war is very sincere," he writes.[16] The novel, now out of print, tells the story of a Marine who, after going through basic training under a brutal drill instructor, is transported to "the shit": the war in Vietnam. Hasford's plot became the basis of *Full Metal Jacket*, and some of the movie's best lines can be found in his book.

Herr and Hasford had been in the shit. Kubrick, for all his fascination with military history, most definitely had not. "I was very lucky," Kubrick said about his lack of war experience. "I slipped through the cracks each time. I was 17 when World War II ended and was married when the Korean War began. I wouldn't have volunteered." Kubrick was, he admitted, a "confirmed coward."[17] On *2001*'s Dawn of Man set he filmed the leopard's attack on the apes from a cage while his actors sweated bullets inside their primate suits. (One can see Kubrick's point: Should Admiral Nelson have shown up on deck during the battle of Trafalgar?)

Kubrick had a severely risk-averse personality, but he loved military history in part because war, like chess, requires the managing of risk. Soldiers become pawns in a great game, parts of a fighting machine rather than individuals. *Paths of Glory, Spartacus,* and *Dr. Strangelove* were all about war, and *Barry Lyndon* contained stunning battle scenes. *Full Metal Jacket* would be Kubrick's boldest war movie yet, the one where he fully explored how the military remakes human beings for tactical purposes. Kubrick's Napoleon screenplay shied away from this subject, downplaying the massive slaughter of the Russian campaign. But Kubrick's Vietnam movie would deal with the absurdity of a war in which more explosives were dropped than during World War II, where civilians were fair game as long as they were in "free fire zones," and where abstract bureaucratic talk about kill ratios and pacified hamlets obscured the grim facts of death and devastation.

During the Vietnam War, Kubrick had kept his distance from the peace movement as he did from all other political side-taking. When he was asked in 1968 whether he would be happy if the United States withdrew from Vietnam, he said only, "Sure."[18] The overt craziness of a futile, unexplainable war was what interested him, not some lesson about American imperialism.

In *Full Metal Jacket* the Marines of the Lusthog Squad are skeptical when interviewed by a camera crew about why they are in Vietnam. Are they fighting for freedom? "If I'm gonna die for a word, the word is poontang," Animal Mother, the most straight-ahead brutal of them, comments. "Do I think America belongs in Vietnam?" another Marine muses. "I don't know. I can tell you one thing, *I* belong in Vietnam." This is one of the movie's choicest lines. The Marines feel bizarrely at home, since the chaos and confusion around them has seeped into their souls.

Kubrick decided on twenty-seven-year-old Matthew Modine for Joker, *Full Metal Jacket*'s main character. He had liked Modine as a Vietnam vet in Alan Parker's *Birdy* (1984). Modine had a friend from acting school, Vincent D'Onofrio, who was working as a bouncer, and D'Onofrio, a newcomer to movies, became Private Pyle, the hapless recruit tormented by his drill sergeant. Lee Ermey, a retired Marine drill instructor, was originally hired as a technical adviser on the film but edged his way into the role, which he played with disturbing perfection. As Kubrick put it, "I mean Lee is not as great an actor as, say, the greatest actor in the world but the greatest actor in the world couldn't be better than Lee in that part."[19]

Filming for *Full Metal Jacket* began at the end of August 1985 and lasted eleven months. The Vietnam scenes, all of the movie after the first twenty-two minutes, were filmed mostly at Beckton, near London, a ruined gasworks scheduled for demolition. "They allowed us to blow up the buildings," Kubrick told an interviewer. "We had demolition guys in there for a week, laying charges. One Sunday, all the executives from British Gas brought their families down to watch us blow the place up. It was spectacular."[20] Palm trees were imported from North Africa. Kubrick and his crew studied advertisements from Vietnamese magazines and used them to make the Vietnamese murals for the streets of Hue. Meanwhile, the actor-recruits got sharper and sharper; they were starting to become Marines. Marching and running precisely in tandem, drilling with their rifles: all this Ermey taught them, while they trained exhausting hours with him. The actors became a corps.

D'Onofrio and Modine spent hours with Kubrick in his trailer bouncing around ideas. "A lot of the time he would let us block scenes. And we worked on the script, in the trailer—a lot." D'Onofrio remembered how Kubrick took the two young actors under his wing:

> We'd come to his house every Saturday night to see movies, Matthew and I. . . . First we'd have dinner, with Christiane and the girls. There was a lot of drinking. Stanley liked those little Heinekens, the ones that look like grenades. Then he would show a movie. There were two projectors, and Stan-

ley would thread the reels himself. Stanley was very kind. He made us feel free to ask any questions. Anything we wanted to know, he'd tell us. I learned so much from him. He showed us Woody Allen, Spielberg. He loved the *Purple Rose of Cairo*, *Annie Hall*, *Manhattan*, and he loved early Woody Allen. He was a big fan of Spielberg. With Scorsese I only heard him talk about *Raging Bull*—he was a big boxing fan.[21]

In *Full Metal Jacket* Modine is game but somewhat squeamish, and Kubrick draws on his uncertain character, neither rebellious nor gung-ho. Modine was uncomfortable at times during the shoot. A family-values Mormon who had just gotten married, he insisted on inserting a towel between himself and Papillon Soo Soo, who played a prostitute in a sex scene that Kubrick later cut.[22] (He retained Soo Soo's famous deadpan come-on, "Me so horny, me love you long time.")

Full Metal Jacket's first sequence, set in the Marine boot camp at Parris Island in South Carolina, is rigid, tunnel-shaped, and full of raw aggression. DI Hartman's face looms too close over the "maggots," his recruits. He hollers insults, slamming the men for being "faggots" and "ladies." Ultrasmooth traveling shots survey the maggots as Hartman berates them furiously, and Kubrick's abusive camera angles trap them.

This first part of the movie is about producing humans who will fit together perfectly in one greater body, "my beloved Corps" as Hartman calls it. Hartman clearly relishes the role, and in Pyle he finds his perfect victim. Private Pyle, slow and dumb, looks like a bug baby with a jelly donut tummy. Basic training will turn him into a drooling automaton, a Section Eight (eligible for psychiatric discharge).

Kubrick's calling cadence sequences shine. The Steadicam smoothly eats up the ground as the recruits run and chant, "I don't know but I been told, / Eskimo pussy is mighty cold."

(Eskimo pussy = death.) The erotic goal of warfare is to blow away someone else, but the soldier's own death is always in sight too. "If I die in a combat zone,/Box me up and ship me home./Pin my medals upon my chest,/Tell my Mom I done my best."

Kubrick was once again meditating on how violence underpins what we are. *Full Metal Jacket*'s basic training segment, like *A Clockwork Orange*'s "Singin' in the Rain," backs up ruthlessness with musical-comedy moves.[23] *2001*'s Dawn of Man has its own version of basic training, the blanket party when the apes take turns beating a rival's corpse with bones. In all three films, viciousness retools humanity.

In *Full Metal Jacket* Kubrick backs up the Marine gospel with a stark-mad theology. Hartman in his Christmas Day sermon delivers a dead-serious parody of religious faith: "God has a hard-on for Marines, because we kill everything we see! He plays His games, we play ours! To show our appreciation for so much power, we keep heaven packed with fresh souls." The Marine and those he kills are expendable, like the victims of atomic holocaust in *Dr. Strangelove*, but the Corps is eternal reality. Here is Hartman: "Marines die. That's what we're here for. But the Marine Corps lives forever, and that means you live forever."

Kubrick ends the basic training sequence with a stupendous set piece. In the middle of the night, Joker finds Pyle, now fully psychotic, in the head, the recruits' bathroom. The head is the one surreal set in *Full Metal Jacket*, comparable to the vibrantly red bathroom in *The Shining*, where Jack has his interview with Grady, the Overlook's old caretaker. Pyle has become a meticulous obsessive about his rifle. As in the case of Norman Bates or Jack Torrance, it's the careful, anal personality that lets loose crazy destruction. Going mad, always in Kubrick, is about losing control *and* being controlled *and* being a control freak. It's a "major malfunction," as Hartman puts it.

The night before the bathroom scene, Kubrick told D'Onofrio, "Just make sure it's big—Lon Chaney big."[24] Coincidentally, D'Onofrio had a few days earlier watched a silent movie with Chaney, and he copies Chaney's leering face of horror when he glowers at Joker and Hartman. Kubrick wanted *Strangelove*-style grotesquerie from D'Onofrio, and he got it.

Ermey remembered, "You know it took seven days to light that bathroom."[25] This head glows with a blue surreal light, unlike any bathroom on Parris Island or anywhere else on earth. We have entered dream space, Kubrick's no-man's-land. Pyle stares us down like Alex at the beginning of *Clockwork*, but where Alex thrilled with his exuberant malice, Pyle menaces, an idiot face over his inert drooling lump of a hunched body.

"What are you men doing in my head?" Hartman yells when he hears Joker and Pyle in the bathroom. And so they are—in his head, that is—contaminating Hartman's hard pure devotion to the corps. Both are as usual in their white T-shirts and boxers. Pyle holds his loaded rifle. "What is this Mickey Mouse shit?" Hartman bellows, steel-hard superego to the last until his heart is blown open by his troubled child Pyle. Joker fears he is next, but instead Pyle points the rifle to his open mouth, sitting slackly on the john. He fires, and his brains blow out the back of his head. We are now ready for Vietnam.

Full Metal Jacket has a precise, sonata-like structure: the twenty-minute scene at the end featuring a teenage Vietnamese sniper matches the twenty-minute basic training episode at the beginning.

To elaborate, the movie divides into:

twenty minutes for basic training at Parris Island
two minutes for the bathroom scene
forty-five minutes for Joker and the other Marines in
    Vietnam, everything before the encounter with the
    sniper

twenty minutes for the sniper scene

two minutes for the coda, in which the Marines sing the Mickey Mouse song and we hear Joker's voice-over

Structure is sometimes hard to see in *Full Metal Jacket*'s drifting, episodic Vietnam section. This is deliberate. Basic training is straitjacket-tight in its form, a regimented, collective insanity. But war means wildness, lack of control. After the deaths of Hartman and Pyle, never mentioned in the rest of the movie, madness becomes routine, rather than fervent and over the top, as in the Parris Island sequence. Everything falls apart, and all you know is this chaos, inside and out. (A joke from writer Phil Klay: "How many Vietnam vets does it take to screw in a lightbulb?" "You wouldn't know, you weren't there.")

The spectacular, dreamlike coordination of Kubrick's basic training section, with its rows of recruits standing at attention swaddled in their white skivvies, yields to a series of discrete episodes, where no visible plot propels the movie forward. Like the Marines it depicts, the last half of *Full Metal Jacket* seems a little lost, narrative-wise, but really Kubrick is on top of every smoke-bomb explosion and every tracking shot. Without looking virtuosic or self-consciously beautiful, the sky during the battles glows with precisely planted fires and smoke clouds.

Joker, quizzical as ever, stands at the center of it all, deep in the shit yet not completely of it. Like the narrator Lyutov's glasses in Isaac Babel's story "My First Goose," Joker's wire-rim glasses stand for a tenderness that is liable to be mocked by tougher men like Animal Mother (Adam Baldwin), whose helmet forthrightly reads, quoting Oppenheimer quoting Krishna, "I Am Become Death." In Babel, wearing eyeglasses is code for being a Jew, someone weighted by ambivalence, the antithesis of the Cossack's brute readiness. Animal Mother has the thousand-yard stare, stoned and numb: he looks far beyond you to the unspeakable core of the matter. Joker, by contrast, is still alive to uncertainty. His heart has not yet turned to stone.

Kubrick makes Joker's ambivalence come to a head in the film's last scenes. Huddled behind a low wall, the squad is being targeted by a sniper from a group of ruined buildings. One by one the men, as if caught by bad magic, get drawn into the sniper's trap. The Marines are cursed: this place is their Overlook Hotel.

So begins one of Kubrick's greatest set pieces, the sniper sequence of *Full Metal Jacket*. Jay Cocks remarks that this section of the movie, like Sam Fuller's small-scale Korean War classic *The Steel Helmet* (1951), "gets its ruthless tension from its simplicity." Here Kubrick is "very focused and precise and very unadorned," Cocks continues. Like Peckinpah, he uses slow motion when the sniper picks off the Marines one by one, their blood shooting out like a fountain. The pressure is close to unbearable. "And this from somebody whose idea of a life and death situation was getting on a commercial airline," Cocks marvels.[26] When Cowboy, the squad's leader, is killed by the sniper, Kubrick stays with a master shot of the Marines clustered around the dying man: no emotion-drenched close-ups here. The masterly Arliss Howard, who plays Cowboy, dies in their arms.

Now comes an utter shock, an even stronger one than Cowboy's death: the sniper is a teenage girl. She whirls around, spraying bullets like crazy. Meanwhile, Joker fumbles his gun like Jimmy Stewart in Ford's *The Man Who Shot Liberty Valance* (1962).

Then Rafterman (Kevin Howard, playing a gung-ho greenhorn, Joker's foil) shoots the sniper. Surrounded by the Marines and dying slowly, she begs to be killed. Joker, after hesitating, at last does what she asks.

The best comment on Joker shooting the sniper was written long before *Full Metal Jacket,* by Herr in *Dispatches:*

> The problem was that you didn't always know what you were seeing until later, maybe years later, that a lot of it never made it in at all, it just stayed stored there in your eyes. Time and information, rock and roll, life itself, the information isn't frozen, you are.
>
> Sometimes I didn't know if an action took a second or an hour or if I dreamed it or what. In war more than in other life you don't really know what you're doing most of the time, you're just behaving, and afterward you can make up any kind of bullshit you want to about it, say you felt good or bad, loved it or hated it, did this or that, the right thing or the wrong thing; still, what happened happened.[27]

Watch Joker's eyes just before he shoots, and then just after. As when Dave talks to the murderous HAL in *2001,* everything is in that gaze. Joker, tongue in cheek as usual, earlier told a news crew that he wanted to "be the first on his block to get a certified kill." This is his certified kill, a notch in his belt that also carves a notch in his skull. During basic training Hartman, who is later shot in the heart, rammed home the point that "your rifle is only a tool, it's a hard heart that kills." Joker kills from a hard heart and a pitying one too.

The movie's startling epilogue follows. As fires blaze spectacularly on the dark heath, the wasteland they have helped create, the Marines sing the Mickey Mouse Club theme song. Then we hear Joker's voice: "I am so happy that I am alive, in one piece and short. I'm in a world of shit. Yes. But I am alive. And I am not afraid."

Maybe Joker, the wild card, is joking in this final monologue (though he's never *only* joking). We can't tell whether he is actually happy and reconciled in his world of shit. His initiation ritual complete, he achieves what the historian Richard Slotkin called regeneration through violence—or so he tells us.

Kubrick said of Hasford's *The Short-Timers*, "I love the Homeric honesty when Joker says I never felt so alive."[28] But in the movie an irony suffuses Joker's claim to aliveness. Joker says he is no longer afraid, and we might wonder whether this resembles Pyle's lack of fear when he shoots Hartman and himself. For the moment he sounds perfectly sane, unlike Pyle, but then again this is Vietnam, so all bets are off.

Kubrick said that he used the Mickey Mouse Club song because he realized it had only been seven or eight years since these young men had been kids sitting in front of their television sets. Marching through ruined terrain, the Marines seem like boys again, innocents enjoying a rebirth after the cataclysm of the sniper's attack, thinking now about getting laid instead about getting wasted by bullets. They are cured, all right. Or are they?

Critic Georg Scesslen writes that this ending is "the moment of highest comedy and deepest hopelessness" in the movie. Here is the saddest fact of all, Scesslen adds: "It is forever the free mind that keeps the madness" of the war going.[29]

Joker stands alone in this ending, as he has all along. *Full Metal Jacket* differs from the typical war movie: it is about isolation rather than camaraderie. This is Kubrick's strike against the typical Hollywood war movie, like *Sands of Iwo Jima* (1949) (the butt of a few derisive yucks in Kubrick's movie). Kubrick here presages *The Thin Red Line* (1998), in which Terrence Malick isolates his soldiers inside their own heads, though Kubrick's casual-seeming grace in *Full Metal Jacket* contrasts with what Janet Maslin calls Malick's "innate momentousness": Mozart, rather than Wagner.

That studied classical quality required much work from Kubrick the perfectionist. The smallest details mattered, as Kubrick scrutinized not just his actors and sets but also the weather, which needed to be precisely suitable for the smoke-bomb explosions. Every sunset, every cloud formation even, had to look just right. This required hours and days of waiting. On *Full Metal Jacket* Kubrick insisted on taking his time, more so than ever. The Warners quartet of Frank Wells, Ted Ashley, John Calley, and Terry Semel had given him permission to do things his own way, as slowly as he wanted. D'Onofrio recalls Kubrick's careful method of filmmaking on *Full Metal Jacket*. At times the actors got fidgety:

> He'd just sit up on the crane with his lenses and figure out what he was going to do. He would look at the clouds, the time of day, and figure it all out. So once Stanley is sitting up there on the crane and there are three hundred extras on the ground, all sitting on yellow tires, waiting. No talking. Stanley's on the crane, about a hundred feet up, and we've been sitting there for an hour or so. One of the natives starts to curse him: "Get off the crane." Terry Needham, a wonderful, great guy [Kubrick's assistant director], comes over and says to us, "Alright, who said it, listen guys, you'll never get another chance like this, you're working with *Stanley Kubrick*, so watch it. No talking." Terry goes away, Stanley keeps on working up there, and again someone says, "Get off the fucking crane." This time Stanley comes down. He clears his throat and he says, "Okay, who said it? Who fucking talked?" And a voice comes from the back: "I am Spartacus." And another: "I am Spartacus." Three hundred extras burst out fucking laughing. Stanley too.[30]

"Why Stanley waited, I never knew," D'Onofrio says.[31] *Full Metal Jacket* was released in June 1987, six months after Oliver Stone's *Platoon*. Stone's movie was a huge moneymaker: it cost only $8 million, with a domestic gross of $138.5 million. *Full Metal Jacket*, which cost $17 million, grossed $38 in its first two months of release. This was not bad at all, but coming on the heels of Stone's massive hit hurt *Full Metal Jacket*.

Kubrick and Stone in fact argue against each other, with Stone providing the traditional Hollywood catharsis that Kubrick refuses. Kubrick's movie is an anti-*Platoon:* think of the portentous voice-over in Stone's film, or the too easily iconic depiction of Elias (Willem Dafoe) as a Christ figure shot by the Vietcong, arms stretched out as if on the cross. Stone's taste for the grandiose contrasts with Kubrick's understated manner, both satirical and sensitive.

In place of the giant heroic-scale dramas in *Platoon, Apocalypse Now,* or Michael Cimino's *The Deer Hunter* (1978), *Full Metal Jacket* is about a sheepish, regular-sized character. Significantly, Joker looks steadily at what he does as he kills the sniper. We have moved from Pyle's insane glare to Animal Mother's thousand-yard stare to Joker's newly mature eyes, which he keeps open. Yet the epilogue, with its too-plain claim to happy life, suggests Joker's retreat from his act of slaughter.

Kubrick's final movie, *Eyes Wide Shut,* will also be about looking. It presents another version of the boyish hero who, like Joker, is not sure how much he dares to see, or how much he wants to know. Like *Full Metal Jacket, Eyes Wide Shut* is about coming to maturity, and in both films Kubrick asks how a free grown-up mind reckons with what happened, what it did and what it saw.

9

Frightened of Making the Movie:
Eyes Wide Shut

KUBRICK DIDN'T MAKE a movie for twelve years between
Full Metal Jacket in 1987 and *Eyes Wide Shut* in 1999. He was
happily ensconced in Childwickbury, busy with young grand-
children, Katharina's and Anya's children. (His first grandchild
was born in 1985, the same year both his parents died.) On the
cusp of late middle age, Kubrick was thinking hard about what
movies he wanted to make next. He devoted himself to caring for his old films. Kubrick and Vitali restored *Dr. Strangelove*
by photographing each frame of Kubrick's print with a Nikon
camera. Kubrick was as usual taken up with his many cats and
dogs, worrying incessantly if one got sick. He would often drift
down to the lawn to watch Christiane paint. Her portraits of
Kubrick frequently show him with a book in his lap, absorbed
in reading. "I literally go into bookstores, close my eyes and
take things off the shelf," Kubrick told a *Rolling Stone* interviewer. "If I don't like the book after a bit, I don't finish it. But
I like to be surprised."[1]

Kubrick eagerly kept up with new movies and, on the phone, with Hollywood gossip. "Knowledge is power," the agent Sandy Lieberson said about Kubrick's phone habit, adding that Kubrick didn't pursue scurrilous details, but had to know everything significant that was happening in the industry. Warner Bros executive Steve Southgate commented that Kubrick "was the one person who knew how the film industry worked—in every country in the world. He knew all of the dubbing people, the dubbing directors, the actors."[2]

Kubrick was concerned with the industry in part because he wanted films shown in more ideal conditions. He complained as usual about the bad state of movie projection: "Fifty percent of the prints are scratched. Something is usually broken. The amplifiers are no good, and the sound is bad. The lights are uneven," he groaned. Kubrick's concern with how his movies were shown was not "some form of demented anxiety," he insisted, but a reasonable response to an awful situation.[3]

Kubrick liked to see as many movies as he could, and he admired some directors very far from him in style, like Mike Leigh and Claudia Weill, whose *Girlfriends* (1978) he praised rapturously. A fan of American football, he also much appreciated the Super Bowl ads, especially, he told an interviewer, the Michelob commercials. Kubrick remarked that their editing and photography were "some of the most brilliant work I've ever seen. Forget what they're doing—selling beer—and it's visual poetry. Incredible eight-frame cuts. . . . If you could ever tell a story, something with some content, using that kind of visual poetry, you could handle vastly more complex and subtle material."[4]

The Kubricks' marriage was still a happy one. "I was the best entertained woman ever, and I think I was also the best loved one," Christiane said after Stanley died.[5] Yet Kubrick's final movie shows the trouble and the promise that disrupt marriage. Even after forty years of talking, something still remains unsaid between a couple. Intimacy brings with it the danger of saying too much, saying the wrong thing, or being too silent, and it makes us wonder how much we really want to know about the other person. Kubrick in his last movie fully depicts these grown-up risks, for the first time in his career. The path to *Eyes Wide Shut* wasn't a straight one. Kubrick in the nineties was occupied with two other possible films, *A.I.: Artificial Intelligence*, the movie he finally handed over to Spielberg, and *The Aryan Papers*, his planned Holocaust film. He settled on *Eyes Wide Shut* rather than the others for several reasons, but mostly because he realized that this project was at the core of who he was, something he had to work out before he died. *Eyes Wide Shut* grapples with the adult fantasies of men and women, whereas the other two movies focus on a young boy. Kubrick was leaving childhood behind, and, in the case of *A.I.*, leaving it in Spielberg's hands.

The Aryan Papers absorbed much of Kubrick's attention in the early nineties. He had read Louis Begley's recent novel *Wartime Lies*, based on his experience as a Jewish boy in Nazi-occupied Poland. Begley and his mother saved themselves by pretending to be Polish gentiles. (In his novel, and in Kubrick's planned film, the mother becomes the child's aunt.) *Wartime Lies* is harrowing in its depiction of Jewish helplessness. The shrewdness of the boy Maciek and his aunt Tania is not polished but desperate. There are moments of Jewish defiance in the book, but they lead only to disaster: death is everywhere.

Begley's story ends with uncertainty about what has happened to the boy Maciek, whether he has anything in common with the middle-aged man who remembers his story. The dizzying gap between past and present, between the boy and the man he becomes, testifies to the impossibility of fully grasping the Holocaust's meaning: if you weren't there, you don't know, and even if you were, you still don't know.

The boy in Begley's novel resembles the one in Zweig's *Burning Secret*, another unmade Kubrick film, as well as Danny in *The Shining*. All try to reckon with a dangerous adult world while still keeping their distance. For the child, refusing to understand certain grown-up facts may be the key to survival, Kubrick implies. Just as Danny holds his hands over his eyes, Begley's Maciek relies on the aunt who shields him from the untold looming disaster of the Shoah.

If Kubrick was going to make his long-delayed Holocaust movie, he would have to decide what to show and what to conceal, both from his viewers and from his child protagonist. In some sense Maciek's innocence, like that of the boy in Imre Kertesz's novel *Fatelessness* (1975), reflects our own, since we don't know how to think about such systematic murderousness, and have a hard time imagining a suitable on-screen presentation of it.

Kubrick had read many books on the Holocaust, but he felt, like any serious student of the Jewish catastrophe, far from actually understanding it. Many years earlier, in 1976, Kubrick had sent his brother-in-law Jan Harlan to New York to ask Isaac Bashevis Singer to write a screenplay about the Shoah. The famed Yiddish storyteller admired *Dr. Strangelove* and *Barry Lyndon*, but he told Harlan that there was only one problem with his writing a script about the Holocaust: he knew nothing whatever about the subject. When Kubrick heard this from Harlan, he commented: I know just what he means.[6]

Fifteen years later, Kubrick found *Wartime Lies* and, taking the plunge, wrote the screenplay himself. By the fall of 1993 preparations for *The Aryan Papers* seemed complete. Filming was set to start in February 1994 in Aarhus, Denmark, where wartime Warsaw would be re-created. Kubrick had chosen Joseph Mazzello, who had appeared in Spielberg's *Jurassic Park* (1993), to play Maciek and the Dutch actress Johanna ter Steege to play his aunt. Then suddenly in November 1993 Warner Bros announced that Kubrick's next movie would be not *The Aryan Papers* but *A.I.: Artificial Intelligence*.

Kubrick dropped *The Aryan Papers* because he learned that Spielberg was making a Holocaust movie, *Schindler's List*, guessed that it would be released about the same time as his movie, and didn't want the films to compete. Yet there must have been other reasons too. He was, Christiane remembered, increasingly depressed and troubled by the subject matter. "If you show the atrocities as they actually happened," Christiane said years later, "it would entail the total destruction of the actors. Stanley said he could not instruct actors how to liquidate others and could not explain the motives for the killing. 'I will die from this,' he said, 'and the actors will die, too, not to mention the audience.'" One scene from the master script dated October 5, 1992, depicting women being raped by the Nazis' Ukrainian collaborators, suggests how hard it would have been to film *The Aryan Papers*: "They raped them publicly, singly, in groups, on the ground, leaning them against broken walls of houses. Some women were made to kneel, soldiers holding them from the back by their hair, their gaping mouths entered by penis after penis."[7]

Had he made *The Aryan Papers*, Kubrick would have had to depict an authority more coldly inhuman than any he had imagined so far, and a Jewish scrabbling for survival more dismal and compromised than most movie audiences were ready for. Bresson could have made such a movie, perhaps, but not Kubrick. It would have required an emotional nakedness that he had never attempted. The script that he wrote for *The Aryan Papers* is at times too easily melodramatic to suit the subject matter, and no doubt would have needed much work during shooting.

A.I.: Artificial Intelligence, the project that Kubrick finally decided to give to Spielberg, centers on a child, like *The Shining* and the unmade *Aryan Papers*: it's about a robot boy adopted by a human family. Kubrick worked on *A.I.* on and off for more than a decade, with a series of writers, before he handed the project over to Spielberg in 1995. (Spielberg wound up using six hundred highly inventive storyboards developed for Kubrick by illustrator Chris Baker.)[8] Kubrick gave up *A.I.* in part because he was waiting for CGI technology that could produce the movie's special effects. But he also must have sensed that *A.I.* was in the end more a Spielberg than a Kubrick movie.

A.I. needed Spielberg. Kubrick could never have sustained its heartrending portrait of the robot child David's rivalry with his real-boy sibling, which climaxes when their mother, Monica, is forced to choose between the two, fearing that David might kill her biological son. When Monica abandons David in the woods, Spielberg echoes Hagar placing Ishmael a bowshot away from her so that she will not see the child die: David is an Ishmael, not a favored Isaac. David does not die, but like Maciek in *Wartime Lies* he endures persecution, surviving a Holocaust-like landscape where the Mechas, robots like David, are slaughtered for kicks by brutal humans. In a series of drafts Kubrick made clear the analogy between the Mecha pogrom and the Shoah.[9]

After the nightmarish massacre of the Mechas, *A.I.* moves eventually toward a happy ending. David gets to spend a perfect day with his mother, who has been resurrected as a cyber-image eons after her death. The movie fulfills the wish for perfect union between mother and son, and there is no ironic distancing. The poignant sense that this is all just our dearest fantasy means we cling to it even more strongly.

We want this ending desperately, holding it tightly to our defenseless moviegoing selves. *A.I.* is the most heartbreaking of films because it so fully conveys a child's wish for complete parental love. Of all the films I have seen, it is the hardest for me to watch without crying. *A.I.* is finally a Spielberg movie, one of his best, rather than a Kubrick movie, because it makes sentiment work.

Yet Kubrick was apparently the source of *A.I.*'s conclusion.

According to Spielberg, "the whole last twenty minutes of the movie," the blissful day that David enjoys with his mother, "were completely Stanley's." Kubrick scribbled a note in the margin of screenwriter Ian Watson's treatment (dated June 10, 1991). "Tomorrow we'll have a wonderful day," Monica tells David during their reunion. But "there isn't enough time," Kubrick writes: Watson was picturing the reunion as eternal, while Kubrick, it seems, knew it had to end. Sara Maitland took over from Watson in May 1994. She remembered that "Stanley and I talked endlessly about mother love."[10]

With the end of *A.I.*, which recovers childhood innocence, Kubrick looked back to his earlier portraits of the imperiled, lonely child. He rewrites the disillusioned final moments of *Barry Lyndon*, where Barry and his mother, like Bullingdon and Lady Lyndon, share an all too mature bond born of hard experience. *A.I.* also revises the ending of *2001*. Instead of the godlike Starchild ascendant all alone, ready to shape worlds, this child wants only for the mother who rejected him to tell him how much she loves him.

Kubrick had been reading Proust, who begins *In Search of Lost Time* with the most famous goodnight kiss in literature. But David's love for his mother is not like the boy Marcel's. Monica seems like his child, or his toy, saying just what he wants her to when he tucks her in at night. Monica is simply, completely pleased by David, suggesting that the parent is herself a kind of robot. We know that this is all only make-believe, and that David's day has to end. Yet clinging to this one artificially created memory is all he has ever wanted. There is no hint of playful argument between mother and son, of the kind that animates real parent-child relationships.

David's need for his mother's love in the closing scene of *A.I.* is so simple and open that, as the critic Molly Haskell points out, we are disconcerted.[11] Is this something from a fable or are its roots in human life? Spielberg lets us be unsettled even as we embrace David's feelings, which give us a window into our deepest, most vulnerable child selves.

A.I., the *Aryan Papers*, and *Eyes Wide Shut* all present characters who are locked into their roles and cannot be authentic: the robot boy who yearns to be accepted as real, the Jewish child forced to masquerade as a gentile, and the man Bill Harford who cannot quite dare to break through from dreaming about a sexual adventure to actually having one. Like Barry Lyndon, Bill remains on the outside looking in even when he's at the center of the action.

The source for *Eyes Wide Shut*, *Dream Story* (*Traumnovelle*) by Arthur Schnitzler, a Viennese Jew and a rough contemporary of Freud, had for decades been one of Kubrick's obsessions.

In his interview with Robert Ginna just after he finished making *Spartacus*, Kubrick revealed that he was already a passionate Schnitzler enthusiast nearly forty years before *Eyes Wide Shut*. "For my part it's difficult to find any writer who understood the human soul more truthfully," he told Ginna. Schnitzler, he said, "had a very sympathetic, if somewhat all-seeing cynical point of view." He predicted that *Lolita* would resemble Schnitzler, with "a surface of comedy and humor and vitality, and only gradually, as the story progresses, do you penetrate beneath this surface."[12] He said that after *Lolita* he was going to make a movie based on one of Schnitzler's works. He probably meant *Dream Story*, which is among the hundreds of books that Kubrick shipped from London when he moved to New York with Christiane and his daughters in 1964.

The Schnitzler novella centers on a couple with a small daughter. The husband, Fridolin, and his wife, Albertine, exchange stories about their sexual fantasies, and Fridolin, struck by jealousy, sets out to have sex with another woman. He doesn't succeed: after a series of near-misses, including a visit to a masked orgy, he returns home from this "senseless night with its stupid unresolved adventures."[13] *Dream Story* ends with Fridolin confessing to Albertine the story of his night wanderings. The couple reaffirm their love and, at dawn, hear their daughter's laughter coming from the next room.

The plot of *Eyes Wide Shut* stays close to Schnitzler, with Fridolin and Albertine transformed into Bill Harford, a present-day New York doctor, and his wife, Alice. But the mood of the film differs from that of the novel. The ultradomestic Kubrick makes adulterous letting go look both stifled and stifling, while Schnitzler gives erotic fantasy more room to play.

In a 2012 interview, Kirk Douglas claimed that Kubrick first found out about Schnitzler's novella from Douglas's psychiatrist, Herbert Kupper, during the making of *Spartacus*.[14] This could be true, but it is tempting to think that Kubrick's second wife, Ruth Sobotka, a Viennese Jew from Schnitzler's milieu, gave him the book.

However he discovered it, Schnitzler's *Dream Story* rapidly possessed Kubrick. He was galvanized by it, but also afraid of it, as was Christiane Kubrick. "Stanley was frightened of making the movie when he first read the novel," Nicole Kidman reported. According to Tom Cruise, when Kubrick wanted to make *Dream Story* after *Lolita*, "Christiane told me she said, 'Don't . . . oh, please don't . . . not now. We're so young. Let's not go through this right now.'"[15]

Dream Story has a stylish air that bespeaks the man of the world, the promiscuous, socially adept author Arthur Schnitzler, but also a naked insight into the fantasies that live within a marriage. This nakedness frightened Kubrick, and Christiane too.

By the early seventies Kubrick's third marriage had proven its stability, and it seemed as if he was finally ready to make his Schnitzler movie. In April 1971 Warner Bros production executive John Calley, Kubrick's main patron at the studio, announced that the next Kubrick movie would be a version of *Dream Story*. Yet again Kubrick veered off: he decided to make *Barry Lyndon* instead.

For decades Kubrick was apprehensive about the self-exposure the Schnitzler project would exact from him. *Dream Story* was never far from his mind, but he could not actually commit himself to such an intimate, self-revealing movie. In the seventies he fantasized about casting an actor in *Dream Story* who would have a comedian's resilience, imagining Steve Martin or Woody Allen in the leading role. The film would be in black and white, perhaps a bittersweet romantic comedy like Allen's *Manhattan* (1979). In a notebook from the eighties he listed a series of possible leading men, including Dustin Hoffman, Warren Beatty, Alan Alda, Albert Brooks, Bill Murray, Tom Hanks, and "Sam Shepherd????"[16] Significantly, when Kubrick finally made his version of *Dream Story*, he cast an actor without a comic bone in his body, the earnest, highly deliberate Tom Cruise. Comedy would have been a weapon for the hero's self-defense; Kubrick makes him, in the end, defenseless.

In the early 1980s Terry Southern briefly worked on a comic, quasi-pornographic version of *Dream Story* in which the doctor-hero is a gynecologist. Southern recalled that Kubrick was then thinking of the project as a "sex comedy, but with a wild and somber streak," perhaps reminiscent of *Blue Movie* (1971), Southern's novel about a Hollywood director who makes a pornographic film, which he dedicated "to the great Stanley K." Kubrick's notebooks show that he was contemplating the story of a husband drawn to a "mystery girl," a Linda Lovelace– or Marilyn Chambers–like porn star. Kubrick's notes conclude: "Wife plays porno cassette with her at end to stimulate him."[17]

Kubrick wound up rejecting Southern's broad, *Strangelove*-esque approach to *Dream Story*. A few years later, after finishing *Full Metal Jacket*, Kubrick was again looking for a screenwriter for the Schnitzler novella. John le Carré was summoned to Childwickbury for a talk about adapting *Dream Story* to the screen. He remarked to Kubrick that "Vienna of the twenties may have been a hive of sexual license, but it was also a hive of social and religious bigotry, chronic anti-Semitism and Austrian repression and prejudice," a place of "social as well as physical danger." Kubrick and le Carré discussed where the story should be set. "Well, Stanley, I've thought about this," le Carré said, "and I believe our best bet is: go for a medieval walled city or country town that is visually confining." After a pause Kubrick replied, "I think we'll set it in New York."[18] And Kubrick's New York does resemble a walled city, or a movie set. Like Max Ophüls's Vienna in *La Ronde* (1950) and *Letter from an Unknown Woman* (1948), Kubrick's New York is transparently staged, artificial.

Kubrick's co-screenwriter for *Eyes Wide Shut* ended up being not le Carré but another British novelist, Frederic Raphael. Whereas Kubrick and Herr shared a camaraderie based in part on their Jewishness, the more prickly Raphael, who was also Jewish, felt divided from Kubrick on this score. He bristled at Kubrick's determination to turn this story by a Viennese Jew into a decidedly non-Jewish film, and thought, rather unfairly, that Kubrick was trying to escape from his own Jewishness. Kubrick made at least one joke at Raphael's expense, saying that he wanted a "Harrison Fordish goy" named Harford to play the lead role.[19] Kubrick surely knew, as Raphael did not, that Ford's mother was Jewish.

Raphael's memoir about working with Kubrick has many axes to grind, some of them rather silly: *The Female Subject* was his proposed title for the film, far better, he says, than *Eyes Wide Shut*. Kubrick of course stuck with his striking title, which probably echoes Ben Franklin's line "Keep your eyes wide open before marriage, half shut afterwards": monitor your spouse, but not too closely.

Kubrick insisted that Raphael eliminate all traces of sparkle from *Eyes Wide Shut*'s dialogue. This is a surprising decision, since *Eyes Wide Shut* is what Stanley Cavell calls a comedy of remarriage: a couple who are on the rocks go through a series of trials and finally realize that they belong together. From Shakespeare to the screwball comedies of Howard Hawks and Preston Sturges, the comedy of remarriage features witty, rapid-fire dialogue, replete with one-upsmanship. Not in Kubrick, though. Dreams aren't witty or agile, and neither is *Eyes Wide Shut*, where the pace is slow, sometimes leaden. As in *2001* and *The Shining*, Kubrick relies on banality. There are many instances of "parroting," as critic Michel Chion has noticed: characters echo one another's lines word for word, as if in partial disbelief.[20]

Kubrick's movie is poised and solemn like a dream. The movie's colors usher the viewer into a carefully constructed world. The wonderfully glowing blue light that appears in many of its scenes is, Chion remarks, both "cosmic" and "intimate," and a radiant red pool table stands at the center of the late scene between Bill and Ziegler (played by director Sydney Pollack), the film's arch macher and reality instructor. Though Kubrick didn't live to complete the sound mix for the movie, the music choices show his usual inspired touch: a Shostakovich waltz, dizzying and lush and echt Viennese, an ominous, growling chant for the orgy scene, and a Ligeti piece featuring a repeated note hammered on the piano. The Ligeti "appears inscrutable and unbidden," writes critic Kate McQuiston, with its simple repeated notes evoking Bill's frustrated quest.[21]

Kubrick selected the real-life Hollywood couple Tom Cruise and Nicole Kidman for the film, and in some measure *Eyes Wide Shut* is covertly about the publicity-haunted life of these two stars. The film concerns a secretive cult that stages orgies. Cruise was a Scientologist, and there were persistent rumors that he was gay. The secrets hidden within a celebrity marriage, like the hermetic cult followed by Cruise, are shadowy undertones in Kubrick's movie.

Kubrick, like Kidman, had to contend with a Scientologist in the family. His daughter Vivian, much to her father's distress, left home in the mid-nineties to live in Los Angeles. Ken Adam said, "Stanley became overpowering to her. . . . She really adored Stanley but he tried to control every move she made." Kubrick wanted Vivian to write the score for *Eyes Wide Shut* as she had for *Full Metal Jacket*, but she refused. Later, while he was editing the movie, Stanley and Vivian "had a huge fight," Christiane remembered. "He was very unhappy. He wrote her a 40-page letter trying to win her back. He begged her endlessly to come home from California."[22] Vivian had joined the Church of Scientology in 1995, though the Kubrick family didn't know this until Stanley's funeral four years later, after which she cut herself off from her mother and sisters.

Kubrick picked Cruise and Kidman not just because they were married but because each of them embodied what he needed for *Eyes Wide Shut*. Kubrick had admired Cruise's tour de force against-type performance in Oliver Stone's *Born on the Fourth of July* (1989). In Stone's movie Cruise played a paraplegic Vietnam vet tormented by impotence, showing a gawky, ill-at-ease, masochistic side that cut against his usual cardboard-cutout macho profile. In his earlier movies Cruise had a clear urge to conquer, a slightly fascistic grin, and something falsely bright about his expressions of triumph. But in *Born on the Fourth of July*, as in *Eyes Wide Shut*, Cruise isn't triumphal at all. His gestures resemble those of a bulky marionette. This herky-jerky awkwardness doesn't look like vulnerability at first, but it is. There is a family resemblance between Keir Dullea in *2001*, Ryan O'Neal in *Barry Lyndon*, and Cruise in *Eyes Wide Shut*: all three specialize in reacting to what they see and hear, rather than taking action. This is a challenging task for an actor, especially for one like Cruise, whose face tends to be masklike, with limited emotional range.

Kubrick turned Cruise's limits to good use, but one still wishes that *Eyes Wide Shut* had a leading man who could loosen up at times. The movie conspicuously evokes *North by North-*

west (1959): the orgy is held in Glen Cove, site of Lester Town-
send's mansion in the Hitchcock film, and the two movies share
a theme of retracing one's steps and trying to figure out what
part to play, all the while being manipulated by the powers that
be. But Cary Grant, supple, stylish, and guarded, is a far cry
from Cruise, with his defensive body armor.

Nicole Kidman is the opposite of Cruise. Soft and fluid in
her movements, she has a surprising inward strength. In the
words of her greatest admirer, David Thomson, "This woman
has everything that makes a voyeur dream: a delightful skin, a
small kissable mouth . . . a sensual intelligence. . . . Yet at the
same time she is totally buttoned up. She resists, she is smooth
and much too aesthetic, she is vain and prudish. . . . What is
inside this sweet cake? Nobody can be sure of this woman."[23]
Kidman, who seems happiest playing married, domestic types
like Alice, is no high-rolling femme fatale, but there is, as Thomson says, something in her that makes us unsure. In *Eyes Wide
Shut*'s greatest scene, Bill will be thrown utterly off balance
when she reveals her fantasy about a naval officer she glimpsed
the previous summer at Cape Cod.

Kidman's performance has several glorious high points.
The first occurs near the beginning of the movie, at the elaborate Christmas party given by Ziegler, Bill's wealthy patient.
Dancing with the Hungarian seducer Sandor Szavost (Sky du
Mont) and flirtatiously fending off his sexual offers, she is bemused, titillated, sardonic, a little dreamy. Kidman is superb
near the movie's end, when she wakes up, still shaken, next to
the mask Bill wore at the orgy the night before, chastened, tentative, and full of regret about her harrowing dream, in which
she had sex with a crowd of men while Bill was forced to watch.
A few minutes later, presiding over the movie's final scene, she
is reassuring and provocative at once. What is inside this sweet
cake?

The peak of Kidman's achievement in *Eyes Wide Shut* is the

pot-smoking scene that takes place the night after Ziegler's party. A stoned Alice begins by asking Bill about the two models she saw him with at the party "Did you . . . happen . . . to . . . *fuck* . . . them?"—she tensely ekes out those pauses, a tic that we noticed when she was dancing with Szavost. Bill, flustered and defensive, sputters a lecture about his loyalty to her. Dangerously, he adds that women are not ruled by their desire as men are. This is what sets Alice off. She has a laughing fit, to Bill's disgust, and then boldly faces him down: "If you men only knew . . . ," she says. And she tells him about her summer fantasy of the naval officer: "I thought that if he wanted me, even if it was for only one night, I was ready to give up everything. You, Helena, my whole fucking future." Kidman's acting here is full of expert grace notes that conceal as much as they reveal. She is by turns absorbed, defiant, charged with mockery, and, as she puts it, tender and sad.

Kubrick shut down filming for days to think about the pot-smoking scene. "At certain times he was very controlling," Kidman reported, but not with her stoned monologue: "He allowed me to really get lost in Alice . . . over the course of a year and a half I really just became that woman."[24] For the most part *Eyes Wide Shut* is a studied movie, mimicking in its style Cruise's efforts to manage his emotional reactions. But Kidman's monologues are freer, almost experimental, and emotionally brittle. Every word she speaks puts her at the center of the movie, from which her husband is excluded.

Kubrick became close friends with both Cruise and Kidman, who told *Newsweek* that Kubrick "knew us and our relationship as no one else does." He got to know her "better even than [my] parents," Kidman said.[25] In none of his previous movies had Kubrick pursued such a curious and intense melding of himself with his actors. He was intimately present with Tom and Nicole for all sixteen months of the strangely prolonged shooting. This intensity declares the crucial role that

Eyes Wide Shut played in Kubrick's psyche, as if the movie were the enfolded meaning of his life.

Kubrick's identification of himself with Bill was clear. Young Stanley had imagined becoming a doctor like his father. Like Bill, Kubrick was polite rather than flirtatious with women, but driven to sexual fantasy. The Harfords' apartment was modeled on the Kubricks' own on the Upper West Side in the early sixties, when Kubrick first wanted to make *Dream Story*. *Eyes Wide Shut*, a slow ritual of a movie, was designed to free Kubrick from the obsession with control that it also embodies, to provide a release into renewed relationship with the wife who had been at his side for four decades, with Tom and Nicole standing in for Stanley and Christiane.

Kubrick needed to know everything about Tom and Nicole, both together and separately. During filming Kubrick manipulated his two stars' off-screen relationship so that he could get the performances he wanted from them, frequently conferring with Nicole apart from Tom. And Kubrick took advantage of Cruise's absence from the set for several days while he filmed the dream sequence in which a mostly naked Kidman has sex with the naval officer. Cruise, like Bill Harford, remained on the outside.[26]

Bill wants to stay on the outside, excluded from Alice's fantasy. He turns down Alice's challenge. "If you men only knew," she says, but he doesn't want to know. He refuses to step inside her erotic life. Instead he tries to outplay her, to get rid of his obsession with her fantasy by actually doing what she only dreamed of. She has passed the fantasy on to her husband, forced his eyes open, and in a vengeful spirit he tries to have sex with someone else.

Eyes Wide Shut is about how a man tries to escape from an obsessive fantasy that is not even his. This is a far cry from *Clockwork*'s Alex, who happily enacts his lurid fantasies of rape and murder. If Bill has his own sexual adventure, he thinks, he can forget his glimpse into Alice's inner life, and be enjoyably diverted instead by whatever woman he chooses. The obsession, he hopes, will vanish.

But Bill can't actually choose anyone, as it turns out. His sexual goals are always being supplied by somebody else. Tellingly, Kubrick and Raphael cut from Schnitzler's novella a fantasy that Fridolin has about a Lolita-like girl on the beach. Dr. Bill has no dream life except what others give him. Women come on to him: he initiates nothing. And he completes nothing—he never has sex with any of them. As in *Don Giovanni*, in *Eyes Wide Shut* all erotic encounters are nipped in the bud. And as in Mozart and Da Ponte's opera, sex is shadowed by death.

In *Eyes Wide Shut* seeking extramarital sex also means courting death. The masked men at the orgy realize Bill is an interloper, and they are about to strip him bare and possibly kill him. A woman offers to "redeem" him, allowing him to escape from the orgy, and the next day Bill becomes convinced that she died instead of him. Bill should have been the sacrificial victim, atoning for his sexual waywardness, but the mysterious woman takes his place.

The molten hot emotional center of *Eyes Wide Shut* occurs at the orgy, when Red Cloak (Leon Vitali, in a cameo) commands Bill to remove his clothes. A doctor like Bill, fully uniformed, treats near-naked patients. Now the tables are turned: he is told to expose himself. In the Schnitzler novella the doctor hero aches to prove his manhood by committing some daring act, but in Kubrick, Bill Harford is passive, a pawn in somebody else's game, and he merely freezes instead of defying Red Cloak's order. Here Cruise's surface-oriented performance works well, using the patented Cruise "this is crazy" double take. He acts like someone acting like he's being threatened, a person in a dream trying to wake up.

Bill's passivity is also front and center in the pool table scene, which has no analogue in Schnitzler. Here Ziegler, who

The stoned Alice (Nicole Kidman) with Tom Cruise in *Eyes Wide Shut*
(Courtesy of Photofest/Warner Bros)

has called in Bill for a man-to-man talk, sets him straight.
Ziegler is like Noah Cross in Polanski's *Chinatown* (1974), a
powerful and depraved older man who keeps all the secrets, and
also like Gavin Elster in Hitchcock's *Vertigo* (1958), the man behind the scenes who controls the plot.

Pollack memorably described Kubrick's way of nudging
him into his role as Ziegler. Pollack said, "You have the bound-
aries of this scene in your head but then he sort of gives you a
little push off and sees where you go and then he starts to correct it slowly and then he records it on video." Kubrick micro-
managed Pollack in a way that was unusual for him. He would
then show Pollack the take on video, freeze the frame and say,
"See, where you turned your head like that," or something similar. Pollack added that in the end he "shut up and did exactly
what [Kubrick] said."[27]

Ziegler reminds Bill that he has stumbled into a foreign,

frightening world ruled by the truly powerful men, the ones able to have women and dispose of them at their will. He tells Bill that the scene at the orgy was staged merely in order to scare him away. The prostitute Mandy was not sacrificed at the orgy, Ziegler insists. She was a typical "hooker" and "junkie," according to Ziegler, in whose bedroom she overdosed earlier on, during the Christmas party. The day after the orgy, she died the way everyone knew she would, by shooting up a little too much heroin.

Ziegler's comment on Mandy's death is devastating in its blandness: "Life goes on. It always does—until it doesn't."

For Ziegler there is nothing to see in sex except the fact of it, and the same is true of life and death. He makes sex look grimly devoid of fun. After Bill left the orgy, he says, Mandy "got her brains fucked out"; the pianist Nick Nightingale, who led Bill to the orgy, is probably back in Seattle "banging Mrs. Nick." Ziegler opens Bill's eyes, but this is also a closing of the mind, a cynical reduction. By this point in *Eyes Wide Shut* sex seems both all-important and peculiarly empty.

Kubrick knew he needed to rescue *Eyes Wide Shut* from Ziegler, and he chose Alice to provide the antidote. Her talk with Bill at the end of the film, as they shop for Christmas presents with their daughter, is exactly the opposite of Ziegler's speech. She respects a mystery instead of stripping things down to bare facts, so the awkwardness between Bill and Alice develops a grace of its own.

"Maybe, I think, we should be grateful," Alice now says to Bill, "grateful that we've managed to survive through all of our adventures, whether they were real or only a dream." Her lines have a taste of wonder utterly absent from Ziegler's speech, and are fitting for the end of a Mozart opera or *A Midsummer Night's Dream*.

Ziegler embodies the joyless wish to be in control, to see without being seen. But for Bill seeing is a trap, not a form of power, both at the orgy and with his fantasy about Alice's sex with the naval officer, the scene that replays itself over and over in his head. To be released from fantasy's bonds you must be open to what your wife has to tell you, her unexpected, surprising word. And no word is more surprising than the final one in Kubrick's final movie.

At the end of *Eyes Wide Shut* Alice and Bill have awakened—but awakened to what, we wonder. Alice says to Bill, "The important thing is we're awake now and hopefully for a long time to come." When Bill asks, "Forever?" she responds, "Forever? . . . Let's not use that word. But I do love you and you know there is something very important we need to do as soon as possible." "What's that?" asks Bill. And now comes her last word: "Fuck."

Stanley Kubrick had a piece of advice for the people he made movies with when they faced a problem that needed to be solved: "Keep asking the question until you get the answer you want." In *Eyes Wide Shut* the answer is "fuck," the mostly unseen activity that the whole movie gravitates around. This reunited couple, chastened by new knowledge, more acutely conscious of each other, will seal their reconciliation with the simple animal act whose image has caused them so much trouble. They had sex after Ziegler's party; now they will again after their long night of Odyssean separation. But they are in a new place. Alice has exorcised the mocking laughter that she directed at Bill when she was stoned. To move from the dream of fucking, with all its torments, at least to the reality of it—since the truth of it doesn't exist—that is something. This is the conclusion of *Eyes Wide Shut*, and of Kubrick's work. Alice's "fuck" is surprising, because *Eyes Wide Shut* mostly avoids profanity, except for the Ziegler scenes. When Bill asks the prostitute Domino what she "recommends" they do, she replies, "I'd rather not put it into words." At the movie's end Alice puts it into words, as she did earlier when she asked whether Bill happened to fuck the two models at the party. Those two lovely girls drifted away, never to reappear, a lost chance like all the others in this movie.

The wannabe adulterer Bill suffers from what Schnitzler calls "the treacherous illusion of the missed opportunity."[28] Alice's genius at the end is to dispel the illusion and give back to marriage its sense of healing urgency. Married love becomes a chance that the couple needs to take, instead of letting sterile fantasy and dead-end flirtation with others take over the stage.

All the seductive near misses during Bill's night wandering have been false dramas, climaxing in the words of the mysterious woman at the orgy: "I will redeem him." This too was playacting, words that, we were told, could never be retracted. Now, in the last minutes of *Eyes Wide Shut*, we hear instead the suspense that comes with an open future. Alice makes no promises, which is the only convincing way to reassure someone, especially in marriage. Hopefully, she says, the two of them will remain awake, but she doesn't like the word "forever." Maybe, just maybe, they will redeem each other. In place of the desperate, clinging fantasy of love at the end of *A.I.*, Kubrick expresses a humane realism about it.

A new intimacy steals into Kubrick's work just as it ends, with the conclusion of *Eyes Wide Shut*. "No one in his right mind would mistake Kubrick for a humanist," the critic David Denby wrote about *Full Metal Jacket*. But he is one in *Eyes Wide Shut*, which exorcises Kubrick's earlier pessimism about the chances of individual humans when they are up against the powers that be. The shadowy forces behind the orgy in *Eyes Wide Shut* don't win out, unlike the aliens in *2001*, the ghosts of the Overlook Hotel in *The Shining*, or the regimes of death in *Dr. Strangelove* and *Full Metal Jacket*. "It was a very good film for an older person to make," Christiane said about *Eyes Wide Shut*. "You become softer and more honest with yourself as you grow older. . . . Stanley was much more pessimistic, much more cynical, as a young man."[29]

Just as he took his time, twelve years, between *Full Metal Jacket* and *Eyes Wide Shut*, Kubrick took his time, more than ever, with the filming of his last movie. At sixteen months, the shoot was the longest in film history. The movie cost $64 million to make and brought in a healthy $22.7 million on its opening weekend. But the critics were circling, ready to slice away at Kubrick's final movie, which they mostly labeled stiff, pompous, unerotic, and boring.

Kubrick didn't live to see the disappointed reaction to *Eyes Wide Shut*, partly the fault of a teaser publicity campaign suggesting that it would be an intensely sexy movie. The attacks centered on the orgy scene, which critics mostly found antiquated and phony, with its glossy Helmut Newton–style nudes in high heels: they had perhaps expected real orgasms and a leather dungeon. "Whose idea of an orgy is this, the Catholic Church's?" one reviewer complained. But the orgy was supposed to be grandiose and frigid. Critic Lee Siegel grasped the point when he wrote that with the orgy "Kubrick wanted to show that sex without emotion is ritualistic, contrived, and in thrall to authority and fear": "Compared with the everyday reality of sex and emotion, our fantasies of gratification are, yes, pompous and solemn in the extreme." As Naremore points out, the orgy is both "sinister" and "silly," exactly like a dream, and this is clearly Kubrick's intention.[30]

It is not the orgy but Kidman's final lines that define the movie. What an unexpected finale to a filmic career full of sublime alternate realities: *Eyes Wide Shut* ends on a quiet note, a nod to the everyday.

On March 1, 1999, an anxious Kubrick ordered the projectionist not to watch *Eyes Wide Shut* while showing it in an advance screening. Five days later, he was dead. Terry Semel talked to Kubrick twice on the day he died. "He had called me for about an hour apiece, and he was in great spirits . . . review[ing] millions of details on the marketing. He was more outspoken and more excited than I think I had ever heard him."[31]

Kubrick had been visibly ill during the filming. Christiane said, "I thought he was awfully tired, and he never slept much—ever—in his whole life." While he was making *Eyes Wide Shut*, she added, Kubrick "was sleeping less and less. He was also a doctor's son and he wouldn't see a doctor. He gave himself his own medicine if he wasn't feeling well or he would phone friends. . . . It was the one thing he did that I thought was really stupid." "He would be holding on to the wall he was so exhausted," remembered Steadicam operator Peter Cavaciuti.[32]

By this time the seventy-year-old Kubrick had an oxygen tank in his bedroom; he knew he was dreadfully ill. His perfectionism, his endless focus on details had taken on a compulsive quality during the filming. Kubrick did take after take of seemingly insignificant sequences like Cruise ringing a doorbell, as if he were looking for clues within the surface of ordinary existence, unable, like the trapped Bill Harford, to break through into meaningful action.[33]

During the last four weeks of filming Kubrick had to operate the camera himself, since his cinematographer, Larry Smith, had left. Kubrick was getting up early to prepare for shooting, and the day's work didn't end until three or four in the morning. "It killed him, really, making that movie," said Sandy Lieberson, Keir Dullea's agent and a friend of Kubrick's.[34]

Leon Vitali remembers driving back with Kubrick to his house after a day's filming. "I thought, you're not even going to find your way to the front door, and we're right in front of it. . . . The last Saturday afternoon I was standing leaning up against my car and we were talking for two and a half hours. Everything was natural and gentle and more relaxed than it had been for quite a while, that same kind of gentleness as when I first met him."[35]

Stanley Kubrick was buried on the grounds of Childwickbury, under a favorite tree. At the funeral Julian Senior said Kaddish, and Cruise, Kidman, Spielberg, Jan Harlan, and Terry Semel spoke about their memories of Kubrick. He went into the grave wearing one of the military jackets he loved, full of pockets for notebooks and pens.[36]

Kubrick's range as a filmmaker is not often acknowledged. If Spielberg with his boyish tinkerers and Tarantino with his testosterone-driven maniacs occupy two ends of the American movie spectrum, Kubrick dealt with both extremes, and he brought in as well the gorgeous alienated vistas characteristic of the European art film.

Movies take you over, notoriously, and Kubrick's are among the most possessive and all-absorbing in the canon. Kubrick's characters in their moments of rapture mirror the moviegoer's absorption, sometimes in sinister fashion: Alex listening to Beethoven; Private Pyle with his rifle; slack-jawed, haunted Jack Torrance; Dave Bowman thrust through the Stargate; Bill Harford mesmerized by his wife's fantasy. These solitary transports stem originally from the inner life of the child Stanley Kubrick, so eerily secure in his own head that he rejected school as early as the first grade.

The child Stanley has a future in Kubrick's work, whether deciphering the frightening clues of an adult world like Danny in *The Shining* or, now halfway grown-up, deciding what to do when faced with someone asking for death, like Joker gazing at the sniper in *Full Metal Jacket*. *Eyes Wide Shut* reverses the emphasis of Kubrick's Vietnam film, and it ends not with death but with life. In both movies, a woman shakes a male protagonist out of his transfixed state. Only in *Eyes Wide Shut*, though, does the woman point to a worthwhile future. This is Kubrick's tribute to his wife, Christiane, who played a cathartic role in

Paths of Glory decades earlier. Christiane stands behind Alice Harford's power to bring her spouse back from his obsessive, self-enclosed fantasy. Kubrick barely had time, at the end of his life, to complete this testament to the potential for a fuller relationship between a man and a woman, one built on conversation and self-questioning. His earlier movies had ignored that potential, and this was the missing piece of the puzzle. Kubrick answered the nightmare trap of the wrong marriage—Jack and Wendy Torrance, Barry and Lady Lyndon—with an appeal to the right one, just as his own marriage to Christiane superseded his previous one to Ruth Sobotka. Days later, he was dead, but he had given his audience the solution to his most personal dilemma.

Kubrick's appeal has outlasted his death, even extending to pop music of the 2010s. Frank Ocean recently sampled *Eyes Wide Shut*'s Nicole Kidman on "Love Crimes," and rapper J. Cole name-checked "that nigga Stanley Kubrick."[37]

Mostly, of course, Kubrick has left his mark on film. Denis Villeneuve's *Arrival* (2016) follows after *2001*, and carefully composed epics from Terrence Malick's *Tree of Life* (2011) to Lucrecia Martel's *Zama* (2017) also emulate Kubrick, reminding us that there is no limit to what cinema can accomplish, if you approach it with a chess grandmaster's intuition and skill, and a sense of the screen as a vast canvas, with every detail fully in the director's hands.

Stanley Kubrick asserted total control over his vision, demanding take after take and looking into every last detail. But he also had a sense of how to use chaos, and he clearly enjoyed the bumper car ride that is filmmaking. In his work Kubrick brought together order and madness, mastery and wild defiance, fulfilling a key dream of cinema, to show human energy at its most dangerous and exciting while also presenting a supremely organized world. And so he changed what movies look like.

NOTES

Introduction

1. Kirk Douglas, *The Ragman's Son* (New York: Simon and Schuster, 1988), 186.

2. James Naremore, *On Kubrick* (London: British Film Institute, 2007), 40.

3. Robert Emmet Ginna interview with SK, University of the Arts, London, Stanley Kubrick Archive (hereinafter SKA), SK/1/2/8/2.

4. Dalia Karpel, "The Real Stanley Kubrick," *Haaretz*, November 3, 2005, https://www.haaretz.com/1.4880226.

5. *Stanley Kubrick: A Life in Pictures*, dir. Jan Harlan (2001).

6. Mary Panzer, "Stanley Kubrick: Eyes Wide Open," *Vanity Fair*, January 22, 2007, https://www.vanityfair.com/news/2005/03/kubrick200503 (Marcus quotation); Michael Herr, *Kubrick* (New York: Grove, 2000), 53.

7. Vicente Molina Foix interview with SK, *Cinephilia and Beyond*, 1980, https://cinephiliabeyond.org/interview-stanley-kubrick-vicente-molina-foix/.

8. Pauline Kael, "Stanley Strangelove" (review of *A Clockwork Orange*), *New Yorker*, January 1, 1972, https://scrapsfromtheloft.com/2016/09/18/a-clockwork-orange-pauline-kael/; Alex Ross, "Stanley Kubrick: Take One, Take Two," *Slate*, March 8, 1999, https://slate.com/news-and-politics/1999/03/stanley-kubrick-take-1-take-2.html; Robert Kolker, *The Extraordinary Image* (New Brunswick: Rutgers University Press, 2016), 141, 205.

9. *Stanley Kubrick: A Life in Pictures* (first Herr quote); Dan Richter, *Moonwatcher's Memoir* (New York: Carroll and Graf, 2002), 136; "For Him, Everything Was Possible," Ken Adam interview with SK, *Kinematograph* 20 (2004): 94; Terry Southern, "Strangelove Outtake: Notes from the War Room," *Grand Street* 49 (Summer 1994): 69; Herr, *Kubrick*, 54; *Filmworker*, dir. Tony Zierra (2017) (Leone quote); Vincent LoBrutto, *Stanley Kubrick* (New York: DaCapo, 1999), 348 (McDowell quote); Douglas, *Ragman's Son*, 333.

10. Jay Cocks, "Stanley Kubrick," in *The Making of 2001: A Space Odyssey*, ed. Stephanie Schwam (New York: Random House, 2000), 3; *Filmworker* (Vitali quote).

11. Michael Benson, *Space Odyssey* (New York: Simon and Schuster, 2018), 176 (Unsworth quote); Peter Bogdanovich, "What They Say about Stanley Kubrick," *New York Times Magazine*, July 4, 1999, https://www.nytimes.com/1999/07/04/magazine/what-they-say-about-stanley-kubrick.html (Howard quote).

12. Vincent LoBrutto, *Stanley Kubrick* (1997; New York: Da Capo Press, 1999), 402.

13. Nathan Abrams, *Stanley Kubrick* (New Brunswick, NJ: Rutgers University Press, 2018), 13, 59; Karpel, "The Real Stanley Kubrick" (Christiane Kubrick quote).

14. Naremore, *On Kubrick*, 23–24.

Chapter 1. I Know I Can Make a Film Better Than That

1. Jeremy Bernstein interview with SK, 1965, https://www.indiewire.com/2013/12/listen-rare-76-minute-interview-with-stanley-kubrick-about-his-start-in-films-nuclear-war-chess-strategies-248700/ (first quote); "Kubrick on *The Shining*: An In-

terview with Michel Ciment" (1980), http://www.visual-memory
.co.uk/amk/doc/interview.ts.html?LMCL=gCIFLU.

2. Mary Panzer, "Stanley Kubrick: Eyes Wide Open," *Vanity Fair*, January 22, 2007, https://www.vanityfair.com/news/2005/03/kubrick200503.

3. Peter Bogdanovich, "What They Say about Stanley Kubrick," *New York Times Magazine*, July 4, 1999, https://www.nytimes.com/1999/07/04/magazine/what-they-say-about-stanley-kubrick.html.

4. Nathan Abrams, *Stanley Kubrick* (New Brunswick, NJ: Rutgers University Press, 2018), 7.

5. Robert Emmet Ginna interview with SK, University of the Arts, London, Stanley Kubrick Archive (hereinafter SKA), SK/1/2/8/2.

6. Bogdanovich, "What They Say."

7. Bogdanovich, "What They Say."

8. Bernstein interview.

9. Abrams, *Stanley Kubrick*, 35.

10. Bernstein interview.

11. Vincent LoBrutto, *Stanley Kubrick* (New York: DaCapo, 1999), 94.

12. David Vaughan in Walter Sobotka, ed., *The Book of Ruth* (New York, 1968), 78 (chess); Bogdanovich, "What They Say" (early quote).

13. Gene Phillips, "Killer's Kiss," in *The Stanley Kubrick Archives*, ed. Alison Castle (New York: Taschen, 2004), 282 (first two quotes); Ginna interview (third quote).

14. Sobotka, *Book of Ruth*, 52.

15. Cited in Dalya Alberge, "Newly Found Stanley Kubrick Script Ideas Focus on Marital Strife," *Guardian*, July 12, 2019, https://www.theguardian.com/film/2019/jul/12/newly-found-stanley-kubrick-script-ideas-focus-marital-strife.

16. Brown Wallet E, SKA, SK shelf 11.

17. Brown Wallet E, SKA, SK shelf 11.

18. Romain LeVern interview with James B. Harris, *Chaos*, 2018 (my translation), http://www.chaosreign.fr/james-b-harris-eyes-wide-shut-est-le-moins-bon-film-de-stanley-kubrick/.

19. Bogdanovich, "What They Say."
20. Robert Polito, *Savage Art* (New York: Knopf, 1995), 394.
21. LeVern interview with James B. Harris (first quote); Samuel B. Prime interview with James B. Harris, *Notebook*, November 13, 2017 https://mubi.com/notebook/posts/the-other-side-of-the-booth-a-profile-of-james-b-harris-in-present-day-los-angeles (second quote).
22. Interview with Sterling Hayden, 1984, *The Killing* Blu-ray.
23. Hayden interview.

Chapter 2. Keep Doing It Until It Is Right

1. John Baxter, *Stanley Kubrick* (New York: Carroll and Graf, 1997), 86.
2. Baxter, *Stanley Kubrick*, 86.
3. Romain LeVern interview with James B. Harris, *Chaos*, 2018 (my translation), http://www.chaosreign.fr/james-b-harris-eyes-wide-shut-est-le-moins-bon-film-de-stanley-kubrick/.
4. Author interview with Nathan Abrams, July 16, 2018.
5. Author interview with Jan Harlan, July 6, 2018 (*Chess Story*).
6. Gary Giddins, *Paths of Glory* Blu-ray commentary.
7. Baxter, *Stanley Kubrick*, 93.
8. Giddins, *Paths of Glory* commentary.
9. Alexander Walker, Sybil Taylor, and Ulrich Ruchti, *Stanley Kubrick, Director* (New York: Norton, 1971), 14 (first quote); Raymond Haine interview with SK, 1957, in *The Stanley Kubrick Archives*, ed. Alison Castle (New York: Taschen, 2004), 309 (second quote).
10. Giddins, *Paths of Glory* commentary.
11. Gene Phillips, "Paths of Glory," in *The Stanley Kubrick Archives*, 300.
12. Interview with James B. Harris, Aero Theater, Santa Monica, September 28, 2017, https://www.youtube.com/watch?v=IAQbxkv6vVs.
13. Author interview with Christiane Kubrick, July 8, 2018.
14. Jon Ronson, "After Stanley Kubrick," *Guardian*, August 18, 2010.

15. Valerie Jenkins interview with Christiane Kubrick, *Evening Standard*, September 10, 1972.

16. Author interview with Christiane Kubrick.

17. Author interview with Christiane Kubrick.

18. Author interview with Christiane Kubrick (first and third quotes); Geoffrey Cocks, *The Wolf at the Door* (New York: Peter Lang, 2004), 26 (second quote).

19. Michael Herr, *Kubrick* (New York: Grove, 2000), 48.

20. Calder Willingham letter to SK, December 14, 1959, University of the Arts, London, Stanley Kubrick Archive (hereinafter SKA), SK/10/8/4.

21. Robert Emmet Ginna interview with SK, SKA, SK/1/2/8/2.

22. Baxter, *Stanley Kubrick*, 129.

23. Ginna interview.

24. Danielle Heymann interview with SK, published in *Le Monde*, October 17, 1987, here quoted from SKA, SK/1/2/8/5.

25. Gene Phillips, "Spartacus," in *The Stanley Kubrick Archives*, 318.

26. Ginna interview.

27. Terry Southern interview with SK, 1962, *The Stanley Kubrick Archives*, 343.

28. Ginna interview.

29. Kirk Douglas letter to Stan Margulies, April 27, 1959, SKA, SK/9/4/3.

30. On SK's idea of the "small" *Spartacus* vs. Trumbo's and Douglas's "big" one, see Fiona Radford, "Having His Cake and Eating It Too: SK and *Spartacus*," *The Stanley Kubrick Archives*, 105, 110–11.

31. Peter Ustinov letter to SK, no date, SKA, SK/9/4/2–6.

32. SK letter to Laurence Olivier, June 5, 1959, SKA, SK/9/4/3.

33. Pauline Kael, *5001 Nights at the Movies* (New York: Henry Holt, 1991), 547.

34. Nathan Abrams, *Stanley Kubrick* (New Brunswick, NJ: Rutgers University Press, 2018), 69.

35. Vincent LoBrutto, *Stanley Kubrick* (New York: DaCapo, 1999), 187.

36. LoBrutto, *Stanley Kubrick*, 190.

37. SK letter to Calder Willingham, no date, SKA, SK/10/8/4.

38. Calder Willingham letter to SK, December 14, 1959, SKA, SK/10/8/4.

39. Martin Russ letter to SK, no date, SKA, SK/10/8/7.

40. Brian Boyd, *Vladimir Nabokov: The American Years* (Princeton: Princeton University Press, 1991), 407.

41. James Naremore, *On Kubrick* (London: British Film Institute, 2007), 99.

42. Vladimir Nabokov, *Lolita: A Screenplay*, xii–xiii.

43. Laurence Olivier letter to SK, December 15, 1959, SKA, SK/10/8/4.

44. James Harris letter to SK, December 22, 1959, SKA, SK/10/8/4 (Bardot); LoBrutto, *Stanley Kubrick*, 203 (Kubrick quote); Baxter, *Stanley Kubrick*, 150 (Nabokov quote).

45. Sue Lyon letter to James Harris, November 30, 1960, signed also by her mother and her teacher Bev Westman, SKA, SK/10/8/4.

46. SK letter to Peter Ustinov, May 20, 1960, SKA, SK/10/8/4, cited in Karyn Stuckey, "Re-Writing Nabokov's *Lolita*," in *Stanley Kubrick: New Perspectives*, ed. Tatjana Ljujić, Peter Krämer, and Richard Daniels (London: Black Dog Publishing, 2015), 127.

47. SK letter to Ustinov, May 20, 1960.

48. Stuckey, "Re-Writing Nabokov's *Lolita*," 128 (first scene); Mick Broderick, *Reconstructing Strangelove* (New York: Columbia University Press, 2017), 86; "Stanley Kubrick's Dr. Strangelove," *Cinephilia and Beyond*, https://cinephiliabeyond.org/stanley-kubricks-dr-strangelove-the-sharpest-most-cautioning-hilarious-political-satire/ (quotes).

49. From "Outline of Lolita," included with SK letter to Ustinov, cited in Nathan Abrams, "An Alternative New York Jewish Intellectual," Ljujić, Krämer, and Daniels, *Stanley Kubrick: New Perspectives*, 70.

50. LoBrutto, *Stanley Kubrick*, 204 (Granz); Richard Corliss, *Lolita* (London: British Film Institute, 1994), 47.

NOTES TO PAGES 65–75

51. Roger Lewis, *The Life and Death of Peter Sellers* (New York: Applause, 2000), 346.

52. Lewis, *Life and Death,* 344.

53. LoBrutto, *Stanley Kubrick,* 205.

54. Filippo Ulivieri, "Waiting for a Miracle: A Survey of Stanley Kubrick's Unrealized Projects," *Cinergie,* September 4, 2017, https://cinergie.unibo.it/article/view/7349/7318.

55. Vladimir Nabokov, *The Annotated Lolita,* ed. Alfred Appel (New York: Vintage, 1991), 283.

56. Southern interview, 343.

57. SK letter to Peter Ustinov, May 20, 1960, SKA, SK/10/8/4.

58. Jeremy Bernstein interview with SK, 1965, https://www.indiewire.com/2013/12/listen-rare-76-minute-interview-with-stanley-kubrick-about-his-start-in-films-nuclear-war-chess-strategies-248700/.

59. John Collins letter to SK, May 9, 1961, SKA, SK/10/8/7.

60. Author interview with Christiane Kubrick.

61. Author interview with Christiane Kubrick (first two quotes); Baxter, *Stanley Kubrick,* 166, citing a *Times* of London February 5, 1973, interview with Christiane Kubrick (third quote).

Chapter 3. Total Final Annihilating Artistic Control

1. Jeremy Bernstein interview with SK, 1965, https://www.indiewire.com/2013/12/listen-rare-76-minute-interview-with-stanley-kubrick-about-his-start-in-films-nuclear-war-chess-strategies-248700/.

2. Five-O interview with James B. Harris, 2002, Scraps from the Loft https://scrapsfromtheloft.com/2018/02/16/james-b-harris-interview-2002/; Alex Singer letter to SK, March 28, 1964, University of the Arts, London, Stanley Kubrick Archive (hereinafter SKA), SK/11/9/97.

3. F. X. Feeney interview with James B. Harris, Director's Guild of America, spring 2013, https://www.dga.org/Craft/DGAQ/All-Articles/1302-Spring-2013/James-Harris-on-Stanley-Kubrick.aspx.

4. Romain LeVern interview with James B. Harris, *Chaos*, 2018 (my translation), http://www.chaosreign.fr/james-b-harris-eyes -wide-shut-est-le-moins-bon-film-de-stanley-kubrick/.

5. LeVern interview with James B. Harris.

6. Sharon Ghamari-Tabrizi, *The Worlds of Herman Kahn* (Cambridge: Harvard University Press, 2005), 5 ("immediate peril"); Herman Kahn, *On Thermonuclear War* (Princeton: Princeton University Press, 1960), 34, 91, 94 (statistics and final quote).

7. Ghamari-Tabrizi, *Worlds of Herman Kahn*, 70.

8. Ghamari-Tabrizi, *Worlds of Herman Kahn*, 70.

9. Mick Broderick, *Reconstructing Strangelove* (New York: Columbia University Press, 2017), 58.

10. Ghamari-Tabrizi, *Worlds of Herman Kahn*, 123.

11. Bernstein interview.

12. See P. D. Smith, *Doomsday Men* (New York: St. Martin's, 2007).

13. Eric Schlosser, "Almost Everything in 'Dr. Strangelove' Was True," *New Yorker*, January 17, 2014.

14. Author interview with Christiane Kubrick, July 8, 2018.

15. Christiane Kubrick interview.

16. Christiane Kubrick interview.

17. Speaking during a cabinet meeting on July 25, 1956, Eisenhower was referring to the hysterical behavior likely to follow news of a Russian nuclear strike. http://www.conelrad.com/atomic secrets/secrets.php?secrets=e18.

18. John Baxter, *Stanley Kubrick* (New York: Carroll and Graf, 1997), 181.

19. Richard Hofstadter, *The Paranoid Style in American Politics* (New York: Knopf, 1965), 28, 31.

20. SKA, SK/11/1/9, cited in Nathan Abrams, "An Alternative Jewish Intellectual," *Stanley Kubrick: New Perspectives*, ed. Tatjana Ljujić, Peter Krämer, and Richard Daniels (London: Black Dog Publishing, 2015), 74.

21. Cited in Gene Phillips, "Dr. Strangelove," in *The Stanley Kubrick Archives*, ed. Alison Castle (New York: Taschen, 2004), 351.

22. SK letter to George C. Scott, November 12, 1963, SK 11/9/97.

23. Terry Southern, "Strangelove Outtake: Notes from the War Room," *Grand Street* 49 (Summer 1994): 67.

24. Southern, "Strangelove Outtake," 72.

25. Baxter, *Stanley Kubrick*, 180.

26. Anne Quito, "The Man Who Designed Dr. Strangelove's Apocalyptic Set Shaped Today's Negotiation Rooms," *Quartz*, March 15, 2016, https://qz.com/638778/the-man-who-designed-dr-strangeloves-apocalyptic-set-shaped-todays-negotiation-rooms/.

27. Southern, "Strangelove Outtake," 80.

28. James Mason letter to SK, January 20, 1964, SKA, SK/11/9/77. The PR firm's letter, from Allan, Foster, Ingersoll and Weber, mentions Hedda Hopper, Vernon Scott of UPI, Harrison Carroll, and Phil Schener.

29. SK letter to Robert Murray at the Aspen Institute for Humanistic Studies, no date, SKA, SK 11/9/94.

30. Robert Brustein, "Out of This World," *New York Review of Books*, February 6, 1964; SK letter to Anthony Macklin, August 11, 1964, SKA, SK/11/9/77.

31. SK letter to Herbert Mitgang of CBS News, June 18, 1964, SKA, SK/11/9/77; SK letter to Gilbert Seldes, April 6, 1964, SKA, SK/11/9/97; SK letter to the Actors Studio, December 7, 1964, SKA, SK/11/9/1.

32. Todd Gitlin letter to SK, marked "unanswered," May 29, 1964, SKA, SK/11/9/97; SK letter to SANE, July 9, 1964, SKA, SK/11/9/97; SK letter to Johnson campaign, September 18, 1964, SKA, SK11/9/94.

33. SK letter to Thomas Fryer, August 19, 1964, SKA, SK/11/9/94.

34. SK, undated essay, SKA, SK11/9/94.

35. Author interview with Julian Senior, July 9, 2018.

36. SK letter to Martin Russ, August 20, 1964, SKA, SK11/9/93.

37. SKA, SK/11/9/77.

38. SK letter to Robert Ettinger, August 12 1964, SKA, SK/11/9/94.

39. SK letter to Robert Ettinger, August 20, 1964, SKA, SK11/

9/94. In his *Playboy* interview with Eric Norden (September 1968), Kubrick talked at length about Ettinger's ideas.

40. SKA, SK/11/9/5.

Chapter 4. The Tower of Babel Was the Start of the Space Age

1. Robert Ardrey, *African Genesis* (New York: Dell, 1961).

2. David Thomson, *The Whole Equation* (New York: Knopf), 155; Martin Scorsese, Introduction to Michel Ciment, *Kubrick: The Definitive Edition* (New York: Faber and Faber, 2003).

3. Michael Benson, *Space Odyssey* (New York: Simon and Schuster, 2018), 39, 22.

4. Jeremy Bernstein interview with SK, 1965, https://www.indiewire.com/2013/12/listen-rare-76-minute-interview-with-stanley-kubrick-about-his-start-in-films-nuclear-war-chess-strategies-248700/.

5. Danielle Heymann interview with SK, published in *Le Monde*, October 17, 1987, here quoted from University of the Arts, London, Stanley Kubrick Archive, SK/1/2/8/5.

6. Bernstein interview.

7. Bernstein interview.

8. Benson, *Space Odyssey*, 88 (Christiane Kubrick quote); "Kubrick on *The Shining*: An Interview with Michel Ciment" (SK quote).

9. Benson, *Space Odyssey*, 76 (Clarke quote); Nathan Abrams, *Stanley Kubrick* (New Brunswick, NJ: Rutgers University Press, 2018), 133 (SK quote).

10. Benson, *Space Odyssey*, 211.

11. Abrams, *Stanley Kubrick*, 132.

12. Leo Steinberg, *Other Criteria* (Chicago: University of Chicago Press, 1971), 407.

13. Benson, *Space Odyssey*, 181.

14. Dan Richter, *Moonwatcher's Memoir* (New York: Carroll and Graf, 2002), 38.

15. Richter, *Moonwatcher's Memoir*, 130.

16. Arthur C. Clarke, *2001: A Space Odyssey* (New York: Penguin/Roc, 1968), 297.

17. Benson, *Space Odyssey*, 418.

18. Benson, *Space Odyssey*, 431.

19. Michael Powell, "A Survivor of Film Criticism's Heroic Age," *New York Times*, July 9, 2009.

20. Alexander Walker, Sybil Taylor, and Ulrich Ruchti, *Stanley Kubrick, Director* (New York: Norton, 1971), 162.

21. Ardrey, *African Genesis*, 348.

Chapter 5. Let's Open with a Sicilian Defence

1. SK letter to Ron Lubin, August 18, 1964, University of the Arts, London, Stanley Kubrick Archive, SK/11/9/100.

2. Joseph Gelmis interview with SK (1970), in *Stanley Kubrick: Interviews*, ed. Gene Phillips (Jackson: University Press of Mississippi), 84.

3. A transcript of SK's conversations with Felix Markham is included in *Stanley Kubrick's Napoleon: The Greatest Movie Never Made*, ed. Alison Castle (Cologne: Taschen, 2017).

4. Stanley Kubrick, *Napoleon* screenplay, http://www.raindance .co.uk/site/picture/upload/napoleon.pdf.

5. Gelmis interview, 84.

6. Kubrick, *Napoleon* screenplay.

7. *Kubrick Remembered*, dir. Gary Khammar (2014); see Vincent Canby's review of *Barry Lyndon*, *New York Times*, December 21, 1975 ("Please don't send me any more pictures where the hero writes with a feather").

8. Eva-Maria Magel, "The Best Movie (N)ever Made," *Kinematograph* 20 (2004): 165.

9. Steven Englund, *Napoleon* (Cambridge: Harvard University Press, 2004), xiv.

10. Vincent LoBrutto, *Stanley Kubrick* (New York: DaCapo, 1999), 336.

11. Anthony Burgess, *A Clockwork Orange* (1962; New York: Norton, 1986), 42, 38.

12. LoBrutto, *Stanley Kubrick*, 338.

13. John Baxter, *Stanley Kubrick* (New York: Carroll and Graf, 1997), 247.

14. Julian Rice describes Alex as an overgrown child in *Kubrick's Hope* (Lanham, MD: Scarecrow/Rowman and Littlefield, 2008), 67–74.

15. Robert Kolker, *The Cultures of American Film* (New York: Oxford University Press, 2015), 233–35.

16. Andrew Bailey interview with SK, *Rolling Stone*, January 20, 1972.

17. Burgess, *A Clockwork Orange*, 130.

18. Burgess, *A Clockwork Orange*, 131.

19. Author interview with Tom Courtenay, July 11, 2017.

20. Burgess, *A Clockwork Orange*, 28; see the offhanded racist "throw 'em a basketball" joke in *Full Metal Jacket*.

21. Kolker, *The Extraordinary Image*, 162.

22. *Times* of London obituary of Adrienne Corri, March 25, 2016.

23. Joseph Gelmis interview with SK, cited in LoBrutto, *Stanley Kubrick*, 360.

24. James Naremore, *On Kubrick* (London: British Film Institute, 2007), 158–59.

25. Interview with Malcolm MacDowell, *A Clockwork Orange* Blu-ray.

26. Burgess, *A Clockwork Orange*, 44–45.

27. Burgess, *A Clockwork Orange*, 102.

28. Victor Davis interview with SK, *Daily Express*, January 1972, cited in LoBrutto, *Stanley Kubrick*, 356; see also Robert Hughes, review of *A Clockwork Orange*, *Time*, December 27, 1971.

29. SK, "Now Kubrick Fights Back," *New York Times*, February 27, 1972.

30. Burgess, *A Clockwork Orange*, 172.

31. Pauline Kael, "Stanley Strangelove" (review of *A Clockwork Orange*), *New Yorker*, January 1, 1972, https://scrapsfromtheloft.com/2016/09/18/a-clockwork-orange-pauline-kael/.

32. Kael, "Stanley Strangelove."

33. LoBrutto, *Stanley Kubrick*, 359.

34. LoBrutto, *Stanley Kubrick*, 364.

35. Bailey interview.

36. Author interview with Julian Senior, July 9, 2018.

37. Senior interview.

38. Senior interview.

Chapter 6. You Can Talk for Hours about a Thing with Stanley

1. Emilio D'Alessandro, with Filippo Ulivieri, *Stanley Kubrick and Me* (New York: Arcade, 2012), 70.

2. Peter Bogdanovich, "What They Say about Stanley Kubrick," *New York Times Magazine*, July 4, 1999, https://www.ny times.com/1999/07/04/magazine/what-they-say-about-stanley -kubrick.html.

3. Christopher Anderson, "The Girl Who Has Everything," *People*, March 8, 1976, https://people.com/archive/cover-story-the -girl-who-has-everything-vol-5-no-9/.

4. Geoffrey O'Brien, print essay, *Barry Lyndon* Blu-ray.

5. Bogdanovich, "What They Say."

6. Bogdanovich, "What They Say" (Adam quote); *Filmworker*, dir. Tony Zierra (2017) (Senior quote).

7. D'Alessandro, *Stanley Kubrick and Me*, 59–60.

8. Vincent LoBrutto, *Stanley Kubrick* (New York: DaCapo, 1999), 403.

9. LoBrutto, *Stanley Kubrick*, 402.

10. Author interview with Lawrence Malkin, February 12, 2018.

11. Interview with Michel Ciment, *Barry Lyndon*, Blu-ray.

12. *Filmworker.*

13. Interview with Adam Eaker, *Barry Lyndon* Blu-ray.

14. Julian Rice, *Kubrick's Hope* (Lanham, MD: Scarecrow/ Rowman and Littlefield, 2008), 93.

Chapter 7. Something Inherently Wrong with the Human Personality

1. "For weeks," Emilio D'Alessandro recalled, "the special effects team . . . had tried and tried again to produce fake blood that convinced Stanley, but he was never satisfied with the color."

D'Alessandro, *Stanley Kubrick and Me* (New York: Arcade, 2012), 115.

2. John Baxter, *Stanley Kubrick* (New York: Carroll and Graf, 1997), 314–15.

3. Baxter, *Stanley Kubrick*, 313.

4. *Stanley Kubrick's The Shining*, ed. Danel Olson (Lakewood, CO: Centipede, 2015), 642.

5. Michel Ciment, *Kubrick: The Definitive Edition* (New York: Faber and Faber, 2003), 189.

6. David Thomson, *The Whole Equation* (New York: Knopf), 331; Olson, *Stanley Kubrick's The Shining*, 631.

7. Nathan Abrams, *Stanley Kubrick* (New Brunswick, NJ: Rutgers University Press, 2018), 135, compares Jack and HAL.

8. Jack Kroll, review of *The Shining*, *Newsweek*, June 2, 1980, https://scrapsfromtheloft.com/2016/09/17/shining-stanley-kubricks-horror-show/.

9. Arthur Schopenhauer, *The World as Will and Idea*, trans. E. F. J. Payne (New York: Dover, 1958), 1: 394–95.

10. Arthur Schopenhauer, letter to Johann Wolfgang von Goethe, November 11, 1815, *Gesammelte Briefe*, ed. Arthur Hübscher (Bonn: Bouvier Verlag, 1978), 18.

11. Douglas Luckhurst, *The Shining* (London: British Film Institute, 2013), 79.

12. Vincent LoBrutto, *Stanley Kubrick* (New York: DaCapo, 1999), 445.

13. D'Alessandro, *Stanley Kubrick and Me*, 118.

14. Typed notes and scene outlines from July 11 and August 27, 1977, University of the Arts, London, Stanley Kubrick Archive, SK/15/1/1, SK/15/1/9; "Ending idea . . . saved by cook," SK/15/1/3.

15. Baxter, *Stanley Kubrick*, 319.

16. Olson, *Stanley Kubrick's The Shining*, 526 (Vitali quote); Ciment, *Kubrick*, 301 (Duvall quote).

17. Author interview with Julian Senior, July 9, 2018.

18. Like *Paths of Glory*, *Dr. Strangelove*, and *A Clockwork Orange*, *The Shining* ends with an old-fashioned song and a tableau of return.

Chapter 8. Make Sure It's Big—Lon Chaney Big

1. Emilio D'Alessandro, with Filippo Ulivieri, *Stanley Kubrick and Me* (New York: Arcade, 2012), 135, 139.

2. Dalia Karpel, "The Real Stanley Kubrick," *Haaretz*, November 3, 2005, https://www.haaretz.com/1.4880226.

3. Filmworker, dir. Tony Zierra (2017).

4. D'Alessandro, *Stanley Kubrick and Me*, 170.

5. D'Alessandro, *Stanley Kubrick and Me*, 168, 78–80 (SK quote and guidelines); Karpel, "The Real Stanley Kubrick" (Christiane Kubrick quote).

6. D'Alessandro, *Stanley Kubrick and Me*, 150.

7. D'Alessandro, *Stanley Kubrick and Me*, 74 (phone calls to Barbara); Peter Bogdanovich, "What They Say about Stanley Kubrick," *New York Times Magazine*, July 4, 1999, https://www.nytimes.com/1999/07/04/magazine/what-they-say-about-stanley-kubrick.html (Milius quote).

8. Danielle Heymann interview with SK, published in *Le Monde*, October 17, 1987, here quoted from University of the Arts, London, Stanley Kubrick Archive (hereinafter SKA), SK/1/2/8/5.

9. Michael Herr, *Kubrick* (New York: Grove, 2000), 11.

10. Herr, *Kubrick*, 11.

11. Herr, *Kubrick*, 10.

12. Grover Lewis, "The Several Battles of Gustav Hasford," *LA Times Magazine*, June 28, 1987.

13. Gustav Hasford letters to SK, December 5, 1982, SKA shelf 3, box 5 (*Full Metal Jacket*).

14. Grover Lewis, "The Killing of Gus Hasford," *LA Weekly*, June 4–June 10, 1993 (Hasfor quotes); Hasford letters to SK, January 23, 1984, and May 28, 1983, both SKA, SK/16/1/2/4 (demands for return of photos and screenplay credit).

15. SK letter to Gustav Hasford, no date, SKA, SK/16/1/24.

16. Gustav Hasford, *The Short-Timers* (1979; New York: Bantam, 1983), 175–76.

17. Jeremy Bernstein interview with SK, 1965, https://www.indiewire.com/2013/12/listen-rare-76-minute-interview-with-stanley

-kubrick-about-his-start-in-films-nuclear-war-chess-strategies -248700/.

18. Charlie Kohler interview with SK, *East Village Eye*, August 1968, https://scrapsfromtheloft.com/2017/01/10/stanley-kubrick -raps/.

19. Heymann interview.

20. Tim Cahill interview with SK, *Rolling Stone*, August 27, 1987.

21. Author interview with Vincent D'Onofrio, February 9, 2018.

22. Matthew Modine, *Full Metal Jacket Diary* (New York: Rugged Land, 2005).

23. Heymann interview.

24. D'Onofrio interview.

25. Interview with Lee Ermey, *Full Metal Jacket* Blu-ray.

26. Jay Cocks, commentary, *Full Metal Jacket* Blu-ray.

27. Michael Herr, *Dispatches* (1977; New York: Vintage, 1991), 20–21.

28. From SK's handwritten notes on Hasford's book, cited in *The Stanley Kubrick Archives*, ed. Alison Castle (New York: Taschen, 2004), 471.

29. Georg Scesslen, "Shoot Me, Shoot Me," *Kinematograph* 20 (2004): 221–22.

30. D'Onofrio interview.

31. Vincent D'Onofrio, commentary, *Full Metal Jacket* Blu-ray.

Chapter 9. Frightened of Making the Movie

1. Tim Cahill interview with SK, *Rolling Stone*, August 27, 1987.

2. Author interview with Sandy Lieberson, July 13, 2017; Peter Bogdanovich, "What They Say about Stanley Kubrick," *New York Times Magazine*, July 4, 1999, https://www.nytimes.com/1999/07 /04/magazine/what-they-say-about-stanley-kubrick.html (Southgate quote).

3. Cahill interview.

4. Cahill interview.

5. Christiane Kubrick, interview, *Eyes Wide Shut* Blu-ray.

6. Ulivieri's is the fullest account of Kubrick's unrealized proj-

ects; Filippo Ulivieri, "Waiting for a Miracle: A Survey of Stanley Kubrick's Unrealized Projects," *Cinergie*, September 4, 2017 https://cinergie.unibo.it/article/view/7349/7318.

7. Geoffrey Macnab, "Kubrick's Lost Movie: Now We Can See It . . ." *Independent*, January 27, 2009, https://www.independent.co.uk/arts-entertainment/films/features/kubricks-lost-movie-now-we-can-see-it-1516726.html (*Schindler's List*); Dalia Karpel, "The Real Stanley Kubrick," *Haaretz*, November 3, 2005, https://www.haaretz.com/1.4880226 (Christiane Kubrick quote); University of the Arts, London, Stanley Kubrick Archive (hereinafter SKA), shelf 9, box 3 (*Wartime Lies*) (script).

8. A selection of Baker's storyboards is reproduced in *A.I.: Artificial Intelligence*, ed. Jan Harlan and Jane Struthers (London: Thames and Hudson, 2009).

9. Nathan Abrams, *Stanley Kubrick* (New Brunswick, NJ: Rutgers University Press, 2018), 269.

10. Joseph McBride, *Steven Spielberg* (Jackson: University Press of Mississippi, 2010), 483; SKA, shelf 8, box A (SK quote); Harlan and Struthers, *A.I.: Artificial Intelligence*, 23 (Maitland quote).

11. Molly Haskell, *Steven Spielberg* (New Haven: Yale University Press, 2017), 174.

12. Robert Emmet Ginna interview with SK, University of the Arts, London, Stanley Kubrick Archive, SK/1/2/8/2.

13. Arthur Schnitzler, *Dream Story*, in *Eyes Wide Shut: A Screenplay and Dream Story* (New York: Time Warner, 1999), 235.

14. Scott Feinberg, "Kirk Douglas: 'I Am Always Optimistic,'" *Hollywood Reporter*, June 6, 2012, http://www.hollywoodreporter.com/news/kirk-douglas-pacemaker-helicopter-crash-stroke-330997.

15. Cited in Robert Kolker and Nathan Abrams, *Eyes Wide Shut* (New York: Oxford University Press, 2019), 27.

16. SKA shelf 2, EWS 11.

17. Kolker and Abrams, *Eyes Wide Shut*, 34–35 (Southern quote); SKA shelf 2, box 12 (*Eyes Wide Shut*) (SK notebook).

18. John le Carré, *The Pigeon Tunnel* (New York: Penguin, 2017), 242–43.

19. Frederic Raphael, *Eyes Wide Open* (New York: Ballantine, 1999), 59.

20. Michel Chion, *Eyes Wide Shut* (New York: Palgrave Macmillan, 2002), 25.

21. Chion, *Eyes Wide Shut*, 28; Kolker and Abrams, *Eyes Wide Shut*, 124 (McQuiston quote).

22. Bogdanovich, "What They Say" (Adam quote); Jon Ronson, "After Stanley Kubrick," *Guardian*, August 18, 2010 (Christiane Kubrick quote).

23. David Thomson, *Nicole Kidman* (New York: Vintage, 2008), 248–49.

24. Interview with Nicole Kidman, *Eyes Wide Shut* Blu-ray.

25. Kolker and Abrams, *Eyes Wide Shut*, 89.

26. Kolker and Abrams, *Eyes Wide Shut*, 107. It was not true, as Thomson reported, that Kubrick barred Cruise from the set for two weeks.

27. Kolker and Abrams, *Eyes Wide Shut*, 98.

28. Schnitzler, *Dream Story*, 109.

29. David Denby, "Death Trap," *New York*, July 13, 1987, 54; interview with Christiane Kubrick, *Eyes Wide Shut* Blu-ray.

30. Stephen Hunter, "Kubrick's Sleepy Eyes Wide Shut," *Washington Post*, July 16, 1999 (Catholic Church quote); Lee Siegel, *Falling Upwards* (New York: Basic, 2006), 229; James Naremore, *On Kubrick* (London: British Film Institute, 2007), 239.

31. Bogdanovich, "What They Say."

32. Bogdanovich, "What They Say" (Christiane Kubrick quote); Kolker and Abrams, *Eyes Wide Shut*, 111 (Cavaciuti quote).

33. Kolker and Abrams, *Eyes Wide Shut*, 97.

34. Kolker and Abrams, *Eyes Wide Shut*, 111 (Kubrick operating camera); Lieberson interview.

35. *Filmworker*, dir. Tony Zierra (2017).

36. Emilio D'Alessandro, with Filippo Ulivieri, *Stanley Kubrick and Me* (New York: Arcade, 2012), 330.

37. Yoh Phillips, "Stanley Kubrick's Unprecedented Influence on Hip Hop," *DJBooth*, February 6, 2019, https://djbooth.net/features/2019-02-06-stanley-kubrick-influence-hip-hop.

ACKNOWLEDGMENTS

I want to thank my editor, Ileene Smith, and my agent, Chris Calhoun, for their steadfast support and wise, good-humored counsel. Mike Levine improved the manuscript substantially with his careful reading, as did the wonderful Dan Heaton and Susan Laity, the copyeditors of my dreams. The staff at the Kubrick Archive at the University of the Arts, London, was extraordinarily helpful. Richard Daniels and Georgina Orgill, especially, gave me essential aid. Late in the day Steven Moore generously came to the rescue with his indexing expertise and keen eye for mistakes. Heather Gold of Yale University Press was more instantly helpful than any author ever deserved.

Members of the Kubrick family, Christiane Kubrick, Jan Harlan, and Katharina Kubrick, shared their memories of Stanley Kubrick and graciously trusted me to proceed with this project. I am honored to have met and interviewed them. Julian Senior and Vincent D'Onofrio generously talked to me about their relationships with Kubrick. I am grateful for their warmth and good humor, as well as the brilliant insight into Kubrick they gave me. For various forms of Kubrickian lore and advice, I also thank Robert Kolker, Nathan Abrams, Katie McQuerrey, Noah Isenberg, Michael Benson, Rodney Hill, Sandy Lieberson, Robert Pippin, Dana Polan, Lawrence Ratna, and Phil Blumberg, as well as Mark Lentz and the other members of New York's Stanley Kubrick meet-up. The Garcia Malkins of Mexico City and the Malkins of New York supported me in my Kubrick research, and in other ways too. Yigal and Esme Chazan and Paulette Farsides provided me a home away from home in London, site of the Kubrick Archive, and Jenn Lewin did the same in Haifa. Eric Banks, director of the New York Institute for the Humanities, and the institute's fellows were extraordinarily helpful when I presented my work. Among my students, Quentin Key-Tello, Nicholas Day, and Mandana Naviafar of the University of Houston Honors College were particularly insightful about Kubrick's films.

My editors at *Tablet* magazine, David Samuels and Matthew Fishbane, have made that publication a much-needed intellectual home for me. *Tablet* has kindly given permission for several passages from my essays on Kubrick to appear here in revised form.

I am grateful for a grant from the John Simon Guggenheim Memorial Foundation, which enabled me to write this book. I am grateful too for the help given me by J. Kastely, who brought honesty and generosity to the University of Houston English Department chair's office, and to Bill Monroe, Dean of the Honors College at UH, whose friendship and good humor never wavered. The John and Rebecca Moores Professorship and the Houstoun grant program at UH provided needed funds for the project.

I owe most of all to my wife, Victoria, and my son Ariel, a challenging interpreter of *2001*. Their love kept me going, and enjoying life with them made writing this book possible.

INDEX

Barry Lyndon, 2, 10, 12, 22, 36, 56, 129–42, 143–44, 169, 186; casting of, 130, 192; costumes in, 133, 135; duel in, 138–40; lighting in, 133, 140; plot of, 130, 137–41; source for, 129
Barton Fink, 155
Bass, Saul, 53
Baxter, John, 116
Beatty, Warren, 189
Beauvoir, Simone de, 91
Bedford Incident, 76
Beethoven, Ludwig van, 115, 120–23
Begley, Louis, 11, 40, 182, 185
Benson, Michael, 97
Berenson, Marisa, 130, 133, 135
Berglas, David, 134
Bergman, Ingmar, 3, 13
Berkoff, Steven, 9, 135
Bernstein, Jeremy, 24, 71, 74, 78, 96
Bernstein, Leonard, 16
Bettelheim, Bruno, 144
Birdy, 169
Bogart, Humphrey, 36
Bolívar, Simón, 110
Bondarchuk, Sergei, 113
Bonnie and Clyde, 119
Borges, Jorge Luis, 159
Born on the Fourth of July, 192
Bowie, David, 119
Brando, Marlon, 51–52, 85, 116
Braun, Wernher von, 105
Brown, Garrett, 147, 158
Bruce, Lenny, 12, 65
Brustein, Robert, 88–89
Bryna Productions, 42, 51, 60
Burgess, Anthony, 114–15, 119, 122, 125, 129
Burstyn, Joseph, 24

Calder, Alexander, 25
Calley, John, 143, 165, 178, 188
Canonero, Milena, 133
Carey, Timothy, 41, 43
Cartier, Walter, 21–22
Cavaciuti, Peter, 202
Cavell, Stanley, 12, 190

Chambers, Marilyn, 189
Chaney, Lon, 162, 173
Chaplin, Charlie, 88, 117, 121
chess: film analogies with, 32, 41, 97–98, 126, 204; Ruth Kubrick and, 25; in SK's films, 35, 100, 103; SK's passion for, 4, 5, 24, 40, 83, 111–12; war and, 168
Chinatown, 197
Chion, Michel, 191
Ciment, Michel, 13, 136
Cimino, Michael, 179
Citizen Kane, 5, 13
Clarke, Arthur C., 95–98
Clift, Montgomery, 16
Cline, Edward, 5
Clockwork Orange, 7, 9–11, 13, 114–27; Alex in, 2, 3, 8, 11, 22, 68, 72, 94, 104, 114–27, 129, 137, 139, 142, 143, 173, 195, 203; casting of, 116; Christiane Kubrick's paintings in, 50, 126; corruption in, 56, 123; music in, 115, 118, 119–21, 123; screening specifications for, 90, 126; "Singin' in the Rain" in, 10, 120, 121–22, 172; source for, 114
Clouzot, Henri-Georges, 144
Cobb, Humphrey, 38
Cocks, Jay, 9, 175
Coen brothers, 155
Cole, J., 204
Colette, 67, 91
Collins, John, 71
Columbia Pictures, 84, 87, 91–92
Conrad, Joseph, 21, 23
Constable, John, 129
Cook, Elisha Jr., 34
Cop, 76
Coppola, Francis Ford, 6, 165–66
Corliss, Richard, 65
Corri, Adrienne, 120
Courtenay, Tom, 118
Crane, Hart, 95
Crawford, Joan, 35
Crothers, Scatman, 146
Crowther, Bosley, 50

Little, Thomas F., 71
Lloyd, Danny, 147
Lockwood, Gary, 98
Lola Montès, 44
Lolita, 2, 11, 13, 41, 59–73, 75, 88, 112, 117, 130, 140, 187; casting of, 17, 61–63, 67, 84; "Condemned" rating of, 71; lack of eroticism in, 69–72; tracking shot in, 34
Look (magazine), 9, 13, 15–21, 22
Love Story, 130
Lubin, Ron, 110
Lucas, George, 7
Luckhurst, Roger, 154
Lull, Raymond, 153
Lust for Life, 42
Lynn, Vera, 87
Lyon, Sue, 17, 62–63, 68–69

Macdonald, Dwight, 6, 20–21
MacGillivray, Greg, 148
Macready, George, 41, 45
MAD (magazine), 7, 12, 79, 94, 117, 135
Magee, Patrick, 120, 134
Maitland, Sara, 186
Malden, Karl, 52
Malick, Terrence, 177, 204
Malkin, Lawrence, 135
Maltese Falcon, 2, 34, 63
Manhattan, 171, 189
Mann, Anthony, 26, 52
Manson, Charles, 145
Mantegna, Andrea, 16
Man Who Shot Liberty Valence, 175
Marcus, Steven, 5
Margulies, Stan, 55
Markham, Felix, 111–12
Martel, Lucrecia, 204
Marx, Groucho, 166
Maslin, Janet, 177
Mason, James, 62, 65–66, 88
Mazursky, Paul, 22
Mazzello, Joseph, 183
McCarthy, Joseph, 56
McDowell, Malcolm, 8, 116–17, 120, 122

McQuiston, Kate, 191
Mead, Shepherd, 91
Meeker, Ralph, 41–42
Melville, Herman, 3, 5, 6
Melvin, Murray, 134, 138
Menjou, Adolphe, 41, 44–46
Metropolis, 84
Metty, Russell, 53
Metz, Toba. *See* Kubrick, Toba (Metz)
MGM (Metro-Goldwyn-Mayer), 2, 38–39, 72, 96, 107–8, 113
Michelangelo, 102
Mies van der Rohe, Ludwig, 94
Milius, John, 165
Miller, Arthur, 40
Minnelli, Vincent, 42
Mitgang, Herbert, 89
Modine, Matthew, 169
Monroe, Marilyn, 60
Morricone, Ennio, 140
Moses, Robert, 4
Mozart, Wolfgang Amadeus, 166, 177, 196, 198
Murnau, F. W., 156
Murray, Bill, 189

Nabokov, Vera, 60
Nabokov, Vladimir, 59–62, 64, 66, 71–72, 117, 156
Naked City, 16
Napoleon Bonaparte, 97; SK's unmade film on, 110–14, 169
Naremore, James, 3, 114, 201
Narrow Margin, 35
Needham, Terry, 178
Nelson, Barry, 148
New Land, 133
Newton, Helmut, 201
Nicholson, Jack, 113, 130, 145, 148, 152, 154–55, 157
Nietzsche, Friedrich, 94, 107
Night and the City, 36
Niven, David, 61–62
Nolan, Christopher, 108
North by Northwest, 192–93
Nosferatu, 156

JEWISH LIVES is a prizewinning series of interpretative biography designed to explore the many facets of Jewish identity. Individual volumes illuminate the imprint of Jewish figures upon literature, religion, philosophy, politics, cultural and economic life, and the arts and sciences. Subjects are paired with authors to elicit lively, deeply informed books that explore the range and depth of the Jewish experience from antiquity to the present.

Jewish Lives is a partnership of Yale University Press and the Leon D. Black Foundation. Ileene Smith is editorial director. Anita Shapira and Steven J. Zipperstein are series editors.

Jabotinsky: A Life, by Hillel Halkin
Jacob: Unexpected Patriarch, by Yair Zakovitch
Franz Kafka: The Poet of Shame and Guilt, by Saul Friedländer
Rav Kook: Mystic in a Time of Revolution, by Yehudah Mirsky
Stanley Kubrick: American Filmmaker, by David Mikics
Stan Lee: A Life in Comics, by Liel Leibovitz
Primo Levi: The Matter of a Life, by Berel Lang
Groucho Marx: The Comedy of Existence, by Lee Siegel
Karl Marx: Philosophy and Revolution, by Shlomo Avineri
Menasseh ben Israel: Rabbi of Amsterdam, by Steven Nadler
Moses Mendelssohn: Sage of Modernity, by Shmuel Feiner
Harvey Milk: His Lives and Death, by Lillian Faderman
Moses: A Human Life, by Avivah Gottlieb Zornberg
Proust: The Search, by Benjamin Taylor
Yitzhak Rabin: Soldier, Leader, Statesman, by Itamar Rabinovich
Walther Rathenau: Weimar's Fallen Statesman, by Shulamit Volkov
Jerome Robbins: A Life in Dance, by Wendy Lesser
Julius Rosenwald: Repairing the World, by Hasia R. Diner
Mark Rothko: Toward the Light in the Chapel, by Annie Cohen-Solal
Gershom Scholem: Master of the Kabbalah, by David Biale
Solomon: The Lure of Wisdom, by Steven Weitzman
Steven Spielberg: A Life in Films, by Molly Haskell
Alfred Stieglitz: Taking Pictures, Making Painters, by Phyllis Rose
Barbra Streisand: Redefining Beauty, Femininity, and Power,
     by Neal Gabler
Leon Trotsky: A Revolutionary's Life, by Joshua Rubenstein
Warner Bros: The Making of an American Movie Studio,
     by David Thomson

FORTHCOMING TITLES INCLUDE:

Judah Benjamin, by James Traub
Franz Boas, by Noga Arikha